OXFORD BROOK UNIVERSITY

BSc (Hons) in
APPLIED ACCOUNTING

Success in Your Research and Analysis Project

T
U
T
O
R
I
A
L

T
E
X
T

In this May 2008 edition

This Tutorial Text has been specially written around the detailed requirements of the Research and Analysis Project you need to complete to earn a BSc (Hons) in Applied Accounting from Oxford Brookes University.

It contains:

- The Information Pack (updated 1 May 2008)
- A self-assessment questionnaire
- Overview of the project
- Advice on how to choose and define the project
- Step-by-step guidance on major project tasks on research and analysis
- Guidance on how to present your Research Project, what to do at mentor meetings, oral presentations and the Skills and Learning Statement

This Tutorial Text is packed with checklists, exercises and examples

APPROVED BY OXFORD BROOKES UNIVERSITY

FOR PROJECTS SUBMITTED FROM AUGUST 2008

BPP
LEARNING MEDIA

First edition 2000
Seventh edition June 2008

ISBN 9780 7517 3309 9
(Previous ISBN 9780 7517 2744 X)

British Library Cataloguing-in-Publication Data
A catalogue record for this book
is available from the British Library

Published by

BPP Learning Media Ltd
BPP House, Aldine Place
London W12 8AA

www.bpp.com/learningmedia

Printed in the UK

We are grateful to Oxford Brookes University for
permission to reproduce in this text Information Pack
guidelines for this project. We would also like to thank
the staff at Oxford Brooks University for their assistance
in developing and updating this Tutorial Text.

Contents

	Page

(iii)

INTRODUCTION

Under the ground-breaking partnership between the ACCA and Oxford Brookes University, students studying for ACCA exams are able, simultaneously to study for a Bachelor of Science (Hons) degree in Applied Accounting. The Research and Analysis Project (RAP) is the final component of this degree. To reach this stage of the BSc degree you will have already successfully completed ACCA exams F1 to F9.

By passing these ACCA exams you have already demonstrated your undergraduate level abilities and the Research and Analysis Project provides you with the opportunity to demonstrate the remaining graduate level attributes necessary for the award of the BSc degree.

Recognising that doing the RAP will be a very different experience from study for professional exams BPP Learning Media has written this Tutorial Text specifically around the type of work that you will have to do for the RAP.

Only you can choose and complete a RAP. However, because the BPP Learning Media Tutorial Text is packed with advice, self-reflection exercises, checklists and examples, it provides an ideal roadmap.

BPP Professional Education Seminars

BPP Professional Education offers a one-day seminar for students embarking on the Research and Analysis Project. It concentrates on focusing the student precisely on the requirements of the project and provides detailed guidance on choosing a topic, research and analysis techniques and the critical skills of report-writing and giving presentations. Please telephone the Customer Services department on 0845 0751 1100 for further details on how to make a booking.

Mentoring

Certain BPP tutors are qualified to act as mentors under the scheme. Please telephone our Customer Service Department on 0845 0751 1100 for further information.

BPP Learning Media
May 2008

Part A:

Official material and skills assessment

chapter 1

The Information Pack

INTRODUCTION

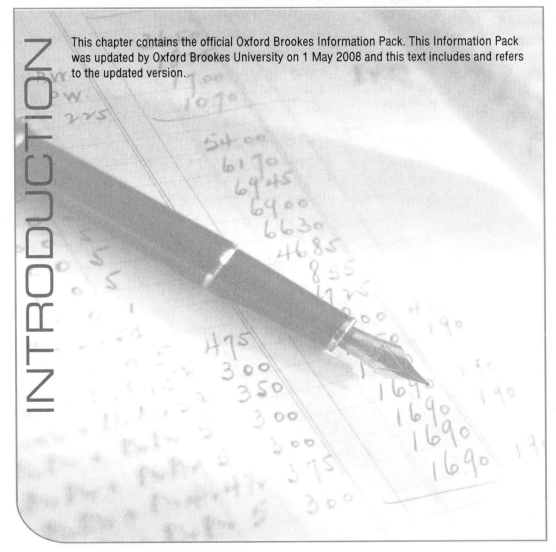

This chapter contains the official Oxford Brookes Information Pack. This Information Pack was updated by Oxford Brookes University on 1 May 2008 and this text includes and refers to the updated version.

BSc (Hons) in Applied Accounting and Research and Analysis Project

INFORMATION PACK

Contents

BPP LEARNING MEDIA

Introduction

The Oxford Brookes University BSc (Hons) in Applied Accounting degree is delivered in collaborative provision with the Association of Chartered Certified Accountants (ACCA). Since the BSc degree was introduced in 2000 over 6,800 ACCA students, affiliates and members worldwide have successfully completed this degree scheme. They have done so by passing the first two stages of the ACCA professional examinations and then passing their Research and Analysis Project which was submitted directly to Oxford Brookes.

Oxford Brookes and ACCA undertook a thorough review of the BSc scheme in 2006 and agreed to make a number of changes to build on the degree's success. The revised BSc degree scheme will be fully implemented on 1 August 2008. This Information Pack provides details about the revised BSc degree programme, and the revised requirements of the Oxford Brookes Research and Analysis Project.

The project continues to be the final component of the BSc degree. To pass, a student must achieve the standards expected of a final year undergraduate in undertaking and presenting an applied piece of research. A student has already demonstrated undergraduate capabilities by passing the ACCA Part 2 / Fundamentals Skills module examinations.

Although the Information Pack is written primarily for ACCA students, I am confident that its contents will be of interest and value to college tutors and employers who provide project mentor support to ACCA students in the preparation of their Research and Analysis Project.

The content of this Information Pack is taken from the BSc degree webpages on the ACCA website. (http://www.accaglobal.com/students/study_exams/qualifications/degree/degree2/). These webpages include the Research and Analysis Project submission form which is specific to each six-monthly project submission period and which is not included here.

The BSc degree webpages will be updated on an ongoing basis. The content of this Information Pack will remain relevant for at least the next two project submission periods, whose deadlines are 3 October 2008 (Period 17) and 3 April 2009 (Period 18). However we may produce additional content for the BSc degree webpages which will provide further support to ACCA students and their project mentors. I recommend that students should visit the BSc degree webpages periodically to check for any new material.

The first seven sections of this Information Pack set out the academic framework of the BSc (Hons) in Applied Accounting degree and the Research and Analysis Project. They also include the Oxford Brookes University rules and regulations for the BSc degree and project. They can be viewed as definitive.

The remaining four sections contain Oxford Brookes advice and guidance to the student and project mentor on how to undertake and present a Research and Analysis Project. These sections include important information on the recommended structure and content of the Research Project and Skills and Learning Statement. I strongly recommend that students should read the Information Pack thoroughly before starting their project work.

I would be pleased to receive any comments that you may have about the content included in the BSc degree webpages and / or this Information Pack. I can be contacted at the email address on page 4.

John Woodley
ACCA Undergraduate Programme Director
Oxford Brookes Business School

Enquiries

If you have an enquiry concerning the BSc (Hons) in Applied Accounting degree or the Research and Analysis Project, please contact the ACCA office at Oxford Brookes University.

CCA Office
Oxford Brookes Business School
Wheatley Campus
Wheatley
Oxford OX33 1HX
United Kingdom

Email: acca@brookes.ac.uk

tel: +44 (0) 1865 485702
fax:+44 (0) 1865 485802

Copyright

© This Oxford Brookes University Information Pack is protected by copyright. No part of it may be reproduced, stored in a retrieval system or transmitted in any form or by any means, electronic, mechanical, photocopied or otherwise, without the written permission of Oxford Brookes Business School.

However, an ACCA registered student and his / her project mentor may download one copy each from the ACCA website for their personal use.

Section 1 Aims and outcomes of BSc (Hons) in Applied Accounting degree

The principal aim of the BSc degree programme is to widen access to Oxford Brookes University (OBU) and enable ACCA students across the world the opportunity to obtain an OBU degree.

The BSc degree aims to enhance and extend the knowledge and skills gained by you in your professional studies, and to improve your effectiveness as a professional accountancy student and future finance professional.

On completing the degree programme, you will have demonstrated a capability to:

Knowledge and understanding

K1   Critically evaluate accounting concepts and principles and their application in solutions to practical accounting problems.

K2   Prepare financial statements of entities, including groups of companies, using relevant financial information, accounting techniques and standards; and to analyse and interpret such financial statements.

K3   Use relevant management accounting techniques with cost information, for planning, decision-making, performance evaluation and control, within different business settings.

K4   Apply financial management techniques to issues affecting investment, financing, and dividend policy decisions of an organisation.

K5   Understand the general legal framework, and apply specific legal principles relating to business, including taxation legislation as applicable to individuals, single companies and groups of companies.

K6   Explain the process of carrying out the assurance (audit) engagement and its application in the context of the professional (audit) regulatory framework.

K7   Describe the organisational context of the accountant and of the development of accounting information systems; to understand the need for the efficient use of resources within an organisation.

K8   Understand the ethical responsibilities of professional accountants, including the principles of the ACCA code of conduct, and to reflect on ethical dilemmas and potential solutions.

Disciplinary and professional skills

D1   Prepare non-complex financial statements using generally accepted accounting principles.

D2   Evaluate and comment on the performance and financial situation of organisations using a range of interpretative techniques.

D3   Select and apply appropriate accounting and financial management techniques to organisational business planning, decision-making and control.

D4   Understand the limitations of accounting techniques and the implications of such limitations.

D5   Understand the limitations of acquired knowledge of legal and taxation issues and recognise the need to seek further specialist advice where necessary.

D6   Communicate analysis of accounting and financial information and recommendations to a variety of different audiences.

Transferable Skills

T1   Solve problems through the identification of key issues, synthesis of information and analytical tools, and the presentation and critical evaluation of a range of options.

T2   Communicate appropriately in writing and through an oral presentation.

T3   Complete a programme of study through independent and self managed learning.

T4   Undertake an independent research project relating to a single organisation or industry sector.

T5   Prepare a written report which meets academic requirements of information collection and referencing of information sources.

T6   Use information technology to record and analyse financial data, to collect information from a range of sources and to present research findings.

T7   To reflect on the learning attained through completing the programme and its impact on future professional development and employment roles.

Section 2 Eligibility

To be awarded the BSc (Hons) in Applied Accounting you must:

- be registered with Oxford Brookes University ie opted-in to the BSc degree scheme before passing any of the three ACCA Fundamentals papers, F7, F8 and F9
- pass the three ACCA Fundamentals papers F7, F8 and F9 and pass other papers as required to successfully complete all nine Fundamentals level papers
- complete the ACCA Professional Ethics module
- complete and pass the Oxford Brookes University Research and Analysis Project
- complete the BSc degree scheme within 10 years of your initial registration onto the ACCA's professional qualification.

Please note that you must successfully complete the Fundamentals level exam papers, F1–F9, and complete the Professional Ethics module before submitting a Research and Analysis Project to Oxford Brookes University.

If you wish to enquire about your eligibility to complete the BSc degree, please contact the ACCA office at Oxford Brookes at acca@brookes.ac.uk. Please include your ACCA student registration number in any correspondence.

ACCA students who passed one or more ACCA professional scheme examinations before, or at, the June 2007 sitting are covered by the conversion arrangements given in Appendix 1.

Determination of class of degree

The class of BSc degree will be based on both:

- the ACCA average mark determined from the exam marks in the Fundamentals Skills papers (F4–F9)
- the grade achieved for the Research and Analysis Project.

The ACCA average mark will be calculated by taking the numerical average of the marks achieved in the Fundamentals Skills papers (F4–F9) that you have sat and passed.

Where the calculated average mark is not a whole number, the calculated average will be rounded up or down accordingly. If you have been given an exemption from any of the three papers F4–F6, no mark is available and so will not be included in the calculation of the ACCA average mark.

The class of degree for each combination of ACCA average mark and Research and Analysis Project grade is shown below.

ACCA average mark	Class of Degree			
	First	Upper Second	Lower Second	Third
68 or more	A, B, C	-	-	-
67	A, B	C	-	-
66	A	B, C	-	-
60-65	-	A, B, C	-	-
59	-	A, B	C	-
58	-	A	B, C	-
54-57	-	-	A, B, C	-
53	-	-	A, B	C
50-52	-	-	-	A, B, C

Examples

- A student with an ACCA average mark of 69 and a grade B for the Project will be awarded the BSc (Hons) in Applied Accounting with First Class Honours

- A student with an ACCA average mark of 67 and a grade C for the Project will be awarded the BSc (Hons) in Applied Accounting with Upper Second Class Honours

- A student with an ACCA average mark of 59 and a grade B for the Project will be awarded the BSc (Hons) in Applied Accounting with Upper Second Class Honours

- A student with an ACCA average mark of 55 and a grade A for the Project will be awarded the BSc (Hons) in Applied Accounting with Lower Second Class Honours

- A student with an ACCA average mark of 53 and a grade C for the Project will be awarded the BSc (Hons) in Applied Accounting with Third Class Honours.

Section 3 Programme regulations

Admission

The minimum academic entry requirements for registering on the BSc degree are two A Levels plus three GCSEs (grade C or above) in five separate subjects including Maths and English. Oxford Brookes University recognises a number of other qualifications which satisfy the minimum English language requirement, including a Pass in ACCA Paper F4, Corporate and Business Law. Further details can be obtained from the ACCA office at Oxford Brookes University.

If you registered with ACCA under the mature student entry route (MSER) and do not have an acceptable English Language qualification, you will be permitted to register for the BSc degree only after you have passed Paper F4, Corporate and Business Law.

If you are a CAT student, and have passed the CAT Advanced level exam papers, you meet all the entry requirements for the BSc degree.

Exemptions

As a registered student, you may be given exemptions from one or more of the nine ACCA specified exam papers. Exemption decisions are made by ACCA and ACCA exemption policy is periodically reviewed by Oxford Brookes University. However, if you wish to achieve the BSc degree you must sit and pass all of the three ACCA subjects F7, F8 and F9.

No exemption can be given from the Professional Ethics Module or from the Oxford Brookes University Research and Analysis Project (RAP).

Progression

When you register with ACCA to undertake the ACCA Qualification, you are automatically registered with Oxford Brookes University for the BSc (Hons) in Applied Accounting, unless you opted-out of the BSc degree programme at the time of initially registering with ACCA.

If you have opted-put, you may re-register for the BSc degree scheme provided you have not passed any of the three subjects – F7, F8 and F9. If you have passed any one of these three subjects you cannot then register on to the BSc degree.

Conversion arrangements have been developed for completion of the BSc degree if you have passed one or more ACCA professional scheme exams by, or at, the June 2007 ACCA exam sitting.

Oxford Brookes University Research and Analysis Project

You must pass or be exempt from the ACCA Fundamentals exams, including sitting and passing all of F7, F8 and F9, and complete the Professional Ethics module before submitting a RAP to Oxford Brookes University.

You will need to find a project mentor to assist you with your RAP, by providing guidance and advice on your RAP and also to verify that you made an oral presentation at the end of your project research. Your project mentor should be a member of staff at an ACCA tuition provider, your line manager or an ACCA qualified member. Please note that this is different role to the role of the workplace mentor you need when completing your practical experience requirements, although you may find that your line manager is the most appropriate person to fulfil both these roles.

Oxford Brookes University has two four-week submission periods each year during which you may submit an OBU RAP. An OBU RAP that is submitted after the end of a submission period will be returned unmarked to you, but it may be resubmitted in the following submission period.

You are required to pay a project submission fee to Oxford Brookes with any project submission. After 1 August 2008, the OBU RAP submission fee will initially be £75 per project submission, though it may be subject to increase in subsequent submission periods.

RAP Submission periods

The next two RAP submission periods, and the dates on which RAP grades and BSc degree results will be despatched, are as follows:

Period 17

Earliest receipt of RAP by Oxford Brookes University	Monday 8 September 2008
Latest receipt of RAP by Oxford Brookes University	Friday 3 October 2008
Oxford Brookes University BSc Examination Board	January 2009
RAP and BSc degree results despatched	Wednesday 4 February 2009

Period 18

Earliest receipt of RAP by Oxford Brookes University	Monday 9 March 2009
Latest receipt of RAP by Oxford Brookes University	Friday 3 April 2009
Oxford Brookes University BSc Examination Board	July 2009
RAP and BSc degree results despatched	Wednesday 29 July 2009

Please note that projects must arrive at the ACCA Office in Oxford Brookes University by the date of latest receipt. Any projects received after the date of latest receipt will be returned to students unmarked.

Students should make appropriate arrangements with postal services to ensure that their project arrives by the submission deadline.

Section 4 Oxford Brookes policies, rules and regulations

You are subject to the following Oxford Brookes University policies, rules and regulations for the preparation, submission and assessment of the Research and Analysis Project and for the award of the BSc (Hons) in Applied Accounting degree. Further details can be found at http://www.brookes.ac.uk/regulations/acadregs1.htm!

Equal opportunities

Please visit the Oxford Brookes website for details of the University's equal opportunities policy. If you have special requirements for completing the Oxford Brookes Research and Analysis Project you should contact the ACCA office at Oxford Brookes University.

Academic appeals

You may not appeal against the academic judgement of an examiner.

You may request a review of the decision to award a particular grade to your Research and Analysis Project. However disagreement with the academic judgement of an examiner is not grounds for such a review, which would normally only consider whether the assessment has been conducted in accordance with the RAP regulations. Further details of the regulations can be viewed on the Oxford Brookes University website.

Complaints procedure

Please visit the Oxford Brookes University website to view the complaints procedure.

Disciplinary procedures

As a student who prepares and submits a Research and Analysis Project, you are subject to the Oxford Brookes University academic regulations, including those on cheating. The details of the regulations can be viewed on the Oxford Brookes University website. The University's Cheating statement, published by the University's Academic Registrar, is reproduced below.

Cheating

All assessments are intended to determine the skills, abilities, understanding and knowledge of each of the individual students undertaking the assessment. Cheating is defined as obtaining an unfair academic advantage and any student found using any form of cheating, attempting to cheat or assisting someone else to cheat may be subject to disciplinary action in accordance with the University's Disciplinary Procedure. The University takes this issue very seriously and students have been expelled or had their degrees withheld for cheating in assessments. If you are having difficulty with your work it is important to seek help from your tutor rather than be tempted to use unfair means to gain marks. Do not risk losing your degree and all the work you have done.

The University's regulations define a number of different forms of cheating, although any form of cheating is strictly forbidden. These are:

- **submitting other people's work as your own** – either with or without their knowledge. This includes copying in examinations; using notes or unauthorised materials in examinations

- **impersonation** – taking an assessment on behalf of or pretending to be another student, or allowing another person to take an assessment on your behalf or pretend to be you

- **plagiarism** – taking or using another person's thoughts, writings or inventions as your own. To avoid plagiarism you must make sure that quotations from whatever source must be clearly identified and attributed at the point where they occur in the text of your work by using one of the standard conventions for referencing. The Library has a leaflet about how to reference your work correctly and your tutor can also help you. It is not enough just to list sources in a bibliography at the end of your essay or dissertation if you do not acknowledge the actual quotations in the text.

Neither is it acceptable to change some of the words or the order of sentences if, by failing to acknowledge the source properly, you give the impression that it is your own work

- **collusion** – except where written instructions specify that work for assessment may be produced jointly and submitted as the work of more than one student, you must not collude with others to produce a piece of work jointly, copy or share another student's work or lend your work to another student in the reasonable knowledge that some or all of it will be copied

- **duplication** – submitting work for assessment that is the same as, or broadly similar to, work submitted earlier for academic credit, without acknowledgement of the previous submission

- **falsification** – the invention of data, its alteration, its copying from any other source, or otherwise obtaining it by unfair means, or inventing quotations and/or references.

Section 5 Research and Analysis Project learning outcomes

The Research and Analysis Project (RAP) is the final component of the BSc degree and consists of two separate documents; a 6,500 word Research Project (RP) and a 2,000 word Skills and Learning Statement (SLS). You are also required to give a presentation on the project to your project mentor.

The learning outcomes of the OBU RAP are achieved through your experience of undertaking a research based project related to a single organisation. The learning outcomes are achieved through completing the two components of the OBU RAP; the Research Project (RP) and the Skills and Learning Statement (SLS). There is no syllabus for the OBU RAP and none of the learning outcomes are based on direct teaching by OBU staff.

The purpose of the OBU RAP is to allow you to demonstrate certain specific **transferable skills** of the BSc degree programme:

T4 Undertake an independent research project relating to a single organisation or industry sector.

T5 Prepare a written report which meets academic requirements of information collection and referencing of information sources.

T6 Use information technology to record and analyse financial data, to collect information from a range of sources and to present research findings.

T7 To reflect on the learning attained through completing the programme and its impact on future professional development and employment roles.

And to use the experience gained by undertaking the OBU RAP to contribute to the development of other BSc programme capabilities:

Knowledge and understanding

K1 Critically evaluate accounting concepts and principles and their application in solutions to practical accounting problems.

Disciplinary and professional skills

D3 Select and apply appropriate accounting and financial management techniques to organisational business planning, decision-making and control.

D4 Understand the limitations of accounting techniques and the implications of such limitations.

D6 Communicate analysis of accounting and financial information and recommendations to a variety of different audiences.

Transferable Skills

T1   Solve problems through the identification of key issues, synthesis of information and analytical tools, and the presentation and critical evaluation of a range of options.

T2   Communicate appropriately in writing and through an oral presentation.

T3   Complete a programme of study through independent and self managed learning.

Section 6 Assessment of Research and Analysis Project

The Research and Analysis Project (RAP) is the final component of the BSc degree and consists of two separate documents; a 6,500 word Research Project (RP) and a 2,000 word Skills and Learning Statement (SLS). You are also required to give a presentation on the project to your project mentor.

You have three attempts to pass the RAP. Unfortunately, if you fail the RAP on three separate occasions you will no longer be eligible to complete the BSc degree. Please note that you can either submit the same project topic three times or three different RAPs.

To pass the RAP you must pass **both** the Research Project (RP) **and** the Skills and Learning Statement (SLS). If you do not pass both components separately within the same RAP submission you will be awarded a Fail grade for the RAP.

You will be given one of three Pass grades (A, B or C) or a Fail grade (F) for the performance in the RP. You will be given either a 'Satisfactory' grade or an 'Unsatisfactory' grade for the performance in the SLS.

If you achieve one of the three Pass grades for the RP **and** the 'Satisfactory' grade for the SLS, then a pass in the RAP will be awarded. The grade awarded to you for the performance in the RAP will be that awarded to you for the RP ie A, B or C. Once you have been awarded one of the three Pass grades for the RAP, then you cannot make any further RAP submissions.

If you are awarded either a Fail grade in the RP or an Unsatisfactory grade in the SLS, then you will be awarded a Fail grade for the RAP. If you are awarded a Fail grade on the first RAP submission you will be allowed up to two further RAP submissions.

The assessment of the Research Project is as follows. This demonstrates the importance of the quality of the understanding of the accountancy / business models used in the RP and their application to the RAP project topic. The student's "graduate" skills will be assessed for a level of competence.

To achieve a pass in the RP a student must gain one of the three Pass grades (A, B or C) for the "Technical and Professional Skills" and demonstrate Competence in the "Graduate Skills". The grade for a student who passes the RP is that awarded for the Technical and Professional Skills component of the RP.

	Learning Outcome	Assessment
Technical and Professional Skills		*Grade A, B, C or F*
Understanding of accountancy / business models	K1	
Application of accountancy / business models	D3	
Evaluation of information, analysis and conclusions	T1	
Presentation of project findings	D6	
Graduate Skills		*Competence / Non-competence*
Communication	T2	
Information gathering and referencing	T5	
Information technology	T6	
Research Project assessment		*Grade A, B, C or F*

The assessment of the Skills and Learning Statement is as follows. It considers whether a student has demonstrated competence in the "graduate" skills of self-reflection and communication skills (specifically, the preparation and delivery of a presentation to the student's project mentor). To achieve a pass in the SLS a student must demonstrate competence in both self-reflection and communication skills.

	Learning Outcome	Assessment
Graduate Skills		*Competence*
Self Reflection	T7	
Communication Skills (Including Presentation)	T2	
Skills and Learning Statement assessment		*Satisfactory / Unsatisfactory*

The full assessment criteria for both the Research Project and the Skills and Learning Statement are given in Appendix 2.

Section 7 Research and Analysis Project resubmission

The following rules will apply to RAP resubmissions:

- If you do not pass the RAP after a third submission, unfortunately you will no longer be eligible to complete the BSc (Hons) in Applied Accounting degree

- The requirements to pass the RAP on the second or third submission are the same as those for passing the RAP at the first attempt

- If you pass the RP at the first attempt, but are awarded an 'Unsatisfactory' grade in the SLS, you cannot submit a revised RP in any further RAP submission. Only a revised SLS can be presented in any further RAP submission

- If you pass the RP at the first attempt, but are awarded an 'Unsatisfactory' grade in the SLS, you will carry forward the RP grade awarded in the first attempt (A, B or C) to a second or third submission

- If you fail the RP on the first submission you will be awarded a grade C for any successful subsequent RP, even if the resubmitted RP is initially assessed as being of a higher pass grade.

The impact of these rules are summarised in the two tables below.

Research Project grade	SLS grade	Overall RAP grade	Grade on successful RP resubmission
A	Satisfactory	A	Not applicable
B	Satisfactory	B	Not applicable
C	Satisfactory	C	Not applicable
F	Satisfactory	F	C

Research Project grade	SLS grade	Overall RAP grade	Grade on successful SLS resubmission	Grade on successful RP and successful SLS resubmission
A	Unsatisfactory	F	A	Not applicable
B	Unsatisfactory	F	B	Not applicable
C	Unsatisfactory	F	C	Not applicable
F	Unsatisfactory	F	Not applicable	C

Section 8 Project Mentor meetings

The Role of the Project Mentor

If you wish to submit a Research and Analysis Project (RAP) to Oxford Brookes then you must have a Project Mentor. The Project Mentor has two different roles. The first which is focused on you is to support your preparation of your RAP, by providing advice and feedback to you at appropriate times during your RAP activities.

Secondly, the Project Mentor will confirm to Oxford Brookes that he or she has been your Project Mentor and that your RAP is your own work. Your Project Mentor will certify this on your RAP submission form and Oxford Brookes will check a sample of Project Mentor certifications.

You will have three meetings with your Project Mentor. These meetings provide your Project Mentor with the opportunity to guide your RAP work and provide feedback to you. The meetings also provide you with the opportunity to develop your personal skills including questioning, listening and giving a presentation. You will reflect on this graduate skills development in your Skills and Learning Statement.

Your Project Mentor is not expected to have specialist knowledge within your project topic area or of academic research methods. Your Project Mentor does not play any part in the assessment of your RAP beyond the certification provided to Oxford Brookes. You should not have to ask your Project Mentor what you have to do to pass – this is given in the assessment criteria for the RAP. You should not expect your Project Mentor to give you detailed advice on the structure and content of your Research Project or to write any of your RAP for you. Those decisions and actions are solely your own responsibility.

However it will be very helpful for your Project Mentor to understand what is required of you to prepare your RAP to the highest standard of which you are capable. You should provide your Project Mentor with as much information as you think useful about the Oxford Brookes Research and Analysis Project and what is required of you. This could include the contents of this document.

Your Project Mentor should encourage you to think about what you propose to do in your RAP work, challenge you to demonstrate that you are meeting your project objectives and that you will be able to meet your timetable for submission of your RAP to Oxford Brookes. Your Project Mentor may also ask you to demonstrate your understanding of the issues that have arisen during your research, and may wish to question you on your conclusions and recommendations.

Choosing your Project Mentor

It is your responsibility to find someone to act as your Project Mentor and to arrange three meetings with him or her. It is not possible for Oxford Brookes to provide a Project Mentor for you but Oxford Brookes has identified three categories of individuals from which you should choose your Project Mentor.

The person you choose should be one of the following:

- Your tutor at College or University
- A senior colleague at work e.g. your line manager
- A qualified Chartered Certified Accountant.

If you identify somebody as a potential Project Mentor who does not fall into any of these three categories, then you should contact the ACCA office at Oxford Brookes and provide a copy of your suggested Project Mentor's CV for approval. If the proposed Project Mentor is a member of a recognised professional body or institute and / or holds a recognised degree equivalent qualification then it is likely that approval will be given.

Oxford Brookes has identified the following characteristics of an effective Project Mentor. You may wish to reflect on this list of attributes when making your own choice of Project Mentor.

- Is approachable and has genuine interest in helping student to succeed

- Listens and actively questions

- Respects confidentiality and is trustworthy

- Acts as a sounding board to explore ideas and issues arising from research

- Provides positive and constructive feedback on research being carried out

- Challenges and discusses effective communication

- Offers support and encouragement

- Helps the student meet their objectives

- Helps the student ask the right questions, to think systematically, to learn to apply appropriate evaluation techniques and to analyse and interpret the findings

- Remains neutral and not judgmental

- Provides subtle guidance but ensures student makes the decisions

- Is knowledgeable and competent

- Grasps the essence of the technicalities without becoming a subject matter expert.

Meetings with your Project Mentor

Oxford Brookes requires that you have at least three meetings with your Project Mentor, each of which would normally be about 30 minutes in length. If your Project Mentor agrees, you could have additional meetings, or longer meetings, but you should negotiate this before you start your RAP work. We suggest a framework for the three meetings below.

The Project Mentor meetings should focus not only on the planning and research needed to prepare a good Research and Analysis Project (RAP), but also on the opportunity for you to develop skills in listening, questioning and presenting your findings. We suggest that your planning for each meeting includes the preparation of an agenda of issues which can be covered in the time available to you. Focus on the key issues and identify the desired outcomes from the meeting. Take notes to record the actions needed to progress your Research Project and to contribute to your reflection for your Skills and Learning Statement.

The first meeting – planning and your RAP title

Before your first Project Mentor meeting you should identify possible project topic areas and / or the organisation that you wish to study. You should also think about the way in which you plan to undertake your research work and prepare a draft RAP timetable.

Remember that to get the best out of your Project Mentor, you need to give your Project Mentor some of your ideas so that they can provide you with some useful feedback. Give your Project Mentor sufficient time to read what you have written and be ready to give clarification of your ideas.

You can use the first meeting to discuss your possible choices of topic area and project objectives with your Project Mentor. It is very important to have a clear idea of the aims and objectives of your RAP at the beginning of your research work. This will determine how you collect information and how you evaluate data. Getting a robust structure within which the project research will be conducted is crucial to your success.

Your Project Mentor may focus on the following issues in the first meeting:

- Have you a clear view of what you want to do?
- Are your project ideas realistic given your previous learning?
- Do you know how you will undertake your research?
- Is your information gathering approach robust?
- How will you demonstrate your analytical and evaluative skills?
- Is your RAP timetable realistic?

Your desired outcomes from the first meeting may include the following:

- An agreed Research and Analysis Project title
- Clarification of your Research Project aims and objectives
- An agreed approach to undertaking your project research
- A robust and realistic timetable for completing your Research and Analysis Project
- Reflection on your personal skills for your Skills and Learning Statement.

The second meeting – Research Project progress update

The second meeting is the opportunity for you to get feedback from your Project Mentor on the indicative findings of your Research Project. Before the second meeting you should have gathered your information and data and done some evaluation to give you some insight into how well you are meeting your Research Project aims and objectives.

You should provide an update on your progress to your Project Mentor. This could include a word-processed document with the structure of your finished Research Project. This draft report could include the early chapters covering aims and objectives, why you have chosen to apply particular accounting or business techniques and how you have chosen to undertake the project research. Your findings may be provisional at this point but such a document will give your Project Mentor a very clear idea of your progress.

Your Project Mentor may focus on the following issues in the second meeting:

- Does your written work contribute towards meeting your aims and objectives?
- Does your written work meet the Research Project assessment criteria?
- Have you been able to do everything you planned?
- If you have had to change your approach, is it still consistent with your objectives?
- Is your evaluation of information and data in sufficient depth?
- What further work do you still have to undertake?
- Are you still confident that you will meet your RAP deadline?

Your desired outcomes from the second meeting may include the following:

- Reassurance that your Research Project is progressing well
- You are confident that you are fulfilling the Research Project assessment criteria
- You can identify changes that you will make following your Project Mentor feedback
- You can identify possible improvements to the quality of your work to date
- You feel confident that you know what else is required of you to complete the RAP
- Realisation that you are able to meet your RAP timetable
- Reflection on your personal skills for your Skills and Learning Statement.

The third meeting – the presentation

By the time you get to the third meeting, you should have completed your research and nearly finished writing your Research Project. You should provide a copy of your draft Research Project to your Project Mentor before the third meeting. This meeting includes a 15 minute presentation that you give to your Project Mentor and perhaps also to other students who have undertaken their own RAP.

You will need to investigate how to prepare an effective presentation, using PowerPoint or overhead slides. A copy of your presentation must be submitted as part of your Skills and Learning Statement. You will also gain experience of giving a presentation to an audience and responding to questions.

Your Project Mentor may focus on the following issues in the third meeting:

- Is the content of the presentation consistent with the Research Project findings?

- How effective was the presentation? Did it make sense?

- Are there satisfactory links between the different parts of the project, from objectives through to findings and conclusions?

- Is the quality of the analysis and evaluation sufficient to meet the required standard?

- If you were to do the RAP again, what might you do differently?

- Given the feedback and questions, will you make any changes to your Research Project before it is submitted to Oxford Brookes?

Your desired outcomes from the third meeting may include the following:

- You are confident that you have produced a good Research Project which meets the assessment criteria

- You can identify further improvements to the quality of your Research Project

- Reflection on your presentation skills for your Skills and Learning Statement

- You have the required presentation to include in your Skills and Learning Statement.

Following the third meeting you will finalise your Research Project and Skills and Learning Statement. You will submit the completed Research and Analysis Project to Oxford Brookes. Your Project Mentor will be required to complete a section of the Oxford Brookes RAP submission form, so you may wish to have a copy of the RAP submission form available for your Project Mentor to sign at the third meeting if this is both convenient and acceptable for your Project Mentor.

Contribution to Skills and Learning Statement

You are required to respond to four different questions in the preparation of your Skills and Learning Statement. Two of these are directly related to your meetings with your Project Mentor:

- 'What did you learn from the meetings with your project mentor, including the presentation that you gave to your project mentor?'

- 'How have you demonstrated your interpersonal and communication skills during the project work?'

To pass the Skills and Learning Statement you have to show your ability to reflect on judgments that you have made and / or actions that you have taken during your project work. You also have to provide evidence that you recognise your own strengths and weaknesses.

It is very important that you think carefully about what you want to achieve in each of the three meetings. It is equally important to reflect after each meeting on what happened during the meeting and how effective you were in meeting your meeting objectives. If you make a note after each meeting, or keep a personal diary of reflections, then you will have developed some content for possible later use in your Skills and Learning Statement.

Section 9 Research and Analysis Project preparation

Introduction

The Oxford Brookes Research and Analysis Project (RAP) is the final component of the Oxford Brookes University BSc (Hons) in Applied Accounting degree. To reach this stage of the BSc degree you have already successfully completed at least nine demanding ACCA professional exams.

You have already demonstrated your undergraduate level abilities by passing the ACCA exams; the RAP provides you with the opportunity to demonstrate the remaining graduate level attributes necessary for the award of the BSc degree. Please read the RAP learning outcomes and assessment criteria carefully before you start your RAP work. This will help you understand what is expected of an ACCA student who wishes to submit a RAP to Oxford Brookes.

You should understand that your research work and preparation of the RAP is covered by the Oxford Brookes University academic regulations. This includes the University's regulations on cheating which can be found elsewhere in this document. If an ACCA student or member is found guilty of breaching these regulations this could lead to permanent expulsion from Oxford Brookes University and disciplinary action by ACCA.

In particular, your submitted RAP must be your own work and your research must have been undertaken specifically for the RAP. You cannot take a workplace research or consultancy report and adapt it for your RAP. Neither can you submit a piece of research work that has previously been submitted to another educational institution for a different academic award.

The RAP is very different to an ACCA written exam. You have many choices to make in order to produce a good quality RAP. You have to choose which organisation to study, what you want to find out, which information sources you will use and how to present your research findings. Each RAP is different and there is no 'model' answer to your project objectives. Your research findings may depend on how you collect and analyse information, and your findings may not be wholly definitive. Your conclusions may be unexpected or not what you might have anticipated before starting the RAP work. This is the nature of applied research.

In order to produce a successful RAP you have to evaluate and / or analyse information from a range of sources. This means creating some meaning of what you have found, or making a judgement or coming to a conclusion. If you only report the information that you have found or generated, you will not pass the RAP. The ability to evaluate and / or analyse information is a very important graduate attribute and the grade that you are awarded for your RAP will be significantly influenced by 'how well' you demonstrate your evaluative and / or analytical skills in your RAP.

You may be one of the many ACCA students whose overall class of BSc degree will not be directly affected by the grade awarded to your RAP (provided you pass). However, a good performance in the RAP will demonstrate to your family, friends, colleagues, tutors and employers that you are capable of undertaking good quality research. If your ACCA average mark puts you in a position where achieving a high grade in the RAP will gain you a higher class of degree, then you must aim for your first project submission to be the highest quality research work of which you are capable. You cannot resubmit a passed RAP and the RAP grade will be capped for a resubmitted Research Project that originally failed.

Your RAP will focus on accounting and / or business issues within an organisation. It is very important to remember that the reported financial performance of an organisation – whether in the private or public sector – is the outcome of the organisation's business activities. A private sector company usually competes against other companies to sell its goods and services and its success in doing so is reflected in the company's financial statements and financial performance indicators. Therefore in order to explain why a company's financial performance has changed, you must look into the company's business environment and identify those actions taken by the company, its competitors, government etc which have led to changes in the company's business performance. To understand change, you may need to look outside of the organisation chosen for your RAP.

The remaining sections of the Information Pack provide further guidance on the preparation of your Research Project and your Skills and Learning Statement. However, there some other general issues that you should think about before starting your RAP work:

- The suggested RAP project topic areas are based on different aspects of the ACCA Qualification syllabus. The RAP is an opportunity for you to apply some of your learning from your ACCA exams. You may have to develop this learning in more depth to prepare a high quality RAP and this will enhance your knowledge and skills in accounting and business.

- You should consider your own strengths and weaknesses when considering what to do for your RAP. If you prefer financial accounting to management accounting, then would it be better to choose a RAP topic which is based on financial reporting? Or do you want to improve your knowledge and skills in your weak areas? If you want to use advanced statistical techniques, then do you really understand how to apply them and to explain the output in business terms?

- Your RAP must have a single organisation as its focus. However you do not have to work for an organisation in order to choose it for your RAP. If there are substantial external information sources for you to undertake a RAP then you may not need to contact individuals within your chosen organisation. If you are working for an organisation, then you may, if you wish, choose your own organisation as the basis for your RAP. However be sure that necessary internal information will be made available to you and can be included in your project report.

- Do not start your research work without having spent some time thinking about what you propose to do, how you propose to do it and when you propose to do it. Although Oxford Brookes does not require you to submit an RAP outline for approval, we strongly recommend that you prepare a short outline for your RAP and a timetable within which you show when you expect to complete the different phases of the research work and how you will meet the Oxford Brookes RAP submission deadline. Be realistic about what information may be available to you, what you can achieve and how long it may take you to complete the RAP documents.

- You must be independent and unbiased when undertaking research. You may think very favourably about a company and / or its products. However if you choose this company for your RAP you have an obligation to look at the range of differing views about the company that exists and to evaluate all of these views within your Research Project. You should not only use those information sources that support your own view of the company.

Please read all of the RAP information in this document before starting your RAP work. It is easier to make changes to your proposed project work before you have collected all of your information rather than to try to make significant changes when writing your Research Project and Skills and Learning Statement.

Research and Analysis Project topic areas and titles

If you intend to submit a Research and Analysis Project (RAP) to Oxford Brookes after 1 August 2008, Oxford Brookes strongly recommends that you should choose one of the following twenty approved project topic areas as the basis for your RAP.

1. An organisation's budgetary control system and its links with performance management and decision making

2. How the introduction of a new technology can assist an organisation in achieving its business objectives

3. The impact of an aspect of impending legislation on the operations and financial position of an organisation

4. The impact of e-business on an organisation

5. The effects of globalisation on an organisation

6. The key factors or indicators in the motivation of employees in an organisation

7. The restructuring of an organisation's operational activities and the effect on the organisation's financial performance

8. The business and financial performance of an organisation over a three year period

9. The planning and implementation of an information system in an organisation

10. The effectiveness of the use of costing techniques within an organisation

11. The financial and operational costs and benefits of the internal audit / internal review activities within an organisation

12. The possible effects of a proposed accounting standard on the financial statements and business activities of an organisation

13. The relationship between an organisation's human resources activities and its business objectives

14. The business and financial objectives of a strategic investment decision made by an organisation and its impact on key stakeholders

15.   The management of an organisation's working capital over a three year period and its impact on the organisation's funding strategies

16.   The financial and operational risk management within an organisation

17.   The quality of the corporate governance within an organisation and the impact on an organisation's key stakeholders

18.   The marketing strategy of an organisation and its effectiveness

19.   The financial and operational consequences of a merger between two organisations or of the acquisition of one organisation by another

20.   An organisation's corporate social responsibility policies, including business ethics, and their impact on business practice and key stakeholders.

Research and Analysis Project Title

Your RAP must be focused on one organisation. The main focus of your project research must be an analysis / evaluation of the project topic area issues in the context of your chosen organisation.

You should combine the analysis / evaluation requirement of the RAP with the project topic area and with your chosen organisation to produce your Research and Analysis Project Title.

For example, if you have chosen an organisation called 'OBU Co' for your research work, then some possible Research and Analysis Project titles are as follows:

- An analysis of the key factors that influence the levels of motivation of staff within OBU Co. (Topic 6)

- An evaluation of the business and financial performance of OBU Co between 1 January 2005 and 31 December 2007 (Topic 8)

- OBU Co: A case study for the evaluation of the use of different costing techniques in the pricing of consultancy services (Topic 10)

- A business and financial analysis of the entry of OBU Co into the market for online postgraduate degree courses and the impact on teachers and learners (Topic 14)

- An evaluation of the quality of corporate governance within OBU Co and the impact on OBU Co professionally qualified accountants. (Topic 17)

Your actual choice of project topic area and organisation will depend on the access you have to internal and external sources of information about the organisation. This is discussed elsewhere in this document.

Study of other project topic areas

If you believe that you face exceptional circumstances and cannot identify a suitable project from the list of approved project topic areas, then Oxford Brookes will consider your request to undertake a RAP based on a different area of your previous academic study.

However you must obtain permission from the ACCA office at Oxford Brookes before you start your RAP research work. You must provide an outline (minimum one page in length) of your proposed project research work, which includes the project title, the objectives of your research and how you will undertake your research to meet your objectives. The outline should also state how you will be able to demonstrate your evaluative and / or analytical skills. Please email acca@brookes.ac.uk with your one page outline and allow 10 working days for a response.

Section 10 Research Project

Before you start work on your Oxford Brookes Research Project, you should read all of the information included in these web pages. In particular it is important that you have a good understanding of, or have finalised, the following matters before you start your research work:

- What is expected of you in preparing your Research Project?
- How will your Research Project be assessed?
- Who will be your Project Mentor?
- How do you ensure that your Research Project submission reflects your full abilities?
- What is the link between the Research Project and the Skills and Learning Statement?
- How do you ensure that you do not breach the Oxford Brookes regulations on cheating?

The purpose of the Research Project is to give you an opportunity to demonstrate a range of *Technical and Professional Skills* in:

- Understanding of accountancy / business models
- Application of accountancy / business models
- Evaluation of information, analysis and conclusions
- Presentation of project findings

and *Graduate Skills* in:

- Communication
- Information gathering and referencing
- Information technology

All of these make a significant contribution to the learning outcomes of the BSc (Hons) in Applied Accounting degree programme. You will demonstrate this range of skills by applying some of your previous ACCA learning in an approved project topic area to a specific, identified organisation. There is a maximum of 6,500 words for the Research Project.

In this section we provide some guidance on how you could proceed to undertake your project work. We also give a recommended structure for your Research Project which should ensure that you have provided sufficient evidence for Oxford Brookes to come to a judgement in each of the assessment criteria for the Research Project.

The Oxford Brookes recommendations are not the only way in which a Research Project could be undertaken. It is your decision as to how you manage your project work and produce your Research Project. However in doing so you must be aware of how your Research Project will be assessed. If you do not include content which is relevant to one or more of the Research Project assessment criteria then you risk not meeting the required standards. Similarly, if you include content that is not relevant, then you risk not providing sufficient evidence for Oxford Brookes to assess your abilities under one or more of the assessment criteria.

There are a number of issues that you must consider before you start your Research Project as they could have a significant impact on both the way in which you develop your project objectives and research questions and how you conduct your research activities.

Information gathering

Every Research Project requires information as the basis for analysis. Information sources can be categorised as either primary or secondary data. There is no requirement for you to collect primary data within your Research Project; it is wholly acceptable to undertake your Research Project using only secondary data. The difference between primary and secondary data is identified below.

Primary data is original data that has been collected by a researcher by whatever means appropriate in the answer of a specific research question. i.e. it has been collected specifically for the Research Project. Examples of primary data include questionnaires, interviews, e-mail contacts and surveys.

If you decide to collect primary data as part of your research work, then you should state and justify the following:

The data collection techniques you intend to use e.g. questionnaires, interviews.

Your sample size and an outline of your sampling strategy.

The method you will use to select your sample and the likely response rate.

If you intend to collect primary data from staff within your chosen organisation you must obtain permission to do this from a senior member of staff within the organisation. You should do this as early as possible during your Research Project, since if you are denied access to your desired information sources you may have to reconsider how to meet your project objectives and research questions.

Secondary data is data that has been collected by others for their own purposes, but which may be used by a researcher for his or her different purposes. Examples of secondary data include reference material, books, CD ROMs and financial statements. You should always evaluate the appropriateness and relevance of secondary data sources. Information included in internet sources may not be reliable from an academic perspective and may not be appropriate for use in your Research Project.

If you decide to use secondary data as part of your research work, you should state and justify your choice to do so. Where you use published secondary data you must provide precise references using the Harvard Referencing System. This is discussed in more detail in the following section.

You must retain all of the information that you collect during your project research work until you have received official notification of your RAP grade from Oxford Brookes. This includes any questionnaire responses, copies of financial statements, extracts from journals, reports, magazines etc. Oxford Brookes may wish to ask you to provide additional evidence of your information gathering following the marking of your Research and Analysis Project.

Referencing of information sources

You are required to reference information sources in your Research Project. This is part of the graduate skills that you must demonstrate in preparing your Research Project.

Referencing is essential for the following reasons:

- To acknowledge other people's ideas.
- To allow the reader of your work to locate the cited references easily, and so evaluate your interpretation of those ideas.
- To avoid plagiarism (i.e. taking other people's thoughts, ideas or writings and using them as though they are your own).
- To show evidence of the breadth and depth of your reading.

You must use the **Harvard Referencing System** for your referencing in your Research Project. This system and how you apply it to individual references in the text of your Research Report, and the preparation of your 'List of References' at the end of your Research Project, is explained in the following Oxford Brookes University document.

"A guide to citing and referencing for Business School students". This can be found on the BSc degree webpages. A brief introduction to referencing is given in Appendix 3.

You should read the Oxford Brookes document very carefully. You must comply with its requirements to demonstrate your graduate skills in information gathering and referencing. If you identify the correct reference for every source that you use, at the time that you first identify the source, then it will be straightforward to prepare your list of references when you complete your research work.

Research ethics

Oxford Brookes University requires all students undertaking research to comply with the University's Code of Practice 'Ethical Standards for Research involving Human Participants'. This document is available on the BSc degree webpages. Before starting your Research Project you should consider the following questions:

- Does your proposed research involve any of the following:

    – Deception of participants,
    – Financial inducements,
    – Possible psychological stress,
    – Access to confidential information,
    – Any other special circumstances?

    If you have answered 'yes' to any of the issues identified above, how will you deal with these issues?

    - Are you likely to need to preserve participants' anonymity and/or confidentiality?
      If you have answered 'yes', how do you intend to do this?

Even if your Research Project will only use secondary data sources and will not involve any interaction with staff within your chosen organisation, you should still read the University's Code of Practice to ensure that you understand the possible ethical issues associated with undertaking research.

Confidentiality and anonymity

In principle, Oxford Brookes University requires your Research Project to contain full details of the organisation that you have investigated in your research, the information sources that you used and the actual data that you collected. This provides reassurance to Oxford Brookes about the originality and the genuineness of the information gathering and analysis in your Research Project.

We have already noted that if you intend to collect primary data from staff within your chosen organisation you must obtain permission to do this from a senior member of staff within the organisation. However, although you may gain such permission, the organisation may request that your research findings remain confidential because of concerns over confidentiality and / or commercial sensitivity.

If you want your Research Project to be considered as confidential or to make specific adjustments to the organisation's data in order to hide the 'true figures' then you must write to the BSc programme director at acca@brookes.ac.uk and request permission. You should give the reasons behind your request and how you intend to resolve such issues in the preparation and presentation of your Research Project. In your request you will have to identify the organisation which is the focus of your Research Project. The BSc programme director will decide whether to give approval to your request.

This issue must be resolved before you submit your Research Project to Oxford Brookes otherwise your project will be returned to you unmarked. Any such correspondence between yourself and the BSc programme director will not be passed on to the Oxford Brookes staff involved in the marking of your Research Project.

Information Technology

As part of your demonstration of graduate skills you have to show reasonable evidence of having accessed online information sources and having used a spreadsheet and / or other software in preparing your Research Project.

It is important that you consider how you will meet this requirement in your initial planning for your Research Project. Your choice of information sources may be influenced by this requirement and you should carefully consider the possible impact on your project objectives and research questions.

You have to word process your Research Project document and this contributes towards meeting this requirement. However Oxford Brookes also needs evidence of the use of other software used to process data. For example, this could be done by using a spreadsheet to prepare financial ratios / performance indicators or by the preparation of graphs / tables / pie charts from a database that records questionnaire findings. You should include sample printouts of spreadsheet formulae or database queries to illustrate how you processed your data.

As part of your Skills and Learning Statement, you may wish to reflect on how you have used your existing IT skills or how they have been improved by doing your project research work.

Preparing your Research Project

Oxford Brookes has prepared a process model which identifies the key activities and their timing in undertaking the Research Project. It also shows links to the meetings with your Project Mentor. You do not have to follow this approach but we stress the importance of preparing a plan for how you will undertake your research and prepare your Research Project by the deadline that you have set yourself. This Oxford Brookes process model can be found in Appendix 4.

Structure, word count and presentation

The word limit for your Research Project is 6,500 words. Oxford Brookes recommends the following structure and approximate word distribution for your Research Project. We believe that this will allow you to demonstrate all of the required technical and professional skills, and graduate skills in sufficient depth.

TITLE PAGE

CONTENTS PAGE

PART 1 – Project objectives and overall research approach – 1,000 words

The first part of your Research Project 'sets the scene' It should include the following:

- The reasons for choosing your project topic area and choosing the particular organisation that was the focus of your research work

- What you wanted to find out in your research work. i.e. your project objectives and research questions

- An explanation of your overall research approach. This should provide the reader with a understanding of the overall framework that you developed to meet your project objectives and answer your research questions.

PART 2 – Information gathering and accounting / business techniques – 1,500 words

The second part of your Research Project should provide more detail about (i) the information that you have gathered and (ii) the accounting and business techniques you have chosen to apply to this information. It should include the following:

- The sources of information from which you have obtained relevant data

- A description of the methods used to collect information, including online access

- A discussion of the limitations of your information gathering

- Identification of any ethical issues that arose during your information gathering and how they were resolved

- An explanation of the accounting and / or business techniques you have used, including a discussion of their limitations.

PART 3 – Results, analysis, conclusions and recommendations – 4,000 words

The third part of your Research Project should provide a detailed account of what you have found from the application of your chosen accounting and business techniques to the information that you have gathered. It should include:

- A description of the results you have obtained and any limitations

- Presentation of your results in an appropriate form e.g. tables, graphs, pie charts

- A critical analysis / evaluation of your results which includes an explanation of your significant findings

- Your conclusions about your research findings and how well you have met your project objectives and research questions

- If appropriate, recommendations on specific courses of action to identified individuals within your chosen organisation.

LIST OF REFERENCES

APPENDICES

Word count and appendices

You must stay within the specified maximum word count. Oxford Brookes University reserves the right to fail Research Projects which contain more than the maximum 6,500 words. You will be asked to declare your word count of your project on the Oxford Brookes RAP submission form.

The 6,500 word limit excludes the Title Page, the Contents Page, the List of References and the Appendices. Words used in tables and graphs and other forms of data presentation are not included in the word count. However, words used in section headings are included in the word count.

If you choose approved topic area 8 'The business and financial performance of an organisation over a three year period' then it is likely that you will use the published financial statements of the organisation as an information source. You must include appropriate extracts from the organisation's financial statements in either the main text of the Research Project or as an Appendix. However, these extracts are not included in the word count.

You should use appendices only for supporting data and information. You should not include written text that properly belongs in the main body of your Research Project. You should keep the number of appendices as low as possible and no more than 8 sides excluding any extracts from financial statements.

Presentation

Your Research Project must be word processed using A4 size pages. You should use black text on a white background. Avoid background graphics or pictures behind the text and remember that italics and heavy bold type are less easy to read.

You should use an appropriate standard business font such as Arial with a font size of 11 or 12. You may use a larger font size for section headings. We recommend a maximum of 1.5 line spacing. When using a spelling and grammar checker, be careful to ensure that you do not unintentionally change the meaning of your text.

Oxford Brookes does not wish to prescribe all of the different aspects of presenting your Research Report and you should identify best practice in business report writing as part of your information gathering activities.

Section 11 Skills and Learning Statement

The Skills and Learning Statement (SLS) is the opportunity for you to demonstrate that you have developed the key 'graduate' skills of self-reflection and communication. You will provide evidence of self-reflection by answering a number of questions. Your communication skills will be developed through the preparation and delivery of a presentation to your Project Mentor. You will submit a copy of the PowerPoint presentation or overhead slides that you used in your presentation to your Project Mentor as evidence of skills development.

Your SLS must be based on the following four questions:

* What did you learn from the meetings with your Project Mentor, including the presentation that you gave to your Project Mentor?

* How well do you think that you have answered your research question(s)?

* How have you demonstrated your interpersonal and communication skills during the project work?

* How has undertaking the RAP helped you in your accountancy studies and/or current employment role?

What do we mean by reflection?

Self reflection, or critical reflection as it may also be called, is a key academic and professional skill. Reflection requires you to review and evaluate the experiences you have had and the learning you have acquired. You should note the emphasis on evaluation. Your Skills and Learning Statement should not be a description of what you did – it must be an evaluation of your experiences of doing your project work. You must try to make some meaning of what you have experienced, and make a judgement of how well you have achieved your objectives, and come to a conclusion about the value of undertaking your RAP.

Your evaluation should be honest. There is no model answer or right answer to any of these four questions. Not all your experiences will necessarily be positive, as things may not always go to plan or happen in the way that you might want them. Your evaluation should reflect on what actually happened, not an idealised version of what you might want Oxford Brookes to think did happen. We know that applied research can be messy and unsatisfying at times, though we strongly believe that what you learn from doing this research will be valuable to you. We hope this will be reflected in your Skills and Learning Statement.

Preparing your SLS answers

An important aspect of study or working life is to actively evaluate your own performance and to identify your own personal development needs. Have you achieved what you intended to achieve? If not, then why not and what do you need to do better in the future? You may have to work with others to achieve your work or study objectives and your ability to make the best use of your resources – and to communicate effectively – are important personal attributes. Your ACCA education will give you knowledge of accountancy and business, and undertaking research will enhance your practical skills. What have been the benefits for you of doing the RAP?

By answering the SLS questions you will gain some important personal insight into these issues. Although there are four questions with a total word limit of 2,000 words, you do not have to write exactly 500 words to answer each of the four questions. You may find that you want to write more about one or two particular questions. You may write between 350 and 650 words on each question within the total word limit of 2,000 words.

SLS assessment

Your Skills and Learning Statement will be assessed as 'satisfactory' or 'unsatisfactory', it will not be given a grade. However you should give it equal importance to the Research Project since you must submit a 'satisfactory' SLS in order to pass the Research and Analysis Project overall.

To pass the 'self-reflection' component of the SLS, you have to make a reasonable attempt to address all of the four SLS questions. If you do not, then you will not pass the SLS. You must demonstrate your ability to reflect on the judgements that you have made and the actions that you have taken while undertaking your RAP work. We want to see you provide evidence that you recognise your strengths and weaknesses. If you only provide a description of what happened while you were doing your RAP, then you will not pass the SLS.

Sources of SLS evidence

When you plan your project research work you should also plan to collect evidence to contribute to your Skills and Learning Statement, so that some of your self-reflection will 'fall out' of the activities undertaken for your Research Project. One important set of activities will be the three meetings with your Project Mentor. If you think about what happened in each of these meetings soon after they have taken place and record your thoughts, then you will be well on the way to writing your responses to two of the four questions.

Other sources of evidence could include meetings with individuals who you may interview as part of your project research or conversations / correspondence that you may have during your information gathering. You should think of every aspect of your project research work and how this may provide evidence for you to write your Skills and Learning Statement.

Communication skills

You will give a presentation on your Research Project to your Project Mentor in your final meeting. The preparation of this presentation will further develop your ability to present the concepts and findings of an accounting / business research report to an audience. As evidence of this you must submit a copy of your presentation in your Skills and Learning Statement.

You will pass 'communication skills' if a copy of the Research Project presentation is included in the SLS and your presentation's structure and content is clearly linked to the Research Project findings. There are many sources of advice (online and hard copy) on how to prepare an effective presentation and we recommend that you follow best practice.

It is possible that your Project Mentor may comment on the quality of your presentation and suggest that improvements would be possible. If you wish to revise your presentation after the meeting with your Project Mentor, then that is acceptable to Oxford Brookes. You should include a reference to this process and what you learned in your response to the first SLS question.

Appendix 1 Conversion arrangements

ACCA exam conversion arrangements

Oxford Brookes will recognise any passes or exemptions from Part 1 and Part 2 exams in the ACCA Professional scheme that are converted to the Fundamentals level of the ACCA Qualification, as contributions towards the award of the BSc degree after 1 August 2008.

Please note that if you still have to pass any of the three papers F1, F2 and F3 at the December 2007 sitting you cannot complete the BSc degree programme before 31 July 2008.

ACCA Professional Scheme exam passes before June 2000

If you passed one or more of ACCA's Professional Scheme exams before June 2000, and opted-in before November 2001, you may complete the BSc degree before 31 July 2008 – provided that you fulfil the requirements of the 'transitional arrangements' published when the degree was introduced. You should contact the ACCA office at Oxford Brookes to seek advice on your eligibility for the BSc degree.

If you intend to complete the BSc degree after 1 August 2008 you will be subject to both the requirements of the 'transitional arrangements', and the requirements of these conversion arrangements.

Completion of ACCA Part 1 and Part 2 exams at June 2007 sitting

If you registered before 1 January 2007, and completed the ACCA Part 1 and Part 2 exams at the June 2007 sitting, you may complete the BSc (Hons) in Applied Accounting before 31 July 2008 by passing the 'current' Oxford Brookes Research and Analysis Project.

You will not be required to complete the Professional Ethics module before submitting the Research and Analysis Project, and the class of degree will be based on the ACCA average mark, determined from the exam marks in the Part 1 and Part 2 papers that you sat and passed.

If you do not complete the BSc (Hons) in Applied Accounting degree by 31 July 2008, then you may do so after this date, but a Research and Analysis Project that is submitted after 1 August 2008 (first attempt or resubmission) must be presented under the requirements of the Research and Analysis Project effective from 1 August 2008.

After 1 August 2008, you must complete the Professional Ethics module before submitting the Research and Analysis Project, and the degree class will be based on the ACCA average mark determined from the exam marks in the Part 2 papers that you sat and passed, and the grade achieved for the Research and Analysis Project.

Completion of ACCA Fundamentals Level at December 2007 sitting

If you registered before 1 January 2007, and completed the ACCA Fundamentals level exams at the December 2007 sitting, you may complete the BSc (Hons) in Applied Accounting before 31 July 2008 by passing the current Research and Analysis Project. However, if you passed any of the three papers, F1, F2 and F3 at the December 2007 sitting then you cannot complete the degree before 31 July 2008.

You will not be required to complete the Professional Ethics module before submitting the Research and Analysis Project, and the class of degree will be based on the ACCA average mark, determined from the exam marks in the Part 1, Part 2 and Fundamentals papers you sat and passed.

If you do not complete the BSc (Hons) in Applied Accounting degree by 31 July 2008, then you may do so after this date, but a Research and Analysis Project that is submitted after 1 August 2008 (first attempt or resubmission) must be presented under the requirements of the Research and Analysis Project effective from 1 August 2008.

After 1 August 2008, you must complete the Professional Ethics module before submitting the Research and Analysis Project, and the degree class will be based on the ACCA average mark determined from the exam marks in the Part 2 and Fundamentals Skills (F4–F9) papers you sat and passed, and the grade achieved for the Research and Analysis Project.

Please review the example below

Example

After the June 2007 exam sitting, an ACCA student has the following results:

| Paper 1.1 | 62% | Paper 1.2 | 60% | Paper 1.3 | Exempt |
| Paper 2.1 | 66% | Paper 2.2 | Exempt | Paper 2.3 | 59% |

Under the ACCA conversion arrangements, passes in Papers 1.1, 1.2, 2.1 and 2.3 will be converted to passes in F3, F2, F5 and F6 respectively. The exemptions in Papers 1.3 and 2.2 will be converted to exemptions in F1 and F4 respectively.

If the student subsequently meets all of the BSc degree requirements after 1 August 2008, the ACCA average mark will be determined from the exam marks in Paper 2.1 (F5), Paper 2.3 (F6) and the three papers F7, F8 and F9. This will be combined with the grade awarded for the Research and Analysis Project to give the class of degree.

After 1 August 2008, the student will be given credit for the passes in Papers 1.1 and 1.2 (F3 and F2). The student will be given credit for the exemptions in Papers 1.3 and 2.2 (F1 and F4).

Appendix 2 Research and Analysis Project assessment criteria

Research Project	Pass - Grade A	Pass - Grade B	Pass - Grade C	Fail - Grade F
Technical and Professional Skills				
Understanding of accountancy / business models	Highly appropriate choice of theory/concepts. Very clear relevance and shows evidence of wider reading	Appropriate choice of theory and concepts. Significant evidence of understanding.	Some, but limited choice and use of theory and concepts. Some evidence of understanding.	Poor choice of theory / concepts, very limited understanding. Reliance on narrow range of material.
Application of accountancy / business models	Insightful and critical application of models to the project topic.	Mostly correct application of theory to the project topic.	Some application of theory, but lacking a coherent approach.	Poor use of theory / models and confused understanding of application.
Evaluation of information, analysis and conclusions	High level of critical thought shown in the analysis and a rigorous approach to the evaluation of information.	Strength shown in some areas of critical review of the information. Good evaluation of information.	Some analysis but a tendency towards description rather than analysis and evaluation	Descriptive and lacking in analysis. Inaccuracies. Little or no critical evaluation
Presentation of project findings	Can engage reader in a professional manner and produce a relevant and coherent project report with appropriate structure.	Can communicate effectively in a format appropriate to the report. Clear and concise manner with all relevant information.	Some communication is effective. Can report practical applications in a structured way.	Communication is only partially effective and project is poorly structured.
Graduate Skills	**Competent**	**Not competent**		
Communication	Language mostly fluent.	Meaning often unclear.		
	Grammar and spelling mainly accurate.	Grammar and / or spelling contain frequent errors.		
Information gathering and referencing	Clear evidence of a range of relevant information sources.	Very few and / or irrelevant information sources used.		
	Clear evidence of correct referencing methodology.	Referencing is mostly absent or unsystematic.		

	Competent	Not competent		
Information technology	Shows reasonable evidence of having accessed online information sources and having used a spreadsheet and / or other software in preparing the project report.	Little evidence of use of IT during preparation of project. Little online access, no evidence of spreadsheet / other soft ware use.		
Skills and Learning Statement	**Competent**	**Not competent**		
Self reflection	Makes a reasonable attempt to address all four questions. (see below *)	Overly focused on only one or two questions.		
	Shows ability to reflect on judgements made / actions taken during project work.	Emphasis on description of events, little evaluation of self-development etc.		
	Evidence of recognising own strengths and weaknesses	Little discussion of own strengths and weaknesses		
Communication skills	A copy of the presentation to the project mentor is included.	A copy of the presentation to the project mentor has not been included.		
	Presentation has appropriate structure. Content is clearly linked to project report findings.	Presentation is poorly structured and / or content is not relevant to project report findings.		

* In the SLS, the student will be asked to reflect on the following four questions.

1. What did you learn from the meetings with your project mentor, including the presentation that you gave to your project mentor?
2. How well do you think that you have answered your research question(s)?
3. How have you demonstrated your interpersonal and communication skills during the project work?
4. How has undertaking the RAP helped you in your accountancy studies and / or current employment role?

BPP
LEARNING MEDIA

Appendix 3 How to reference your work

This is an introduction to how to reference your work. You should read the full Oxford Brookes document "A guide to citing and referencing for Business School students" which is published on the ACCA BSc degree webpages.

Referencing

Whenever you are directly quoting or referring to one of your sources of information, you should acknowledge this in the text as you go along. References should be clearly set out using the Harvard System. It is important to double check that all references in your text appear in the List of References.

List of References

Your List of References comes at the end of your Report. It is a list of all the sources you have used in compiling your Report e.g. books, articles, company publications, newspaper articles etc. The List of References should be set out alphabetically using the Harvard System. It is not sufficient to merely include your sources of information in the List of References without including the proper reference in the text. Failure to do this will result in failure of the Research Project.

How to reference your work and construct a List of References

Correctly referencing your work is simple, and compulsory. You must reference all your sources of information. We do advise you to reference as you go along, rather than leaving it until the end of your research work. There is nothing more time consuming than constructing a List of References retrospectively.

References within your text

In the Harvard system references within the text are set out as follows:

Example

In any organisation made up of different interest groups some conflict over goals is inevitable (Needle, 1994).

In the List of References the reference shown above would appear in this way:

Example of a book reference

Needle, D. (1994) *Business in Context*. 2nd Edition, London, Chapman & Hall

---

NB: You only cite the edition if it is not the first. Please note that the title of the book is either underlined or emboldened.

Example of a journal or newspaper reference

Buxton, J. (1998) Management: The Growing Business: Co-operative's Wheels of Fortune. *The Financial Times*, February 24

NB: It's the title of the journal or newspaper that is either underlined or emboldened

---

Example of journal article where no author is given

The Economist (1997) 'New technology is no snap', October 11, p125

Citing Electronic Sources

No standard agreed method has yet evolved for citing electronic sources. Electronic sources may include ftp sites, Telnet addresses, WWW and gopher pages, newsgroups and e-mail messages.

A simplified solution might be:

Author's last name, First name. Title of work. *Title of complete work if applicable in italics*. [protocol and address] [path] (date of message or visit).

Example

Walker, Janice R. MLA-Style Citations of Electronic Sources.
http://www.columbia.edu/cu/cup/cgos/idx_basic.html (visited 1 April 2008)

Appendix 4 Oxford Brookes Process Model

BPP
LEARNING MEDIA

chapter 2

Test your skills:
self-assessment questionnaire

INTRODUCTION

There are many students who will feel confident about tackling the project element of the Applied Accounting degree and will need to be guided only by the Research and Analysis Project Information Pack.

There will also be many students who have never undertaken a project like this before, and know that they will therefore need to learn and practise the techniques and skills involved. This book should prove to be invaluable for those students, as it is designed to provide further support and guidance in developing your skills and completing the Project.

There will also be a middle group: the students who are not sure whether or not they already have the necessary skills, and are not quite confident enough to launch into the research required for the production of the Project without doing some preparatory work. If you feel that you fall into that middle category, this chapter is for you. It will allow you to test your knowledge of some of the concepts and principles which you are expected to have in order to do the Project, and to assess whether you have the skills that you are expected to display.

This chapter contains a self-assessment questionnaire. Once completed, it will indicate to you which areas you can feel comfortable about and which areas you will need to work on, by reading the relevant sections of this book.

1 Eligibility for the degree

To be awarded the BSc (Hons) in Applied Accounting you must:

- be registered with Oxford Brookes University ie opted-in to the BSc degree scheme before passing any of the three ACCA Fundamentals papers, F7, F8 and F9

- pass the three ACCA Fundamentals papers F7, F8 and F9 and pass other papers as required to successfully complete all nine Fundamentals level papers

- complete the ACCA Professional Ethics module

- complete and pass the Oxford Brookes University Research and Analysis Project

- complete the BSc degree scheme within 10 years of your initial registration onto the ACCA's professional qualification.

Please note that you must successfully complete the Fundamentals level exam papers, F1–F9, and complete the Professional Ethics module before submitting a Research and Analysis Project to Oxford Brookes University.

If you wish to enquire about your eligibility to complete the BSc degree, please contact the ACCA office at Oxford Brookes at acca@brookes.ac.uk. Please include your ACCA student registration number in any correspondence.

2 IT and word processing skills

Part of the assessment procedure will focus on your IT skills. It is a specific requirement of the Project that you produce some of your material in spreadsheet format, and the Information Pack guidelines advise you to provide a sample printout of the formulae you use in producing your spreadsheet. Additionally you may wish to reflect on your usage of IT skills in your Skills and Learning Statement.

Exercise 1

(a)	Can you produce a spreadsheet and show the formulae you have used?	**YES/NO**
(b)	Can you present data in both tabular and graphical form?	**YES/NO**
(c)	Can you use spelling and grammar checkers?	**YES/NO**
(d)	Do you need to bring your word-processing skills up to date?	**YES/NO**
(e)	Do you feel comfortable using the Internet for research purposes?	**YES/NO**

2.1 Self assessment

The tutorial text will provide some brief guidance on the use of spreadsheets but you should consider whether you are fully competent at other aspects of word processing. If not, you should attend a short course or perhaps buy one of the available manuals to teach you some of the basic skills.

3 Report writing and the structure of reports

Your ability to write clearly and succinctly is of paramount importance here. Try these exercises to assess your skills.

Exercise 2

Put what follows into report format.

'The first criterion is whether this will be profitable over the estimated life cycle of Product A. Another criterion which is related to the first criterion is that of estimated volume sales at the proposed price. A third criterion which needs to be considered when deciding whether or not to launch Product A is....'

Answer

Decision criteria in rank order

(i)	Profit (ROI) over product life cycle
(ii)	Sales volume at proposed price
(iii)	...

Exercise 3

Put these headings into the order in which you would expect to see them in a report.

Methods of research selected
Analysis of results
Conclusion
Terms of reference
Appendices
Observations
Bibliography
Executive summary

Answer

Terms of reference
Executive summary
Methods of research selected
Observations
Analysis of results
Conclusion
Appendices
Bibliography

Exercise 4

Use the information set out below to produce the heading of a report.

Hugh Mountolive the Managing Director can see both sides of the arguments presented by Melissa and Clea regarding closing down the Alexandria factory and moving to Port Said, but is uncertain about how to evaluate such an important issue.

He has asked you, Justine Nessim the management accountant, to write a report covering all the major factors that need to be considered in relation to the closure and move, with a recommendation.

Answer

To: Hugh Mountolive, Managing Director

From: Justine Nessim, Management Accountant

Date:

Re: Analysis of and recommendations regarding the proposed closure of the factory in Alexandria and the move to Port Said

Exercise 5

You have a very tight word constraint in writing the Research Project and Skills and Learning Statement, which means that you will have to demonstrate the two skills of:

- prioritisation of issues arising from your research
- concise and succinct use of words

Test your ability here by attempting this exercise.

BMW pulled out of car manufacturing in the UK, by selling its investment in Rover cars to another firm, although some parts of it were sold to Ford.

Here are some of the factors underlying the decision.

- Rover lost £750m in 1999.

- £150m of aid from the UK government to BMW was under threat from the European commission, given its concern over state subsidies.

- The pound was for some time very high compared to the euro, making exports from the UK to Europe very expensive.

- 10,000 jobs in Rover were at risk, as were 40,000 supplier jobs in the West Midlands. BMW had spent a lot of time and money on 'the English patient' since buying it.

- BMW had invested in Rover to enable BMW to become a volume car manufacturer as opposed to a niche maker of executive cars.

- BMW is the 14th largest motor manufacturer in an industry that has been consolidating recently.

- The UK is unlikely to join the euro for some time.

- Rover lost market share in the UK from 13.5% to 6% over 5 years. Not enough British buyers were buying Rover cars.

- BMW could be vulnerable to a takeover.

- The main BMW brand is suffering.

What were BMW's priorities in reaching the decision? Show a rationale.

BPP
LEARNING MEDIA

Answer (1)

Rationale

Survival of BMW. BMW's management wished to preserve BMW as a successful, independent company, and considered that future involvement with Rover would jeopardise this aim.

Key issues underlying the decision

Priority – importance	Justification
1 Stem losses: no prospect of future profitability	**Future**. BMW had invested a lot in Rover, but what concerned them was the future – future incremental cash flows were negative. Rover had been losing market share in the UK. Exports had tailed off because of the high level of sterling. New products had not been successful.
2 Concentrate on BMW brand	**External**. Too much management attention had been focused on Rover. No evidence existed that this had hit BMW brand yet, but managers were concerned about this.
3 Compete elsewhere: consolidation of motor industry	**External**. Motor firms are merging into larger groups – the reason why BMW bought Rover.

The answer above has a clear rationale and the relative importance of each item has been shown. It demonstrates good use of words and good prioritisation.

Answer (2)

- Rover lost £750m in 1999.
- The exchange rate is not favourable and so cars are expensive.
- Rover has been losing market share recently.
- BMW want to concentrate on building the BMW brand.

This sort of style would probably lead to a narrow fail because it does not clearly specify the **rationale** behind the decision, which is that Rover will be a **future** drain of cash for BMW, and that investing in Rover will prevent BMW from protecting its brand. In short, while the list is appropriate there is no underlying rationale.

3.1 Self assessment

It is up to you to judge your performance in the four exercises in the section of this questionnaire on report-writing skills, and you must be honest with yourself.

If you felt that the exercises were straightforward, you felt comfortable handling the material and your answers were roughly similar to ours, you have probably already got adequate report-writing skills.

However, if you felt that you were out of your depth in some of the exercises, or you did not fully understand what they required, you might find it helpful to practise, in order to improve your technique.

4 Referencing material

The Research and Analysis Project Information Pack guidelines emphasise that you must reference your sources professionally and prepare a List of References.

Exercise 6

(a) George Franklin published a book in 1999, with a new edition in January 2003. The book was called 'Analysing the Retail Industry' and was published in Manchester by Business Publishers Ltd.

Show how you would acknowledge the most recent edition in the text of your Research Project and in the List of References.

(b) In the March 2008 issue of Accountancy magazine there is an article by Andrew Lennard entitled 'Up for discussion' regarding proposed accounting rules for pensions.

Show how you would acknowledge the article in the text of your Research Project and in the List of References.

(c) The Financial Times contained a comment on the of inflation in Britain on page 33 of the issue of March 27th 2008. The comment had no attributable author name.

Show how you would acknowledge the comment in the text of your Research Project and in the List of References.

(d) On June 24th 2003, it was possible to read a comment by Anthea Rose on the ACCA's website (www.acca.co.uk) to the effect that the government is imposing too much red tape on small businesses. The comment was included in an article entitled 'Raising the audit threshold – raising the risk of fraud' which was originally posted on May 15th 2003.

Show how you would acknowledge this in the text of your Research Project and in the List of References.

Answer

(a)   In the text:

(Franklin, 2003)

In the List of References:
Franklin, G. (2003) <u>Analysing the Retail Industry</u>. 2nd edition, Manchester, Business Publishers.

(b)   In the text:

(Lennard, 2008)

In the List of References:
Lennard, A. (2008) Up for discussion. <u>Accountancy</u>, March

(c)   In the text:

(Financial Times, 2008)

In the List of References:
<u>Financial Times</u> (2008) June 27th, p.33

(d)   In the text:

(Rose, 2003)

In the List of References:
Rose, A. Raising the audit threshold – raising the risk of fraud. <u>www.acca.co.uk</u> 15th May 2003. Accessed on 24th June 2003

4.1 Self assessment

If you are familiar with the Harvard system of referencing, you will be perfectly capable of referencing your Research Project in exactly the way specified by Oxford Brookes in the Project Information Pack guidelines.

If you were not familiar with the means of referencing shown above, you should either study the Project Information Pack guidelines in detail, or refer to the relevant section of this book.

5 Questioning techniques

In your Research and Analysis Project and Skills and Learning Statement, you may be required to consider appropriate questioning techniques.

Exercise 7

Which questioning techniques would you think are most likely to be relevant to your work?

Answer

You are most likely to employ (or at least discuss)

- Open
- Closed
- Leading
- Probing
- Multiple

5.1 Self assessment

If you are not familiar with the above terms, you should do some work on questioning techniques. These are all covered in the Tutorial Text.

6 Listening techniques

In your Research and Analysis Project and Skills and Learning Statement, you maybe required to consider appropriate listening techniques.

Exercise 8

List the different methods (or styles) of listening which may be of significance when you are considering listening techniques.

Answer

- Listening for content
- Critical listening
- Empathetic listening
- Attentive listening

Exercise 9

Do you think that listening is an active or a passive activity?

Answer

It is an active process. It is not the same as hearing, which is passive. Effective listening requires the deployment of specific skills.

6.1 Self assessment

If you are not familiar with the concept of active listening, or the terms used to describe different types of listening, you should do some work on listening techniques. These are covered in the Tutorial Text.

7 Self reflection

The Skills and Learning Statement is the opportunity for you to demonstrate that you've developed one of the key "graduate" skills of self reflection. This is done by answering a number of questions.

Exercise 10

What do we mean by reflection?

Answer

- also known as critical reflection
- key academic professional skill
- review and evaluate experiences
- review and evaluate learning acquired

7.1 Self assessment

If you are not familiar with the concept of self reflection return to the Skills and Learning Statement guidance which indicates how you should approach the answers to the four questions set.

8 Presentations

As a part of your Research and Analysis Project, you will be required to deliver a fifteen minute presentation on your Research Project to your mentor and possibly a group of fellow students.

Exercise 11

Answer these questions:

(a)	Have you delivered a formal presentation before?	**YES/NO**
(b)	Do you feel confident about public speaking?	**YES/NO**
(c)	Can you handle questions from an audience?	**YES/NO**
(d)	Are you terrified at the thought of the presentation?	**YES/NO**

8.1 Self assessment

If you answered 'yes' to questions (a) to (c) and 'no' to question (d) you should feel confident about preparing for and delivering your presentation, and you need no coaching in techniques.

If you answered 'no' to questions (a) to (c) and 'yes' to question (d) you should read about presentation techniques before you reach that stage in the Research and Analysis Project.

Chapter roundup

- You are the person who knows your skills the best. If you have been scrupulously honest with yourself, you should by now have come to a conclusion as to whether you need to read about the required skills for the preparation of your project.

- If you feel that you need more guidance and support, you should find that in the relevant sections of this Tutorial Text.

Part B:

The Research and Analysis Project

chapter 3

The project in outline

INTRODUCTION

This chapter gives you a general overview of the project. Section 1 highlights the differences between the project (for a degree) and sitting exams for a professional qualification. You need only read this if you do not already have a degree – or if you feel you need to be reminded of the difference. Section 2 details the skills covered, by linking it to the requirement of other accountancy-based degrees. Section 3 expands the overview of the work you will have to do; Section 4 covers the issues involved in writing the Research Project and the Skills and Learning Statement.

1 The Research and Analysis Project (RAP): Its role in your degree

1.1 What is so special about this project?

You are doing this Research and Analysis, the related Research Project and Skills and Learning Statement to obtain a **degree** from a respected UK awarding institution: a Bachelor of Science (Hons) in Applied Accounting from Oxford Brookes University.

This is what you must do in the project.

Output	Process
The **Research Project**	Choose a topic, research and analyse data, come to a conclusion. Write the Research Project of 6,500 words based on your research and analysis.
The Skills and Learning Statement based around four key questions.	Find a mentor; arrange and reflect upon three meetings; reflect in particular upon the way you have answered your research questions, how you demonstrated your interpersonal and communication skills during the project work and how undertaking the RAP has helped in your studies and/or employment; give a presentation; write a 2,000 word Skills and Learning Statement.

Think about the list above. This is very different from studying for ACCA exams, which are focused on satisfying the examiner in a three hour exam.

Exercise 1

Write down the key differences between the Research and Analysis project and studying for ACCA exams.

Answer

ACCA exams	Research and Analysis Project
Questions are precisely defined.	The topics chosen are very general and you must narrow them down to a Project objective.
Questions are precisely structured, with defined tasks clearly outlined and marks allocated.	You have to provide a structure and define what you are trying to discover.
You only have three hours.	You can take as long as you like.
Pen and paper.	You have to demonstrate familiarity with IT, such as use of word processing, spreadsheets etc: your report must be word processed.
You are working to a syllabus.	There is no syllabus.
Exam technique is your business only.	You have to reflect and report on the process of doing the Research and Analysis Project.
For many of the papers, the data is given. All you have to do is a read a question and answer it.	You will have to draw conclusions from reviewing your data, but this depends on: • Identifying the right data in scope and depth • Asking the right questions of the data Your conclusion may not support what you set out to prove.

1.2 What's so different about a degree?

A **degree** is not the same as a **professional qualification,** even though the subject matter may overlap and the degree and professional qualification may be taught in the same institution (and by the same people!).

For example, you may have a degree in accounting, but there are certain things you cannot do – such as sign audit reports – simply because you have a degree. Or again, to become a member of the ACCA, you not only must pass exams, but you must also undergo training and experience directly related to your practical work.

A degree and a professional qualification are both stretching – but the **focus** is different.

(a) The **focus of a professional qualification** is working for others in a public role; the ACCA is checking – as part of its quality control procedures – that you are fit to be let loose on the fee-paying business community.

(b) The focus of a **degree is** not only the world of work. It offers you personal fulfilment, by stretching you to achieve a personal goal. The university is assisting you in this, but is also measuring you against your contemporaries: at college, in the country where you live, and around the world.

A degree typically involves testing certain abilities that may not be the focus of the examinations for your professional work. The context of a degree is the wider academic community.

(a) Degrees in one subject must in some respect be **comparable** with degrees in other subjects. A BSc in Applied Accounting should, all other things being equal, be worthy of the same esteem as a BSc in Engineering or a BA in Media Studies – a huge scope of subject matter. (It is insulting to suggest that some areas of study are 'easier' because they are different – but there has to be some common benchmark for achievement.)

(b) Degrees awarded by universities throughout the country should be of **comparable worth**. A first class honours should be a first class honours wherever this is earned.

(c) To be awarded a degree, you generally need to show that you have the knowledge and skills required by the degree programme.

(d) A BSc or BA is merely the first in a hierarchy of qualifications related to academic work. Therefore, **rigour** and **method** in approaching and understanding a topic are essential.

If you have acquired the necessary knowledge you are well on the way. However, knowledge is not really enough. Here is an extract from the **Benchmark Statement in Accountancy** published in 2007. This is produced by the Quality Assurance Agency for Higher Education, a UK-based body whose role is to promote public confidence that the quality of provision and standards of awards in UK higher education is safeguarded and enhanced. All accountancy degrees awarded in the UK should follow this benchmark and your degree must deal with these issues.

The current Benchmark Statement for an Honours level degree in Accounting, which was published in 2007, identifies the following attributes of an honours graduate in accounting.

Cognitive abilities and generic skills

- The capacity for the critical evaluation of arguments and evidence

- The ability to analyse and draw reasoned conclusions concerning structured and, to a more limited extent, unstructured problems from a given set of data and from data which must be acquired by the student

- The ability to locate, extract and analyse data from multiple sources, including the acknowledgement and referencing of sources

- Capacities for independent and self-managed learning

- Numeracy skills, including the ability to manipulate financial and other numerical data and to appreciate statistical concepts at an appropriate level

- Skills in the use of communications and information technology in acquiring, analysing and communicating information (currently these skills include the use of spreadsheets, word processing software, online databases)

- Communication skills including the ability to present quantitative and qualitative information, together with analysis, argument and commentary, in a form appropriate to the intended audience

- Normally, an ability to work in groups, and other interpersonal skills, including oral as well as written presentation skills.

The benchmark statement suggests a variety of **assessment activities** to test not only your **understanding** of conceptual and applied aspects of accountancy but also **'the cognitive abilities and non-subject specific skills they have developed as a consequence of [your] studies'.**

1.3 So this is what the Research and Analysis Project is for?

Oxford Brookes University receives independent assurance that the first nine ACCA professional examinations are appropriate for an Honours level degree in Accounting. The Research and Analysis Project is the final component of the BSc (Hons) in Applied Accounting degree. It allows you to demonstrate some of the above cognitive abilities and non-subject specific skills in addition to enhancing your learning from your ACCA studies. The combination of the nine ACCA examinations, Ethics Module, and Oxford Brookes Research and Analysis Project meets the requirements of the UK Accounting Benchmark Statement.

What about the class of degree?

In the UK, undergraduate degrees fall typically into the following categories or classes 1st, 2:1, 2:2, 3rd.

The class of BSc degree will be based on both:

- the ACCA average mark determined from the exam marks in the Fundamentals Skills papers (F4–F9)

- the grade achieved for the Research and Analysis Project.

The ACCA average mark will be calculated by taking the numerical average of the marks achieved in the Fundamentals Skills papers (F4–F9) that you have sat and passed.

Where the calculated average mark is not a whole number, the calculated average will be rounded up or down accordingly. If you have been given an exemption from any of the three papers F4–F6, no mark is available and so will not be included in the calculation of the ACCA average mark.

The class of degree for each combination of ACCA average mark and Research and Analysis Project grade is shown below.

| ACCA average mark | Class of degree | | | |
	First	Upper second	Lower second	Third
68 or more	A, B, C	–	–	–
67	A, B	C	–	–
66	A	B, C	–	–
60-65	–	A, B, C	–	–
59	–	A, B	C	–
58	–	A	B, C	–
54-57	–	–	A, B, C	–
53	–	–	A, B	C
50-52	–	–	–	A, B, C

1.4 Be a self-starter

Doing the Research and Analysis Project will be a very different **experience** from studying for ACCA exams. Hopefully, you will find it an interesting – if challenging – experience, one which will equip you with forensic skills in the world of work and which will broaden your horizons.

To some degree it is original work, not based on learning from Study Texts (no matter how good they are), nor is it based on rigorous and repeated question practice from Practice & Revision Kits (no matter how good they are).

Moreover, you will have to drive yourself. If you are used to a taught course, you may miss the structure of course exams, mocks and so forth – although you do have to conduct mentor meetings. It is **your** project, it is open-ended and, to an extent, you can follow your interests.

2 The abilities to be tested

For the Research and Analysis Project the **technical knowledge** you need is covered in the rigours of your ACCA exams. Let us examine the skills that the Research and Analysis Project is designed specifically to deal with.

2.1 Critical examination of arguments and evidence

Consider the following scenario.

Exercise 2

Let us say you are doing **Project Topic 6**: **The key factors or indicators in the motivation of employees in an organisation**. As part of your research, you want to assess the relationship between reward schemes and motivation.

Four months ago, the sales manager at Saramago plc replaced a salary based scheme for 30 sales staff with a commission only scheme. He says: 'The new scheme has been a big success for the company and staff: they seem a lot happier. I mean, Bill came to see me last week and said he was really looking forward to his bonus, after all the work he'd put in. Money talks doesn't it?'.

How would you **critically examine** the arguments and evidence in this statement?

Answer

By **critical**, this does not mean saying to the sales manager 'That's rubbish, you're no good'. It means that, tactfully, you hold up the statement for review; you do not take it at face value. By **examine** it means that you have to inspect the data, tease out its meaning, test it and so on.

(a)   What does the sales manager mean by **'big success for the company'**? This is his argument. He has not presented you with any **evidence**.

   (i)   More **sales revenue** for the company? Is this quantified or measured? Are there sales reports? You'd need to see some figures.

   (ii)   Has this been accompanied by problems of credit control and bad debts?

   (iii)   Has the increase in revenue over the past four months **really** been affected by the bonus scheme?

   –   What about seasonal factors? Compared to a similar period last year, is the increase really so wonderful?

   –   Was revenue significantly up **before** the scheme was introduced?

(b)   **'Big success'** for staff? Are they earning more? In fact, is the company paying more than is really warranted by the increase? Are they happier?

(c)   His **argument** 'money talks' is that people are motivated mainly by money. Quite possibly, this is true in this case, but you need to put this in a context. His staff may be motivated by other factors, as suggested by a whole host of motivation theories.

(d)   His **evidence** about staff feelings is impressionistic: nothing wrong with that as such, but given he only mentions one person – Bill – this seems anecdotal. (Furthermore, Bill could have been complaining.)

(e)   The sales manager has every reason to praise a system he introduced himself.

If the sales manager were to unveil a detailed report with all the variances explained, proof that bad debts were not increasing and so on, you would see this in a different light.

Analyse and draw reasoned conclusions concerning structured and to a more limited extent unstructured problems from a given set of data and data which must be acquired by the student.

There's quite a lot going on here. Let's look at what this means – from the end first.

2.1.1 Given data/data which must be acquired

As the Research and Analysis Project is not an exam, neither the ACCA nor Oxford Brookes will give you data. They suggest some project topics, but the data gathering work is yours. We cover this later – but it is for **you** to **define** what you need to know, to **plan** how to **obtain** data and to **implement** your plan.

2.1.2 Structured/unstructured problems

You will have already learnt about structured and unstructured problems elsewhere in your ACCA studies, but here is a recap.

(a)   A **structured problem** is one in which there is a defined number of elements, and it is possible to go about solving the problem in a systematic way.

(b)   An **unstructured problem**, on the other hand, is less easy to analyse as it appears to lack any obvious logic, underlying procedures or rules for solving it.

An example of a relatively **structured** problem might be as follows.

2.2 Example: sole trader

A sole trader decides to incorporate his/her business as a limited company and asks your advice as to whether this is a good idea and how to go about it.

(a)   Is it a good idea? It is relatively easy to model the effect of the change on:

(i)   The legal position of the business
(ii)   The tax position

and so on, as there are defined rules as to how companies work.

(b)   How to go about it? Incorporating a company is a relatively routine procedure and the legal steps are easy to identify.

An example of a relatively unstructured problem is one which there are no simple steps to reach a result: it cannot simply be deconstructed into its components, if people disagree fundamentally as to the nature of the problem.

2.3 Example

Many organisations draw up a **mission statement**. This aims to describe what the organisation is 'for' and its aspirations. The mission statement is used as a communication tool to employees, shareholders and customers and so on.

Drawing up a mission statement is an 'unstructured' problem because:

(i)   There are no clear rules as to what a mission statement should be.

(ii)   Many 'stakeholders' have completely different perspectives on what organisations are for. These perspectives are not always easy to incorporate in one over-arching mission.

2.4 Ability to locate, extract and analyse data from multiple sources, including the acknowledgement and referencing of sources

This needs to be pulled apart.

2.4.1 Locate data

Where should you look to find what you want? Obviously, this depends on the type of data that you need to find.

2.5 Example

Let's say, for example, that you are interested in **Project Topic 12: The possible effects of a proposed accounting standard on the financial statements and business activities of an organisation.** Where would you find data?

(a) Some of the data may be necessary **theoretical background**. You would need to find out details of the proposed standard. You could for example, obtain them the International Accounting Standards Board website www.iasb.org.

(b) Some data may be directly obtained from employees of the company, for example in general discussions or formal interviews.

(c) Some of the data would result from analysis and modelling. You could for example, try to see what would happen if you **re-stated** the accounts of a company originally prepared according to local GAAP according to IASs.

(d) Some data could be provided by a review of relevant professional journals, such as Certified Accountant, the ACCA's Student Accountant, Accountancy – accounting standards are the subject of some debate, and even hit the business pages of some of the major newspapers on occasion.

(e) Some data could be located by identifying and selecting a sample of respondents for a questionnaire.

 Exercise 3

Jot down as many ways you can think of to 'extract' data in relation to, the items (a) to (e) in the example above.

Answer

Just to give you an idea:

(a) Taking notes (eg from a Study Text covering UK)

(b) Some dates may be directly obtained from employees of the company, for example in general discussions or formal interviews.

(c) Making a tape recording of an interview with the Finance Director in which he/she describes her opinions in full and details in broad terms, the costs involved of preparing accounts under the proposal.

(d) Inputting data on to a spreadsheet for further analysis

(e) Articles can be obtained by library visits or visits to relevant websites where a 'search' facility might enable you to review and print out certain articles

(f) Designing a questionnaire, and getting answers to it

2.5.1 Analyse data

Here is an example of what we mean.

- Make sense of the data
- Apply theoretical concepts to it
- Compare it with other data for consistency

Exercise 4

Taking Exercise 3 and the example above, we can identify analytical tasks you could use.

Answer

Locate (Example)	Extract (Exercise 3)	Analyse
(a)	(a)	Determine principal differences between current practice and proposed standard.
(b)	(b)	Need more detail as to costs. FD's response is likely to be personal and focused on his job and department
(c)	(c)	Provides numerical proof of effects on reported profits. Model effects on reported earnings
(d)	(d)	Identify current areas of controversy
(e)	(e)	Get a wider industry view

Exercise 5

You have a set of published financial accounts for the past three financial years and copies of relevant International Accounting Standards. What initially could you do to analyse the data?

Answer

The most obvious tool would be ratio analysis. From such data, you can easily calculate receivables, payables and inventory turnover, the total cash cycle and related trends, the proportion of working capital to total net assets, gearing and so on. You could then get an idea of the total performance of the company.

Of course the **significance** of your calculations will depend on other matters gleaned from other areas of your research. If, for example, the proposals regard differ, you would want to conduct your analysis with a purpose.

(a)   Effect on reported profits and earnings per share.

(b)   Your research must reveal industry peculiarities that lead to some treatments of goodwill being preferred over others.

2.5.2 Analyse and draw reasoned conclusions from

Effectively, this means that you have, as suggested earlier, to review your data, do things to it and come to a judgement about what the data may actually mean. A simple example may be correlation. But many examples are not so simple.

You are shown a graph showing sales of product X in the summer of 2004.

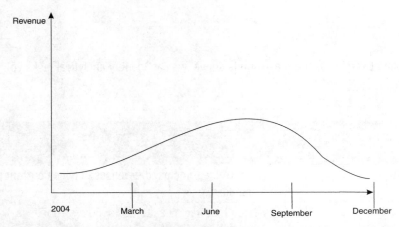

More of product X is sold in the summer of 2004 than in the winter. Without, for the time being, knowing what product X is you might **assume** that product X is sold when the temperature gets hotter.

(a)   If product X is ice-cream, then you can draw a reasoned analysis that high sales volumes relate to hot weather.

(b)   If product X is however, the Harry Potter books, their release will almost definitely not relate to the hot weather, more to the fact that there is huge demand for these anyway, and a new book was published in the late spring.

Other examples in a business context, are these.

(a)   If a company invests in new technology, and if labour productivity increases soon afterwards, you could reasonably conclude (all other things being equal), that the new technology enabled the workforce to become more productive.

(b)   One company's managers may invest in a high-risk project which offers a high reward if successful. In another company, managers are more cautious. A reasoned conclusion is that managers' attitude to risk depends on various different factors.

2.6 Example

This is directly related to **Project Topic 11: The financial and operational costs and benefits of the internal audit/internal review activities within an organisation**. Managers might be reluctant to employ an internal audit team because of the salary cost. However, such a team may be able to identify improvements in the system, which will save money, and also will reduce internal audit costs.

A **reasoned conclusion** would be that an internal audit department should, for the sake of argument, be brought in, as it would have benefits (firmly derived from the data).

2.7 Capacity for independent and self-managed learning

Independent and self-managed: this effectively means that you have to have the necessary skills to complete the project by yourself; in other words, you have the resources you need to learn without being spoon-fed by a tutor, and that you have to plan and manage your learning.

If you are one of the many students who have no tutorial support, you will by now, have had plenty of experience in this. We will cover some scheduling techniques in Chapter 5.

You should be able to show that:

- You can identify what you need to learn
- You can plan your learning time
- You will identify techniques to help you learn

You should be able to demonstrate numeracy skills, including the ability to manipulate financial and other numerical data and to appreciate statistical concepts at an appropriate level.

The Research and Analysis Project is **not** designed to **test** these skills as such: the work you have done sitting the ACCA exams so far is evidence that you have these skills in abundance. However, the Project is an opportunity to demonstrate that you can apply these skills or use them.

Look at the business situation below.

Exercise 6

You are doing **Project Topic 14: The business and financial objectives of a strategic investment decision made by an organisation and its impact on key stakeholders**. The company is lolinda Ltd, your employer, and you have a lot of data to use.

lolinda Ltd is a biotechnology company about to be listed on a stock market. It has used genetic manipulation (GM) technology to generate a species of rose that is impervious to aphids. The company is very confident that the new rose will be a huge market success, but needs to conduct trials in plant nurseries. Of course, these trials may fail or have unintended consequences. There is a risk that the trials may fail and/or that environmentalists will disrupt them. lolinda does have some other valuable patents, in GM technology for farmers, but this is the first time it will market directly to a consumer products industry (not food). Consumers and the gardening public will be propagating GM plants.

The venture capital firms that have financed lolinda want to recover their investment by selling shares. Other biotechnology companies have no difficulties in raising equity. However, the share prices of biotechnology firms have been quite volatile in relation to the market as a whole, with some spectacular successes and failures. lolinda intends to float whether or not the rose project fails or succeeds.

Required

What **numerical analysis** could you do on data items (1) to (6) below?

(1)   Historic data on likely success/failure of trials of GM products (ie failure rate pre launch)

(2)   Cash flows required for the trials pre-launch

(3)   Proposed pricing strategy (eg penetration or skimming strategies) and sales forecast; distribution and marketing costs assuming launch is successful; comparative volumes in relation to other products

(4)   Projected earnings per share for the company as a whole, or similar information from the prospectus

(5)   Interest rates

(6)   Market values, dividend levels and yields, and betas of similar companies

Answer

Here are some ideas.

The **historic success rate** for GM product trials can be used to develop **probabilities** of the success of the trials, and so you can then calculate **expected values** of the future cash flows. These might give an idea of **risk**. However, you may also need to consider the risk that the **political climate** opposed to GM products may significantly reduce the sales turnover. All this will be relevant to **investment appraisal**.

If significant cash flows are involved, you may be required to prepare **cash budgets** and to monitor **working capital**.

The proposed pricing strategy will give an idea of what cash flows might be expected and hence you could estimate the significance of the rose trial in the **overall product portfolio**.

With suitable information you might analyse the **risk** of the project, and use the **beta**, if it meets the relevant tests.

Note that there is a **limit** to the technical knowledge you need apply. (For example, you are unlikely to have come across beta valuation in your ACCA exams to date.)

Skills in the use of communications and information technology in acquiring, analysing and communicating information, including the use of spreadsheets, and word processing software, the world-wide web and email.

Here are some examples.

Acquiring	Conducting a web search using a search engine
	Visiting relevant websites
Analysing	Modelling using spreadsheets, such as 'what if?' analysis
Communicating	Emailing responses
	Communicating in a chat-room
	Joining a group
	Word processing your report
	Using graphics in spreadsheets

2.8 Communication skills including the ability to present quantitative and qualitative information together with analysis, argument and commentary in a form appropriate to different audiences

Communications skills are covered in Part C of this Tutorial Text. The Research and Analysis Project tests your skills in:

- Research Project writing (the Project)
- Oral presentation (Skills and Learning Statement)

You have to present **analysis, argument and commentary**.

(a)   **Analysis**: in the Research Project, you need to be able to explain the analytical work you have done, and to describe your method. In fact, thinking how you would explain and justify your analytical work to an audience (eg friends) is a good way of testing whether you have done enough work.

(b)   **Argument**: stating a case, and justifying it with reasoned argument.

(c)   **Commentary**: a commentary could include adding detail, adding context and so on.

Exercise 7

The data below is taken from an unpublished undergraduate dissertation project.

Required

Each sentence is numbered. The ten sentences below contain a mix of **analysis**, **argument** and **commentary**.

Pick **one** example of each type of sentence.

(1) Sales people rarely consider a car as a perk; instead it is a pre-requisite for accepting a job. (2) However, the potential for a company car to motivate a sales force can be considerable if structured thoughtfully and is most powerful in satisfying higher social needs. (3) Within X plc cars are given to all salesman and better models are allocated according to the progress a salesman makes. (4) Some managers felt that a set of standards should be disclosed so that sales people know on what basis cars are allocated. (5) Survey results revealed that a car signifies financial status and social standing. (Packard, 1980). (6) Therefore, company cars have a significant motivational capacity, as well as being a cause of contention or jealousy especially taking Equity theory into account. (7) Hence this perk must be controlled with integrity and firmness. (8) A survey showed that for some sales people in London a car is of little practical usefulness in the selling task, as the London Underground is more practicable. (9) At present all X plc's sales staff are still issued with a car. (10) With reference to the Cafeteria reward system mentioned in Chapter 3, it may be more satisfactory for sales people to have a choice of a higher salary, a car or some other benefit.

Answer

(a)	**Argument**	Sentence (2): says why a car can motivate a sales force. Sentences (6) and (7): sentence (6) is based on facts described earlier.
(b)	**Commentary**	Sentences (3) and (4): descriptive about X plc
(c)	**Analysis**	There is little analysis in the extract given but it does confirm some of the data. Sentence (5) applies theory to reported results of a survey.

(*Note.* The reference to (Packard, 1980) would be fully described in the List of References to this project. If you have not read through Appendix 3 of the Information Pack on referencing, do so now.)

Finally, the Research and Analysis Project deals with your ability to put over a point in person. It is not an exercise in public speaking, but throughout your work you will have to be an effective oral communicator.

3 Outline and overview of the work involved

Oxford Brookes University has provided useful guidelines in the Information Pack. We will briefly go through each stage as outlined by Oxford Brookes University in the description of the project. This section is a **summary. Detailed coverage of research, mentor meetings etc is found in later chapters.**

3.1 Choosing a mentor

The suggested framework below offers a useful description of the key tasks involved in completing the project. If you already have a degree, you almost certainly have encountered these before but in outline there are two issues: **content** and **process**.

First of all, you should choose a mentor. This person can be your employer or line manager, a tutor or any member of the ACCA. You must do this first of all because you have to **report** on three meetings with your mentor in the Skills and Learning Statement.

Steps 1/2 Choose a topic, read around the topic

Chapter 4 outlines the suggested topics in detail with some guidance notes as to how to go about this. There are **twenty topics** in total. They are not like exam questions; they are very open, identifying the **broad area** of your research and analysis. They create a space, as it were, for you to fill.

You do not have to do a detailed literature review, but you may need to explore the issues. Some relevant knowledge may be found in BPP Learning Media study material.

Step 3 Define aims and objectives of the project

We will cover this in more detail in Chapter 4 – but a project objective is very important.

Detailed guidance on defining the project objective is given in Chapter 4, but here is a taster. The project objective outlines **precisely** what you are going to do, the company involved and so on.

The first mentor meeting you have to report on covers the outline proposals, how you intend to research them and your aims. The mentor will act as a sounding board, but does not take a directive role.

3.2 Example

Let us say that you have chosen **Project Topic 10: The effectiveness of the use of costing techniques within an organisation**. Your employer is H plc, a company manufacturing forklift trucks, which markets the trucks and replacement parts through independent dealers in Europe, the Middle East, and Africa.

'The objective of this project is to evaluate the effectiveness of H plc's system for measuring the performance of its dealers and, through analysis and critique to put forward recommendations on how to improve it.' This project evaluates the effectiveness of the measurement system, **not operational performance**.

Defining the project objective is not the same as choosing a topic. The topic outlines a broad field of activity. The objective gives you a target to work towards.

Step 4   **Choose the analytical framework, ie tools, models and theories you will apply**

The aim of the research project is to explore a situation and you will need a map, so to speak, to help you understand the terrain. Your earlier ACCA studies may have given you some ideas as to some of the frameworks you can use. We offer more help in Chapters 6 and 7.

3.3 Example

A project report investigated the effect of reward systems on the motivation of a sales force. The theoretical framework (covered in ACCA paper F1 Accountant in Business) could be motivation theory, for example:

- Maslow's hierarchy of needs
- Expectancy theory and so on
- Equity theory

Step 5   **Plan information gathering**

We cover this in detail in Chapter 5. You have to **plan** for obtaining data: what you want and how you intend to collect it. You are likely to use a variety of research methods (covered in Chapter 6); these include **secondary research** (reading), and **primary research**.

3.4 Example

An Oxford Brookes University undergraduate did some research into whether, how and why companies communicate data about the impact of their operations on the physical environment.

- **What was needed**: a questionnaire to assess whether companies in the survey had a department specifically devoted to environmental issues, whether they had a stated policy, use of environmental schemes and so on.

- **How it was obtained**: the questionnaire had to be designed – not as straightforward as you think – mailed out and completed.

- A **sample** has to be selected.

- **What if it goes wrong**? Frequently, initial research plans go awry. You may need a contingency plan to meet your research objective.

Putting your well-made plans into effect will need skills of **time management**, **scheduling** and organisation. If you are sending out a questionnaire, you may not receive immediate responses. You may have to book meetings with other people. You may not be able to obtain all the books you need at one time.

3.5 Second meeting with your mentor

After you have gathered all the information you need, by whatever method, you should have some idea as to the progress of the project brief and the findings from your data. To gather your thoughts together, you will need to draft a **word processed** document **summarising your findings so far for discussion with the mentor**. This could be:

(a)   A brief description of what you have done to date

(b)   A brief summary of the information you have gathered

(c)   Initial views

You should be about half way through the project. You may for example want to talk about how to interpret some of the data if the results were not quite what you expected. You may feel it is necessary to do further research.

Step 6   **Analysing the information**

This is when a lot of the more difficult intellectual work takes place. You are in effect converting the data you have gathered into usable information. The analysis work involves interrogating the data, applying theory to it and so on, to obtain the information you need to satisfy the project objective.

3.6 Example

To do **Project Topic 6: The key factors or indicators in the motivation of employees in an organisation** your project objective is based on a stationery supplier.

In your data gathering exercise, you have obtained:

- Details of the company's sales figures, for each of the past 36 months, and of receivables ageing
- From a trade body, an index of prices for the industry as a whole

Your analysis phase could – depending on your project objective – start by adjusting the actual sales figures for general price changes in the industry as a whole. This would give you some idea as to the **underlying** performance of the company, to see whether it was doing better or worse than similar companies elsewhere. You could then obtain reports from other companies in the industry, such as key competitors. This suggests that one set of analytical work might generate more work.

Steps 7/8 Reporting findings and drawing conclusions

Here is an example of a conclusion from an undergraduate dissertation.

3.7 Example

The aim of the project was to evaluate the effectiveness of a performance measurement system for dealers. Based on the study and evaluation of this report, the conclusion is that the performance measurement systems work reasonably well. This research aim has been met by meeting four project objectives.

(1)   Through secondary research, a standard for an effective performance measurement system was developed

(2)   The operations of the current system were investigated

(3) The current system was evaluated in the light of the standard outlined in 1. This analysis showed that the system had been developed according to (1), but that there were some areas of dissatisfaction

(4) Three recommendations were made to the company. One of these has already been adopted.

3.8 Third mentor meeting, presentation, report

To expand, the **final stage** of the project involves the following tasks.

(a) The **intellectual labour** of drawing the data together into a **conclusion**, clearly based on the work done.

    (i) You will need to assess what the information you have discerned actually means.
    (ii) You will have to describe your findings in terms of the project objective.

(b) The **communication task of presenting your findings** in a 15 minute presentation to your mentor.

(c) The **communication task of writing a 6,500 word Research Project** (with appendices).

(d) The **communication task of writing a 2,000 word Skills and Learning Statement** based on your communications.

These are covered in the next sections.

4 What you are expected to produce at the end

4.1 The Research Project

It is worth working through the requirements in some detail. Fortunately you are given quite specific guidance as to the length and weighting of the Research Project. Details required for writing the Research Project are given in Chapter 10.

Word length: 6,500 words (plus NO MORE THAN 8 pages of appendices).

Your Research Project must be no longer than 6,500 words: if you write more Oxford Brookes University reserves the right to fail your project.

This is one of the key differences between the Research Project and an undergraduate dissertation: a typical dissertation is often twice as long.

6,500 words sounds a lot – but this depends very much on how concisely you write. (We will be giving detailed hints and tips in Chapter 11.) And remember, you have to put the word count on the title page.

To put this in context:

    At ten words a line, 6,500 words is 650 lines.
    At 50 lines a page, 6,500 words is 13 pages.
    If you double space your document it will be about 26 pages long.

For your information, the **word count in this chapter so far, including headers** is:

6,345

This should give you some idea as to scale.

4.2 Recommended structure

The Information Pack also gives a suggestion as to structure. This is not compulsory but you will be **taking no risks** by following this format.

Part 1 – Project objectives and overall research approach

- The reasons for choosing your project topic area and choosing the particular organisation that was the focus of your research work
- What you wanted to find out in your research work. i.e. your project objectives and research questions
- An explanation of your overall research approach. This should provide the reader with a understanding of the overall framework that you developed to meet your project objectives and answer your research questions

1,000 words

Part 2 – Information gathering and accounting / business techniques

- The sources of information from which you have obtained relevant data
- A description of the methods used to collect information, including online access
- A discussion of the limitations of your information gathering
- Identification of any ethical issues that arose during your information gathering and how they were resolved
- An explanation of the accounting and / or business techniques you have used, including a discussion of their limitations

1,500 words

Part 3 – Results, analysis, conclusions and recommendations

- A description of the results you have obtained and any limitations
- Presentation of your results in an appropriate form e.g. tables, graphs, pie charts
- A critical analysis / evaluation of your results which includes an explanation of your significant findings
- Your conclusions about your research findings and how well you have met your project objectives and research questions
- If appropriate, recommendations on specific courses of action to identified individuals within your chosen organisation

4,000 words

List of references

Appendices

The 6,500 word limit excludes the Title Page, the Contents Page, the List of References and the Appendices as well as words used in tables and graphs and other forms of data presentation.

4.3 Skills required for the Research Project

Remember that you will be given one of three Pass grades (A, B or C) or a Fail grade (F) for the performance in the Research Project. We consider how you need to use various skills required by Oxford Brookes in order to achieve each grade.

Research Project	Pass-grade A	Pass-grade B	Pass-grade C	Pass-grade F
Technical and professional skills				
Understanding of accountancy/business models	Highly appropriate choice of theory/concepts. Very clear relevance and shows evidence of wider reading.	Appropriate choice of theory/concepts significant evidence of understanding.	Some but limited, choice and use of theory/concepts. Some evidence of understanding.	Poor choice of theory/concepts, very limited understanding. Reliance of narrow range of material.
Application of accountancy/business models	Insightful and critical application of models to the project topic.	Mostly correct application of theory to the project topic.	Some application of theory, but lacking a coherent approach.	Poor use of theory/models and confused understanding of application.
Evaluation of information, analysis and conclusions	High level of critical thought shown in the analysis and a rigorous approach to evaluation of information.	Strength shown in some areas of critical review of the information. Good evaluation of information.	Some analysis but a tendency towards description rather than analysis and evaluation.	Descriptive and lacking in analysis. Inaccuracies. Little or no critical evaluation.
Presentation of project findings	Can engage reader in a professional manner and produce a relevant and coherent project report with appropriate structure.	Can communicate effectively in a format appropriate to the report. Clear and concise manner with all relevant information.	Some communication is effective. Can report practical applications in a structured way.	Communication is only partially effective and project is poorly structured.

Other 'graduate' skills and your competence in them can be summarised as follows:

Graduate Skills	Competent	Not competent
Communication	Language mostly fluent Grammar and spelling mainly accurate	Meaning often unclear Grammar and/or spelling contain frequent errors
Information gathering and referencing	Clear evidence of a range of relevant information sources. Clear evidence of correct referencing methodology	Very few and/or irrelevant information sources used. Referencing is mostly absent or unsystematic
Graduate Skills	**Competent**	**Not competent**
Information technology	Shows reasonable evidence of having accessed online information sources and having used a spreadsheet and/or other software in preparing the project report	Little evidence of use of IT during preparation of project. Little online access, no evidence of spreadsheet/other software use.

4.4 The Skills and Learning Statement

The Skills and Learning Statement (2,000 words) is your reflection on your experiences in undertaking the Research and Analysis Project. This will include the meetings with your project mentor. Your Skills and Learning Statement will also include your reflection on how you developed a number of interpersonal skills such as questioning and listening and the success of your oral presentation to your project mentor.

The purpose of this is to enable you to show that you have considered your oral communication skills in the light of what is expected in the **benchmark statement mentioned in Section 1**. You are not expected to be a world-class public speaker, however, but there are techniques you can use to communicate effectively in a face-to-face context. You may have already acquired some of these techniques in other situations requiring communication, such as:

- Meetings with client staff
- Team briefings
- Interviews (both as interviewer and interviewee)
- Meetings with/presentation to other people in the organisation

The Information Pack guidelines helpfully offer you a structure for the Skills and Learning Statement. You are asked to:

- Communicate orally in meetings and in a 15 minute presentation

- Reflect on your oral communication

- Write down your reflections – including a judgement about your own performance – as to how you would do better

Remember that in the Skills and Learning Statement you are asked to reflect on the following four questions:

- What did you learn from the meetings with your project mentor, including the presentation that you gave to your project mentor?

- How well do you think that you answered your research question(s)?

- How have you demonstrated your interpersonal and communication skills during the project work?

- How has undertaking the Research and Analysis Project helped in your accountancy studies and/or current employment role?

The skills that must be evidenced for your Skills and Learning Statement to be satisfactory can be summarised as follows:

Skills and Learning Statement	Satisfactory	Not satisfactory
Self reflection	Makes a reasonable attempt to address all four questions.	Overly focused on only one or two questions.
	Shows ability to reflect on judgements made/actions taken during project work	Emphasis on description of events, little evaluation of self development
	Evidence of recognising own strengths and weaknesses	Little discussion of own strengths and weaknesses
Communication skills	A copy of the presentation to the project mentor is included	A copy of the presentation to project mentor has not been included.
	Presentation has appropriate structure. Content is clearly linked to project report finding.	Presentation is poorly structured and/or content is not relevant to project report findings.

5 Other people involved: your peer group and your mentor

5.1 Your peer group

First of all, the project is to be your own work. It is not a group project, and Oxford Brookes University **will FAIL projects that show evidence of syndication**.

Here is an extract from Oxford Brookes University guidance for undergraduate dissertations about 'syndication'.

Syndication

You must also take care that, unless you are specifically instructed that a piece of work for assessment is to be produced jointly with other students, the work you submit has been prepared by you alone. If you collude with other students to prepare a piece of work jointly, or copy each other's work, and pass it off as an individual effort, it is syndication and is against the University's regulations. It is also, obviously, against the rules to copy another student's work without his or her knowledge.

That said, if a number of people in your firm are doing the Research and Analysis Project, it would be a shame not to talk things over with them. Here are some suggestions as to how you can make **best** use of a peer group.

(a) **Choice of topics**. One way of ensuring that there is no syndication is to choose different topics from the list provided by Oxford Brookes University. As the list of topics is fairly broad, you may wish to brainstorm ideas.

(b) Colleagues at work might have a good idea as to **your strengths and weaknesses**. Given that written and oral communication are such an important part of the Research Project, it is sometimes good to be told that these are issues you have to work on.

(c) **Presentation**. Your third meeting with the mentor – at which you must give a 15 minute presentation – can take the form of a presentation to your peer group also.

(d) You may be able to share hints and tips about how to plan the project.

5.2 Your mentor's role

Firstly, you have to **find** a mentor. It will be worth your while doing this **before you start the project.**

There are two aspects to the role.

(a) **Formal**

   (i) To be present at three meetings with you
   (ii) To verify to Oxford Brookes University that the meetings took place
   (iii) To confirm that the Research Project has been carried out according to the Information Pack guidelines

(b) **Informal**

   (i) Sounding board for ideas
   (ii) A champion for the degree project within the organisation; a mentor will appreciate that you have **other** demands on your time

(iii)   Give you unbiased constructive feedback about your presentation and communication skills

(iv)   Suggest fruitful avenues of enquiry

(v)   Pull strings on your behalf with other managers

A **mentor's role is not**:

(a)   To act as a tutor throughout the project

(b)   To give detailed instructions on how to tackle the project

(c)   To read and offer a detailed critique of your Research Project

(d)   To act as a progress chaser on the project – you should be motivated enough

5.3 Who can be your mentor?

Your mentor can be:

(a)   A senior colleague at work, your employer or line manager (current or previous) OR

(b)   Your tutor at college or university OR

(c)   A qualified Chartered Certified Accountant (sorry, but this excludes members of all other accountancy bodies unless they are also members of the ACCA). The qualification of your mentor to act will have to be certified on the Submission Form which accompanies your project.

Whoever you choose, you will have to reassure them that your project will not breach commercial confidentiality. More about this in a later chapter.

If your mentor is 'your employer or line manager'

(a)   In theory it could be **anybody** – but you need someone who can give you constructive feedback and take a responsible, but not intrusive, interest in the project.

(b)   You could ask your **immediate line manager** to assume this role – but remember that your line manager has an interest in keeping you working on what you are paid to do.

(c)   You could ask your line manager to recommend someone else in the department or in another department.

(d)   You could ask someone in the human resources department or, if you have a training department, in the training department to be your mentor.

Briefing a mentor

- Ask first of all – do not assume that your choice has the time or inclination to take this role.

- Explain carefully what the mentor has to do – in case he/she is frightened off.

- **Agree a timetable in advance if possible**. You know when the Research Project has to be submitted, and you may have to schedule your meetings and your own time with your mentor's other commitments.

- If you cannot make your appointments, give as much advance notice as possible.

- Make sure that you ask for feedback.

- Explain how important the degree is to you, and that a relatively limited use of mentor's time can help you get a degree.

- Explain how acquiring some of the skills in the project may make you a more effective worker (if this is indeed to be the case).

- You could also ask if the company would pay the £75 submission. After all, if they support your ACCA studies, this is not too much to ask.

Chapter roundup

- This chapter has given an overview of the different skills you need to adopt when doing the project, and a brief overview of what is involved.

- A degree has to satisfy other criteria than a professional qualification.

- The Research and Analysis Project enables Oxford Brookes University to test abilities required for all accountancy degrees.

- Research, analysis and communication skills are required.

- Nothing will be handed to you on a plate.

- You can set your own deadlines.

- We will go into more detail in later chapters.

chapter 4

Choosing and defining your project

INTRODUCTION

This chapter discusses one of the most crucial decisions you will have to make: the choice of topic. Oxford Brookes University has indicated 20 broad topic outlines. However, you have to turn one of these into a project with a defined objective.

In Section 1 we outline the list of topics and the rationale for doing them. In Section 2 we give some hints as to how you can make your choice, following this up in Section 3 by discussing what to do if you have a burning desire to branch out on your own.

In Section 4, we offer some suggestions as to how to convert the choice of project into a genuine objective.

In Section 5 we discuss the complex issue of confidentiality and consider ways of solving potential problems.

In Section 6, we have jotted down some ideas about each topic to get you thinking.

1 Oxford Brookes University's list of recommended project topics

The Information Pack guidelines offer you twenty topic areas to choose from. Read them carefully.

Project topic areas and titles

1   An organisation's budgetary control system and its links with performance management and decision making

2   How the introduction of a new technology can assist an organisation in achieving its business objectives

3   The impact of an aspect of impending legislation on the operations and financial position of an organisation

4   The impact of e-business on an organisation

5   The effects of globalisation on an organisation

6   The key factors or indicators in the motivation of employees in an organisation

7   The restructuring of an organisation's operational activities and the effect on the organisation's financial performance

8   The business and financial performance of an organisation over a three year period

9   The planning and implementation of an information system in an organisation

10   The effectiveness of the use of costing techniques within an organisation

11   The financial and operational costs and benefits of the internal audit/internal review activities within an organisation

12   The possible effects of a proposed accounting standard on the financial statements and business activities of an organisation

13   The relationship between an organisation's human resources activities and its business objectives

14   The business and financial objectives of a strategic investment decision made by an organisation and its impact on key stakeholders

15   The management of an organisation's working capital over a three year period and its impact on the organisation's funding strategies

16   The financial and operational risk management within an organisation

17   The quality of the corporate governance within an organisation and the impact on an organisation's key stakeholders

18   The marketing strategy of an organisation and its effectiveness

19   The financial and operational consequences of a merger between two organisations or of the acquisition of one organisation by another

20   An organisation's corporate social responsibility policies, including business ethics, and their impact on business practice and key stakeholders

The **scope** of topics is very wide and would suggest **different treatments** and a **different scheme of work for each of them**. There are two ways of looking at this issue.

For example, contrast these two projects.

(a) **Project Topic 4: The impact of e-business on an organisation**

    (i) The scope of your **analysis of e-business** can be enormous, as you could cover marketing, its effect on sales volumes and revenues, raising finance, how you value e-businesses, information technology, effect on distribution, risks and costs.

    (ii) **An organisation of your choice.** If you wish to focus on a **particular company**, you might find this easier to grasp; for example if you focus on food retailing, you might concentrate on a supermarket chain, such as Tesco in the UK or Wal-Mart in the US.

(b) **Project Topic 12: The possible effects of a proposed accounting standard on the financial statements and business activities of an organisation.**

    This alerts us to a different set of issues entirely.

    (i) First, you will be limited to **one** organisation (but you can use others for comparison).

    (ii) Second, you are restricted **to an organisation which has to prepare financial statements** according to local accounting standards. You could thus exclude partnerships or sole traders, and much of the public sector.

2 Choosing your project

Your choice of topic is key in ensuring that the project is an interesting and enjoyable experience for you.

2.1 If you find a project topic you like strongly

With luck, you will see one straight away. If you are absolutely convinced of what you want to do, then read this section no further, ignore Section 3, and go straight to Section 4 of this chapter. However, before you do that think carefully whether:

- you will be able to gain **access** to information (for example will there be issues of confidentiality if you are planning to base your research on your own company?)

- you will be able to obtain **enough** material: even if the topic interests you, you may not be able to find enough to say about it

2.2 If you like none of the project topics on the list

The list of topics has been **carefully** designed and developed by the academic staff at Oxford Brookes University. A great deal of thought has gone into this list, and it is appropriate for the BSc (Hons) in Applied Accounting and in the light of your ACCA studies to date. The Research and Analysis Project is not an undergraduate dissertation, but something unique to **this** degree. Therefore you are strongly advised to choose a topic from this list.

(a) **First, look again more carefully**. You may find that with a little more thought, you can find a number of topics that interest you.

(b) Second, if you have difficulty making up your mind, then carry on reading this section.

2.3 If you cannot make up your mind, follow these steps

Step 1   **Cross off the projects that definitely do not interest you**

Even if you cannot find the topic you like, there may be a few that you would definitely want to avoid. This may narrow the field according to key criteria significantly, making it easier to choose from those remaining.

Step 2   **Grade the remaining projects**

In the example to follow we suggest a number of **criteria by which you can grade the attractiveness** of a project. You can decide yourself what the most appropriate criteria are, and give each criterion a weighting (eg 3 marks max, 6 marks max etc). You can of course, change the weightings. (If relevance to your future career is more important to you than what your mentor thinks, then give it a higher weighting.) All we are suggesting is a technique **to help you prioritise**.

For each project you are grading, make a decision on each of the criteria, below.

(a)   **How relevant is this topic to my experience to date**? (Weighting 3 = very relevant; 0 = not relevant – make up your own weighting from now on.)

(b)   **Can my employer benefit from the project topic**? Your employer may have issues worth investigating, which can be adapted for the project. An advantage of taking this into account is that your employer may agree that at least some of the project can be done in **working hours**, as the organisation will benefit.

(c)   **How relevant is the topic to what I would be interested to pursue in my future career?**

     (i)   If you want to work as an accountant for a bank, say, then some topics may be more relevant to the banking sector than others.

     (ii)   You may not have a sector in mind, but may be interested in exploring management accounting issues in a strategic context.

(d)   Some people are happier with a **broad brush**; others prefer a **forensic approach**.

(e)   How far does the topic **build on technical or other knowledge I am confident of using**? The Research and Analysis Project covers particular skills, and most of the technical knowledge you have gleaned from your ACCA studies. But you may have other resources of your own you could bring to bear – for example you may have experience in developing an information system, or there has been an IS project in your department recently.

(f)   Can I define **key issues** and **examples**?

For example, if you are analysing the financial position of an organisation, you might identify cash flow as a major indicator of 'going concern' status.

(g)   Can I **obtain data easily**? You may find that some topics are easier for you to research than others (for whatever reason). This will differ from person to person, but as you will be doing the Research Project while holding down a job, this is worth considering.

(h)   From an informal chat with my **mentor**, how far do I think the project topic will enable me to get constructive **feedback** from him/her?

Step 3   **Total the score**

Add up the scores and you have a result. But then again, you might want to go back and reweight the criteria. Or the result you arrive at may cause you to think seriously and realise that you actually do not want to do this topic, in which case you can then focus on other topics.

2.4 Example

In the example below questions (c) and (e) are of more importance to the student than the other questions so they have a higher weighting. The student would be able to ignore Project Topics 4 and 11 and should, strictly speaking, choose Project Topic 12, with the highest score. However as Project Topics 12 and 15 are very close, the student might consider reviewing this assessment. The exercise at least narrows the choice down to two topics rather than the previous four.

Question		Project number and marks			
		No 4	No 11	No 12	No 15
(a)	How relevant/related is this topic to my experience to date?	3	0	2	1
(b)	Can my employer benefit from the project topic?	3	2	1	1
(c)	How relevant is the topic to what I would be interested in doing in my future career?	0	4	5	6
(d)	How does the topic reflect my preferences for breadth of scope over depth?	0	1	2	3
(e)	How far does the topic build on technical or other knowledge that I am confident using?	2	3	5	4
(f)	Can I define some key issues or examples?	0	0	1	2
(g)	Can I obtain data easily about this topic (eg background reading material, primary data)?	3	0	2	1
(h)	From an informal chat with my mentor, how far do I think the project topic will enable me to get constructive feedback from him/her?	4	3	2	1
Total		15	13	20	19

By now you have chosen your topic. Now you have to define your objective. Go to Section 4.

2.5 Still unhappy?

If you really cannot make up your mind, read Section 3 below.

3 Project topics not on the list

Below we reproduce what Oxford Brookes University has said about choosing topics.

If you believe that you face exceptional circumstances and cannot identify a suitable project from the list of approved project topic areas, then Oxford Brookes will consider your request to undertake a Research and Analysis Project based on a different area of your previous academic study.

However, you must obtain permission from the ACCA office at Oxford Brookes before you start your RAP research work. You must provide an outline (minimum one page in length) of your proposed project research work, which includes the project title, the objectives of your research and how you will undertake your research to meet your objectives. The outline should also state how you will be able to demonstrate your evaluative and / or analytical skills. Please email acca@brookes.ac.uk with your one page outline and allow 10 working days for a response.

4 Defining the project objective

Now we have selected a project topic, this is the next key issue for you to look at: **defining the project objective**. This will be the focus of the project and will direct your research and so it is worth spending a lot of time on this.

As an **analogy**, when choosing a holiday you may be looking for somewhere exciting to go. This is of course a matter of personal preference. You will need to translate 'somewhere exciting to go' into something concrete for you. If your definition of 'somewhere exciting to go' involves partying the night away, you might set yourself a definite objective of going to Ibiza. If 'somewhere exciting to go' means travelling to parts of the world you have never visited before, you might book a trip up the Amazon river.

So, your job is to turn the general nature of the project topic into something specific that you can latch on to, and design a research programme around. The external examiner has commented that the Research Project must be business related and linked to an organisation. Some candidates have not linked their report to an organisation, but have instead written generally about the subject.

4.1 Analyse every word in the project topic

Each of the topics outlined is expressed as a brief sentence – which is why you have to read it carefully. For example, let's take Project Topic 6 and latch on to the **key words.**

Project Topic 6: The key factors or indicators in the motivation of employees in an organisation

Key factors	There is a lot of theory as to what motivates people. But in this **particular** organisation, what is important? **Key factors** are the underlying substance of motivation.
	You could take a theory of motivation and see how it works in practice.
Indicators	An **indicator** is something which shows something (eg a temperature gauge shows how hot it is). For motivation, the same **indicator** mean different things. A person working excessive overtime may be motivated to work late:
	• Because he/she loves the job
	• Out of a strong sense of responsibility to the customer or to other members of staff
	• Out of fear of looking less than committed if everybody else works late – an example of 'presenteeism'
	• Because he/she is inefficient
	• Because he/she needs the money
	• Because he/she has been bullied into it
	• Because he/she is using work as a substitute for dealing with personal problems and so on.

Employees	Technically, **'employees'** means everybody employed by the company, and this includes the Board of Directors.
	Employees need not be taken just to mean 'non-managerial staff', even though this is how the word is often used.
	Are different levels of staff motivated in different ways?

You should now have a much richer appreciation of what could be covered by this project topic.

4.2 Categorisation

This is sometimes known as 'defining the research problem'. Here is an extract from an undergraduate dissertation to show what we mean. It is given in the introduction to a project report. Please note that this is not from the approved list of project topics. (We don't want to give too much away.)

Paragraph

1   This project evolved from a year's work in the Statistics and Finance Department in Q Ltd. During the year I spent much of my time analysing sales and contribution figures for individual areas and for the whole company. The other half of my job was to calculate commission payments each month and to authorise bonuses.

2   I was particularly interested in how the accounting and control systems within Q Ltd influenced behaviour and in turn what result these changes in behaviour had on the firm. At the same time as this it was clear that Q Ltd was experiencing deteriorating sales and declining contribution.

3   Therefore I set myself the aim to explore how effective different reward systems (which require accounting and control systems to operate) have been and could be used to motivate sales staff and sales performance, contribution and ultimately the profit of Q Ltd.

     Conclusions are hard to prove but theory, opinion and logic can lead to some recommendations.

In a nutshell this encapsulates turning the project topic into a project objective.

(a)   Paragraph 1 describes the context.

(b)   Paragraph 2 describes the general area: equivalent to the 20 topics Oxford Brookes University provide. You could rephrase it. 'Describe how accounting and control systems influence behaviour in an organisation of your choice'.

(c)   Paragraph 3 defines the aim of the project. There are other examples of accounting control systems but once you have identified the category the answer should slip in.

General category topic	Example of category example – project aim
Accounting control systems	<ul><li>Reward systems</li><li>Costing systems etc</li><li>Budget systems</li></ul>
Behaviour	<ul><li>Motivation of sales staff to perform better and thus improve **profitability**</li><li>Accurate budgets</li><li>Goal congruence</li></ul>
Organisation of your choice	Q Ltd, in this case

(d)   You can now define the project aim by taking **examples** from the general category.

> Show the influence of accounting control systems on behaviour by describing how commission **reward systems** at Q Ltd contribute to **profitability** in the light of relevant **motivation** theory.

(i)   You could, conceivably, have chosen how **budget** systems influence 'goal **congruence'**, as both are specific examples of the category described.

(ii)   Very sensibly, the author draws attention to **theory** and evidence, underscoring the possible limitations. For most of the Oxford Brookes University research topics, you will have to draw on theory.

If you read through the list of recommended project topics, you can probably find ways of applying this approach elsewhere. We give some pointers in Section 5.

4.3 Still stuck for ideas? Mind maps, tree diagrams etc

You may still feel uncertain and you may wish to explore certain issues. Using a tree diagram or a mind map can help you explore a topic in some detail. Below is a chart covering some of the issues of **Project Topic 3: The impact of an aspect of impending legislation on the operations and financial position of an organisation**.

What you should do is start off with a key word say, and explore some of the issues from there. You may find that you can then link areas together.

4.4 Example

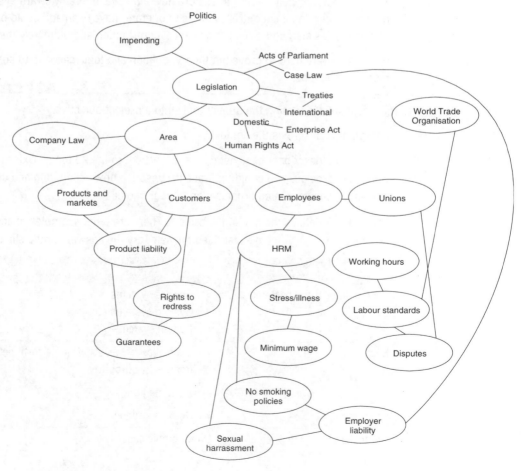

4.5 Testing the project objective: do a reality check

When you have formulated the project aim, you should test it; in other words you should show how it fits together. Here is what you should do.

Step 1   Identify what you would need to do to reach the aim. Is it feasible?

Step 2   Describe the project aim to a friend (this need not yet be one of the three mentor meetings). Does what you have said actually make sense?

You have a little more to do before your first mentor meeting, but for that you need a bit more about your proposed line of research, and the methods you will use.

Section 6 below aims to get you thinking about each of the project topics, to stimulate your creative juices.

5 Confidentiality and anonymity

We reproduce here the relevant section of Oxford Brookes University Information Pack.

In principle, Oxford Brookes University requires your Research Project to contain full details of the organisation that you have investigated in your research, the information sources that you used and the actual data that you collected. This provides reassurance to Oxford Brookes about the originality and the genuineness of the information gathering and analysis in your Research Project.

We have already noted that if you intend to collect primary data from staff within your chosen organisation you must obtain permission to do this from a senior member of staff within the organisation. However, although you may gain such permission, the organisation may request that your research findings remain confidential because of concerns over confidentiality and / or commercial sensitivity.

If you want your Research Project to be considered as confidential or to make specific adjustments to the organisation's data in order to hide the 'true figures' then you must write to the BSc programme director at acca@brookes.ac.uk and request permission. You should give the reasons behind your request and how you intend to resolve such issues in the preparation and presentation of your Research Project. In your request you will have to identify the organisation which is the focus of your Research Project. The BSc programme director will decide whether to give approval to your request.

This issue must be resolved before you submit your Research Project to Oxford Brookes otherwise your project will be returned to you unmarked. Any such correspondence between yourself and the BSc programme director will not be passed on to the Oxford Brookes staff involved in the marking of your Research Project.

6 Thought points on each project topic

Project Topic 1

An organisation's budgetary control system and its links with performance management and decision making

Budgetary control system

- Choose organisation with strong budgetary control
- What is system?
- Relevance to type of business – manufacturing/service
- Consider organisational structure
- Cost centres, profit centres, investment centres
- Responsibility accounting
- Variance reporting

Performance management

- How is system linked with performance management?
- Is it used for performance appraisal and reward?
- How are decisions really taken – is system directly used in performance management?
- Corporate culture
- Behavioural aspects of budgeting
- Comparison with other organisations

Decision making

- How is system linked with decision making?
- Goal congruence
- Management responsibility
- Dysfunctional decision making

Project Topic 2

How the introduction of new technology can assist an organisation in achieving its business objectives

Introduction

- Why is it being introduced?
- Is it new to industry or just new to organisation?
- Competitive pressures

Type of technology

- Equipment
- Techniques and work practices
- Work organisation eg teams
- Physical processes eg manufacturing equipment
- Communication processes eg IT
- Products
- Does not have to be 'hi-tech' – low technology application can be as radical
- Information

Organisation

- Type
- Business
- Public sector
- Non profit orientated
- Size
- Management and departmental structure
- Compatibility of systems
- Location – centralised/decentralised
- Industry sector

Business objectives

- Mission statement
- Financial objectives
- Marketing objectives
- Sales objectives
- Satisfying stakeholders
- Cost vs benefit

Project Topic 3

The impact of an aspect of impending legislation on the operations and financial position of an organisation

We have used UK examples here, but many issues here may be reflected elsewhere.

Impending legislation

- Forthcoming companies legislation
- Regulations against discrimination on grounds of disability, religious beliefs, sexual orientation and age

Choice of organisation

- Depth of knowledge of the organisation
- Confidentiality an issue?
- Own experience?
- How easy to research?

Factors to consider

- State of play before the legislation (or the current situation if discussing impending legislation)
- Need for legislation: problems arising with the current situation
- Why was/is the legislation introduced?
- How effective has the legislation been?
- How can you quantify the impact of the legislation: statistics available/questionnaire appropriate?
- Need for further legislation
- Comparison of the chosen organisation with others
- Financial impact
- Social/environmental impact
- Effect on employees: if beneficial to employees, effect on company
- Ability to avoid legislation: loopholes

Project Topic 4

The impact of e-business on an organisation

Development of e-business

- Very rapid
- Types of business most affected (eg financial services, retail, travel)
- 'Boom or bust' scenario with dot com start-ups, but less impact with established businesses
- High public profile
- Highly topical: good availability of information likely

Features of e-business

- Big cash injections to start or to upgrade
- Need for sophisticated hardware and software: capital expenditure budget
- Highly-skilled, computer literate staff
- Ability to trade in international markets
- Fear among same-industry companies of being 'left behind' in e-commerce
- Risk of abandoning, ignoring or alienating traditional markets
- Well-publicised fears over computer security
- Move to centralised distribution

Organisation of choice

- Organisation includes not just companies: consider charities, partnerships (the firm you work for?) pension funds, schools, universities, doctors' fund holding practices etc.

- Consider own experience

- Consider ease of access to information

- Consider confidentiality

- Negative impact, eg effect on small independent booksellers of internet book-buying

- Could be an organisation which is greatly affected

- Could be an organisation which is not affected at all

- Could consider organisation as a whole or a specific department within it

- Could consider an organisation which is affected by other people's e-business, eg small local bookshop or travel agent

Analysis

- Financial: impact on income/expenditure/profits/losses

- Business valuations: difficulties

- Strategic: marketing, pricing, planning

- Social: impact on employees

- Compare what with what in the analysis? Eg current financial results with others over what period of time?

Project Topic 5

The effects of globalisation on an organisation

Organisation

- Type – manufacturing/service
- Size
- Geographical areas

Globalisation

- Move towards greater globalisation in late 20th century
- More likely due to ease of communications
- Desire for international representation, eg by accountancy firms
- Harmonisation of laws (within the EC)
- Harmonisation of accounting standards (worldwide)
- Impact of use or non-use of the euro
- Impact of exchange rates: weak dollar
- Issues of language and culture

Effects

- Need to consider both positive and negative
- Financial: impact on profits, sales
- Operational: need to start up elsewhere or close down some locations
- Marketing: need to cater to different types of market, and adjust advertising methods
- Social: impact of moving operations to another country, use of cheaper labour abroad
- Management: drawn from different international sources
- Areas of disparity: different attitudes to eg working practices
- Cyclical nature eg Far East's 'tiger economies' in decline
- Greater risk of merger/takeover to create global giants

Project Topic 6

The key factors or indicators in the motivation of employees in an organisation

Choice of organisation

- Might be difficult to obtain information
- Usually an area of confidentiality
- Your own organisation is relevant, but access to information still might be difficult
- Need to devise a questionnaire/survey; risk of low response rate
- Maybe conduct interviews with employees (guarantee their confidentiality)

Key factors

- The underlying substance of motivation
- Desire for recognition and reward
- Greed
- Fear of losing the job/job security
- Job satisfaction
- A way to pass the time/deflect attention from other problems
- Achievability of rewards

Indicators

- Indicators show you something or demonstrate it
- Rates of pay compared with industry averages
- Performance related pay
- Expected benefits
- Levels of overtime
- Levels of absenteeism
- Levels of morale
- Demands made in pay negotiations
- Working conditions
- Rates of staff turnover/ease of recruitment
- Levels of industrial unrest
- Degrees of productivity
- Public perception of the company

Motivation

- Motivation models or theories
- MacGregor's Theory X and Theory Y
- Maslow's hierarchy of needs
- Herzberg's two factor theory
- Vroom's Expectancy theory
- Handy's motivation calculus

Employees

- Everybody employed by the company, including managerial staff and directors (their motivation likely to be different from 'normal' employees)

- May be differences between part and full time

Project Topic 7

The restructuring of an organisation's operational activities and the effect on the organisation's financial performance

Type of restructuring

- Type of business
- Organisational structure
- Physical restructuring – changing manufacturing methods
- Employee restructuring – change in working practices

Operational activities

- What were they?
- How have they changed?
- Why?

Effect on financial performance

- Profit
- Gross profit margin
- Net profit margin
- Tax
- Return on capital employed
- Returns to shareholders
- Dividends
- Working capital
- Operating cycle
- Balance sheet valuations
- Cash flows

Project Topic 8

The business and financial performance of an organisation over a three year period

Financial performance

Meaning

- Per financial statements
- Financial structure (eg debt/equity)
- Solvency

Current position

- Trends leading to current position
- Trends possibly for the future
- Financial position reflecting underlying operating performance
- Working capital
- Ratio calculations
- Industry comparisons
- Competitor comparisons

Reported financial results not reflecting 'true value'

- Fixed asset valuations: market vs historic cost
- Goodwill and intangible assets (eg brands)
- Off balance sheet finance
- Financial reporting vs decision making information

Fluctuations in performance

- Seasonal differences/trends
- Exchange rates

Business performance

- Market share
- Competitor activity
- Industry comparisons
- New products
- Other performance measures
- Balanced scorecard

Project Topic 9

The planning and implementation of an information system in an organisation

Choice of organisation

- Needs not to have a suitable information system at the moment
- Could be your own organisation: suitable depth of knowledge
- Whole tone of answer depends on nature of organisation
- You will need to describe the organisation in some detail, explaining its IT needs and expectations, discussing its products and services, providing a profile of its users

Will depend on the type of business

- Consider the needs of the organisation
- Need for information management (identification of needs, sources and users of information)
- Identification of whether it is a support activity, a key operational activity, a turnaround activity or a strategic activity

Systems theories

- Nolan's stage hypothesis
- Systems Development Lifecycle

Planning

- Expenditure and funding
- Centralisation or decentralisation
- Multi user and distributed systems
- LANs and WANs etc.
- Feasibility studies
- Cost-benefit analysis
- Acquisition procedures
- Financing methods
- Evaluation of proposals and tenders
- Software contracts
- Security, privacy and data protection

Implementation

- Project management: network analysis, Gantt charts, project management software
- Installation and testing
- Staff training
- File conversion and changeover
- Post-implementation review

Project Topic 10

The effectiveness of the use of costing techniques within an organisation

Effectiveness

- Who defines effective?
- Effective for organisation or stakeholders?
- Mission statement
- What is technique expected to achieve?
- Costs vs benefits
- Goal congruence

Costing techniques

- Explain theory of technique
- Record how used in practice
- Evaluate how used in practice
- Relevance to type of organisation
- Manufacturing business
- Service business

Use of technique

- Actual reporting
- Control vs decision making uses
- Performance appraisal and reward
- Budgeting

Organisational setting

- Organisation as a whole
- One department/division
- Part of management information system
- Comparison with other organisations
- Corporate culture

Project Topic 11

The financial and operational costs and benefits of the internal audit/internal review activities within an organisation

Organisation of your choice

- Public sector
- Private sector
- Whole organisation or division/operating unit

Internal audit/internal review

- Different audit requirements

- Scope of audit vs review, from reporting to shareholders to value for money and operational effectiveness

- Integration of financial audit with review of operations

- Controls and processes

- Benefits of internal audit vs external audit

Costs

- Costs to whom?

- Stakeholders in the audit outcome – for example, public sector audits do not report to shareholders and may have different requirements

Types of cost

- Salaries and overheads of internal audit staff
- Costs of time spent by line management
- Costs of controls instituted
- Operational as well as financial

Benefits

- Benefits to whom?
- Reduced costs of external audit
- Value for money audit
- Identified savings
- Reduction of risk
- Management of the department
- Operational as well as financial

Project Topic 12

The possible effects of a proposed accounting standard on the financial statements and business activities of an organisation

Effect on who or what?

- Results as reported in published statements
- Underlying classification of transactions data
- Format of accounts
- Distributable profits
- Asset valuations
- Performance ratios
- Management decision making

Proposed Accounting Standard

- See relevant FA texts for details
- Need to look at exposure drafts

Financial statement

- Pre tax
- Post tax
- Earnings per share

Business activities

- Effect on internal organisation

- Effect on group structure

- Would it affect an organisation's credit rating and interest cost?

- Would it affect types of business the company operates in?

- Asset valuation

- Impact on investors

Project Topic 13

The relationship between an organisation's human resources activities and its business objectives

Relationship

- Meaning
- Two-way relationship

Type of human resources

- Manual labour – skilled/unskilled
- Office staff
- IT experts
- Accountants
- Managers
- Directors

Human resource activities

- Recruitment
- Training
- Redundancies
- Dealing with recession
- Employee development
- Employee motivation
- Remuneration

Business objectives

- Mission statement
- Financial objectives
- Non-financial objectives
- Various stakeholders

Problems to consider

- Anything to do with human resources normally very sensitive issue
- May be difficult to find information
- Data could be very sensitive
- Confidentiality issues
- Difficult to access data
- May need to disguise identity of organisation used

Project Topic 14

The business and financial objectives of a strategic investment decision made by an organisation and its impact on key stakeholders

Business and financial objectives

- Must firstly discover both business and financial objectives of decision
- Mission statement
- Business objectives will include strategic and operational
- Marketing objectives
- Financial vs non-financial objectives
- Financial statements may hold clues ie Chairman's statement etc

Type of investment decision

- Non-current asset expenditure
- Marketing campaign
- New product launch
- Research and development
- New information systems and IT
- Acquisition of company

Key stakeholders

- Investors
- Employees
- Directors
- Loan providers
- Suppliers
- Customers
- Government
- Public

Types of impact

- Financial
- Environmental
- Fiscal – tax implications
- Tangible/intangible benefits
- Risk factors

Project Topic 15

The management of an organisation's working capital over a three year period and its impact on the organisation's funding strategies

Working capital

- Balance sheet definition, current assets and current liabilities
- Degrees of liquidity of current assets
- Current liabilities repayable on demand
- Operating cycle
- Cash cycle
- Working capital ratios such as inventory turnover, receivables turnover, payables turnover
- Inventory levels

Management

- Obtain cash for use elsewhere

- Insolvency arises from lack of liquidity not lack of profitability

- Source of finance – it is sometimes alleged that many businesses rely on bank overdraft finance as a source of long term capital – not appropriate

Areas to consider

- Early payment discounts
- Bank overdraft and loan interest
- Cost of credit control
- Debt factoring (ie selling debts to a collector)
- Discounts
- Credit terms and sales force
- Bad debts
- Obsolete inventory
- Relationships with suppliers and customers (eg trade discounts, credit periods)
- Volume vs profit
- Overtrading

Funding strategies

- Operating cycle
- Overdraft facility
- Loans
- Gearing level
- Short vs long term funding

Project Topic 16

The financial and operational risk management within an organisation

Type of organisation

- Manufacturing/service
- National/international
- Size
- Management structure
- Industry sector

Financial risks

- Interest rate risk
- Foreign exchange rate risk
- Credit risk
- Gearing risk
- Market risk

Operational risk

- Process risk
- People risk
- Systems risk
- Event risk
- Business risk

Managing risks

- Portfolio analysis
- Scenario analysis
- Stress testing
- Swaps
- Futures
- Forward contracts
- Options
- Risk policies
- Risk identification
- Risk assessment
- Risk mitigation
- Risk control

Project Topic 17

The quality of the corporate governance within an organisation and the impact on an organisation's key stakeholders

Corporate governance

- Increasingly important
- Cadbury report
- Hampel report
- Greenbury report
- Combined code (revised July 2003)
- Turnbull committee
- Reasons for its prominence: investor protection
    - public perception
    - good PR
- Contributes to 'openness'
- Impact depends on whether a private or public company or another type of organisation

Financial performance

- Directors' remuneration
- Share price movements
- Impact of corporate governance or practices such as off balance sheet finance and creative accounting
- Conflicts of interest between management and shareholders
- International comparisons

Key stakeholders

- Investors
- Employees including directors
- Loan provider
- Supplier
- Customer
- Government
- Public

Other aspects of corporate governance

- Variety of directors required; executive, non executive etc
- Difficult to find people to act?
- Audit committee
- Reporting requirements; greater bureaucracy?
- Public relations: effect on company if seems to flout regulations with eg 'fat cat' payments to directors

Project Topic 18

The marketing strategy of an organisation and its effectiveness

Strategy

- A course of action to achieve a specific objective
- What is course of action?
- What is objective?

Marketing

- Development of a marketing plan
- Mission statement
- Statement of objectives
- Situation analysis
- Strategy development
- Implementation
- Geographical market
- Social market
- Marketing mix
- Pricing policy
- Promotion

Effectiveness

- Has it met objective?
- Cost/benefit
- Stakeholders
- Goal congruence

Project Topic 19

The financial and operational consequences of a merger between two organisations or of the acquisition of one organisation by another

Organisation

- Merger or acquisition?
- Reasons for merger/acquisition
- National or international expansion
- Vertical or horizontal expansion

Financial consequences

- Economies of scale
- Exchange rates
- Tax implications
- Profitability
- Benefits to shareholders
- Benefits to other stakeholders
- Diversification of risk

Operational consequences

- Business synergy
- Need for new markets
- Employee consequences
- Systems compatibility
- Cultural effects
- Competitiveness
- Change in marketing strategy
- Change in product mix
- Redundancies or recruitment
- Marketing effects
- Conflicts in working practices

General considerations

- Consider both positive and negative effects
- Financial effects
- Non-financial effects
- Areas of conflict
- Size of new organisation
- Effect on share price
- Public perception

Project Topic 20

An organisation's corporate social responsibility policies, including business ethics, and their impact on business practice and key stakeholders

Corporate social responsibility

- Ethical
- Environmental
- Social issues
- Charitable contributions
- Community development
- Mission statement
- Information in financial statements eg Chairman's report

Business ethics

- Integrity
- Responsibility
- Legal factors
- Independence

Business practices

- Operational
- Management
- Financing
- Geographical
- Work force
- Minimum wages
- Conditions
- Suppliers used
- Packaging used

Key stakeholders

- Investors
- Employees
- Suppliers
- Customers
- Government
- Public

Chapter roundup

- This chapter has explored the twenty project topics on the Oxford Brookes University list.

- By applying the techniques outlined, you should be able to narrow the possibilities down to one or two definite probabilities.

- If you choose a topic not on the list, ensure you get approval from Oxford Brookes before starting work.

chapter 5

Planning and managing your project

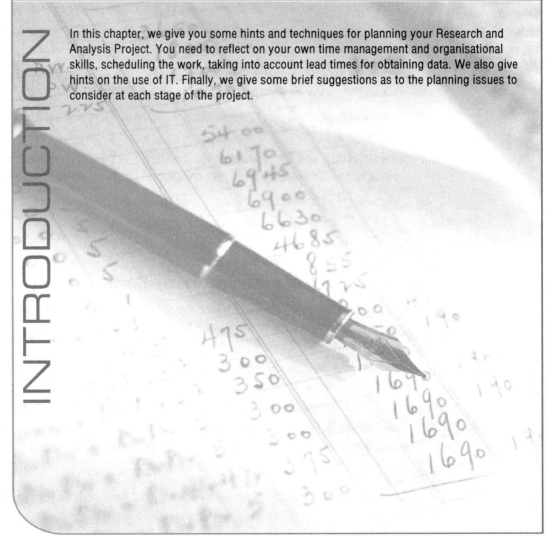

INTRODUCTION

In this chapter, we give you some hints and techniques for planning your Research and Analysis Project. You need to reflect on your own time management and organisational skills, scheduling the work, taking into account lead times for obtaining data. We also give hints on the use of IT. Finally, we give some brief suggestions as to the planning issues to consider at each stage of the project.

1 Project management skills and the Research and Analysis Project

1.1 The Research and Analysis Project

Any project – whether it is developing a new software package, or constructing a new building – is, in many ways, a unique, one-off task. But all **projects** have:

- A defined start. By choosing the project objective, you have started already.

- A defined project objective.

- A number of activities that need to be co-ordinated – some of them depend on earlier activities, some depend on other people.

- A budget (of money, hours, or whatever).

- A defined endpoint – in this case the **Research Project** and the **Skills and Learning Statement.**

In commercial projects, a project is successful if it is completed to the client's objectives, is on time and within budget. Even with commercial projects, this is often easier said than done. A construction project might be delayed by unexpected problems, financing problems or just poor project management.

A research project, whether it be a PhD, an undergraduate dissertation, or the Research and Analysis Project is a special kind of project.

(a)   **Issues of breadth**. You may find that the field is much broader than you thought, and you need to set up some clear boundaries (see below).

(b)   **Issues of depth**. You may find that you need to go into more detail, if matters are not clear (see below).

(c)   **Predictability**. You can research to ask a question; but you cannot predict at the outset what the result will be. The data obtained may not support what you are trying to prove (see Chapter 8).

(d)   **Incomplete outcome**. Your 'result' may be a realisation that you need to do further research (see Chapter 8).

1.2 Example: breadth

Project Topic 4: The impact of e-business on an organisation

Let us assume you have defined your project objective as 'An analysis of the impact of the Internet on the distribution systems of The Books plc (a book selling company)'. Without giving too much away, you could find yourself covering two related but fundamentally distinct issues:

(a)   **Retailing books** – online ordering taking over from bookshops as a delivery mechanism – you might have scores of articles, price lists, website downloads and so on; you might find yourself drawn to wider issues of retailing.

(b)   **Downloading books** – will paper disappear as a medium carrying intellectual property and will people download books from the Internet to PCs, mobile phones, or 'e-book' readers?

Are there different issues involved in different types of books – reference material, fiction and so on?

In practice, if you face this sort of problem, you may not have defined your project objective precisely enough.

1.3 Example: depth

Project Topic 9: The planning and implementation of an information system in an organisation

Let us say that your objective is 'An examination of how a Sage accounting software package was chosen and implemented in X Ltd.'

You may find yourself involved in the detail of how the programme works with certain types of hardware – does it use visual basic and so on? This might be relevant if dealing with implementation or changeover, or with functionality in general – but not really the heart of what you should be doing, which should be about choice and implementation.

In practice, if you face this sort of problem, it is because you are losing sight of the 'big picture' and are departing from the project objective.

1.4 The Research and Analysis Project is not an exam

We've made this point already in Chapter 3. But this difference is just as crucial for **how** you **plan** and **manage** your work as it is for choosing your project.

1.4.1 Deadlines and time pressure – how it differs

Here are some key contrasts about deadlines.

An ACCA exam	Research and Analysis Project
• Takes three hours, typically • You have to plan your time carefully in the exam room	You can take as little or as long as you like to do your research, and write the Research Project and Skills and Learning Statement
• Sat on one particular day • You have to plan your time carefully in the run up to this date: learning, practice and revision	You can submit it whenever you like – the date of submission may affect when it gets marked but if you miss one date, you will not be disqualified from the next one
• Cannot be put off; if you miss one day, you have to resit	You can put it off; the time it takes is up to you
• Exam and studying are done outside the work environment	Depending on the topic you have chosen, some of the work **might** be done at work

You ought to conclude from this that **your deadlines on the project are for you to manage**. You have to set them, especially when they involve others. You have to police them. This is – in part – what is meant by **independent and self-managed learning**.

1.5 Realistically, how much time am I likely to need?

The answer to this question can – if you are not careful – be another question: 'How long is a piece of string?' But this is not good enough, is it? One important way of approaching this issue is by **analysing the work** involved and developing a realistic schedule based around it. There are a number of ways of doing this.

- Analysing the tasks
- Estimating the time you will need
- Developing schedules

2 Analysing the tasks

Identify each task you have to do and note it down.

For example, if you are cooking a meal, there are a number of different tasks, such as 'prepare vegetables' and 'make sauce'. Each of these tasks can be further subdivided. 'Prepare vegetables' can be subdivided into 'Prepare tomatoes', 'Prepare onions' and so on. 'Prepare onions' can be subdivided into 'Peel onions' and 'Chop onions'. Finally you will reach a point where you cannot subdivide the work any further. There is little point in going any further. This technique is called a **Work Breakdown Structure**.

Below is an example from an unpublished undergraduate dissertation. This describes one part of the project, the research method. (We will cover this in the next chapter, but it is a good example of the variety of work that needs to be done.)

2.1 Example

Initially the work I carried out on the project was extremely informal in that whenever I met a salesman or spoke to a manager I would ask them about their feelings towards the present pay scheme or the method by which targets were allocated. When salesmen complained about errors in their commission payment due to faults in the payment scheme I was in an ideal position to suggest to managers changes and refinements in the pay scheme.

Secondary data

Following this initial exploration I decided to familiarise myself with the theory behind targeting specifically and, more generally, how information and control system influence behaviour. At the same time as this I spoke to people outside Q Ltd both from academic backgrounds, so as to develop ideas, and in other selling companies, so as to compare Q Ltd with other selling firms.

Primary data

Once I felt well briefed about the problem I sought permission from the Southern Sales Director, Mr X to interview his sales managers. He requested a questionnaire which I forwarded to him. Mr X made minor adjustments to this in form rather than content. For example, one question I asked was, 'Why do you think Q Ltd has higher turnover of salesmen than other similar companies?', this was changed to: 'Do you think Q Ltd has a higher turnover of salesmen than other similar companies? If so, why? (See Appendix 1).

I developed the questionnaire with the background knowledge I had acquired and discussed some of the questions with Mr A, the Statistics and Finance Manager, my immediate superior.

Over a period of about a month I interviewed five sales managers, each interview lasting about one hour. I felt the questionnaire was a little restrictive, therefore I chose to approach the interviews informally using the questionnaire as a check that I had covered most of the points. This was specifically important as I felt that the psychological atmosphere of the interview would be at least as important as the mechanics of the interview. I realised that this would require me to be flexible, however, I didn't realise how flexible I would have to be. I organised one interview and found that this manager shared his room with another manager so I spent much of the interview making notes on discussion between the two of them, myself acting as a catalyst when discussion waned. This particular interview was especially useful since it uncovered issues such as the education and training of management that would otherwise have been overlooked. I decided to make written notes rather than a tape-recording because I though this might be off-putting to the managers.

During the interviewing and recording process I tried to avoid personal bias and judgement and when incorporating findings into this text I tried to avoid jumping to simplistic conclusions without considering their implications.

2.2 Planning techniques

We will now show you two planning techniques for you to use, and this is best done via by an exercise.

Exercise 1

(a)   Identify the tasks involved in the first paragraph in the example above, and put them in a hierarchy.

(b)   Flesh out paragraph 2 in the example above into a work breakdown strucutre, similar to that given at the start of this section.

Answer

(a)

Task breakdown
1.   Becoming familiar with the outlines at least of the scheme. 1.1   Getting the details 1.2   Reading them
2.   Arranging informal meetings with 2.1   Salesmen 2.2   Managers to discuss the issue and/or remembering to tag the issue on at the end of another meeting, ie 12 meetings
3.   Within each meeting – say 12 meetings 3.1   Asking how salesmen felt about the scheme 3.2   Asking how the targets were allocated 3.3   Taking notes of the response
4.   Developing refinements to the system
5.   Arranging meetings with managers to describe refinements developed

(b)

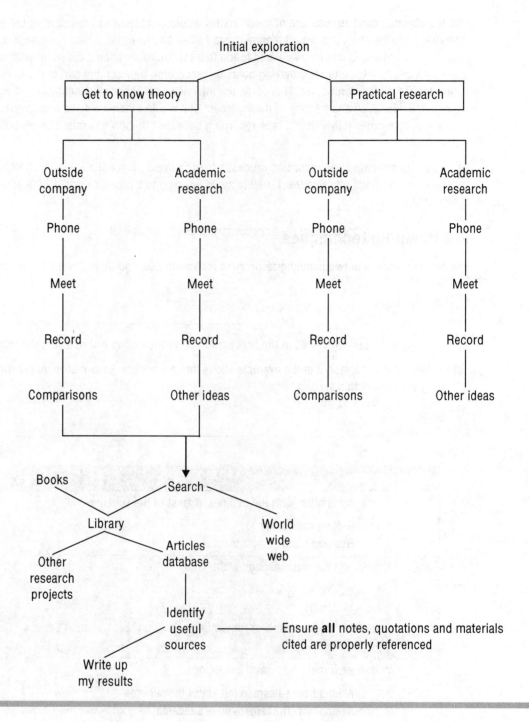

3 Estimating time

The tasks in the example above all take time, especially phoning, e-mailing and paperwork. How good are you at estimating your use of time?

We suggest there are four types of estimators. How do you find out which you fall into?

Type	Key vice and its cause	How do you know it's you?
Over-promiser	Vice: promises things can be delivered sooner than is possible Cause? Unwillingness to sit down and plan hour by hour – 'a month' seems a long time ahead; 20 working days is, in fact, a lot less. Too willing to please a manager who may only be asking for information. Doesn't like asking people to wait for a response. Consequence – unnecessary stress, especially if other people rely on you; reputation for unreliability. Cure? Keep records of how long tasks have taken you in the past (eg reading an article) and use these to plan your projects. Give yourself time to plan.	Your manager routinely makes allowances for the fact that you miss deadlines. You constantly fail to meet deadlines you have set yourself. At least you are consistent in your ways.
Budgetary slacker	Vice: over estimates volume/difficulty of work; builds in budgetary slack to everything. Cause? Excessive fear of pressure; refusal to work at a faster pace than you are capable of; inefficiency. Consequence – fewer learning opportunities; boredom; reputation of being slow or lazy, even though the only problem is estimation. Cure? Set yourself targets to build confidence. Learn speed reading techniques?	Your manager gives you more work than you think you can cope with, even though you get it done and you are given no more work than others.
All over the place	Vice: over- or under-estimates time spent Cause? Cannot relate tasks to time. Consequence: frustration. Cure? Try the over-promiser's cure.	The most frustrating as others cannot predict a pattern of behaviour, and nor can you. Nobody believes anything you say.
Never gets it wrong	The best position to be in. You're perfect.	

(a) If you are an **over-promiser**, you will set yourself (and your mentor?) unrealistic deadlines for completing the Research and Analysis Project. Failing to meet them will depress you – you do not have other people to check your progress. If you do struggle to meet your self-imposed deadlines, you might rush or do inadequately your research or analysis.

(b) If you are a **budgetary slacker**, this is less of a problem, except that you might take longer on the Research and Analysis Project than you really need or you might be insufficiently ambitious.

(c) If you are completely **inconsistent** in your time estimation, you will face both problems at once. Arguably, you should not set yourself a time limit, but plan your work breakdown structure meticulously. Do not arrange meetings until you have finished this task and any preparation.

We have put some very approximate timings into the example in Exercise 1.

Task breakdown	Time guesstimate	Comment
1. Becoming familiar with the outlines at least of the scheme. 1.1 Getting the details 1.2 Reading them	1 hour	Could be longer
2 Arranging informal meetings with: 2.1 Salesmen to discuss the issue and/or remembering to tag the issue on at the end of another meeting, ie 12 meetings	5 minutes to fix up a meeting (phone, leave message etc) = 1 hour, approx Chase up if no response	Use IT? Email may be quicker. Microsoft Outlook allows you to book meetings by issuing a meeting request. Even so, with 12 private meetings, there are twelve different messages to be sent and responded to.
3. Within each meeting – say 12 meetings: 3.1 Asking how salesmen felt about the scheme 3.2 Asking how the targets were allocated 3.3 Taking notes of the response	45 minutes per meeting, around 9 hours	How about tape recording? Note that 1 hour of tape recording takes about 6 hours of typing to transcribe it. Note taking is probably quicker and should be sufficient.
4. Developing refinements to the system	2 hours	A lot of thought to go in to this; could well be longer.
5. Arranging meetings with two managers to describe refinements developed	10 mins	
6. Within each meeting	2 × 1 hour	

Total time – Over 15 hours? Almost certainly an underestimate. Only two days work? How about adding in interruptions, cancellations or postponements? If you are an over-promiser, **look carefully** at **task 2 Arranging informal meetings**: in the absence of email, arranging twelve meetings could take an hour to set up.

3.1 Dealing with your estimation problems – particularly for over-promisers

The best solution is to keep a **record**, on an experimental basis, of the time you spend on the activities below. They are related to the Research and Analysis Project.

Activity	Relevance	Note down how long you spent doing this
Read, absorb and **take notes** of an article in the ACCA *Student Accountant* on a subject that is unfamiliar to you – count the words first.	The Research and Analysis Project is about research, and you will have to do the reading required – skim reading may not be enough. Furthermore, the data you have to read and absorb may not be written or structured in a way you are familiar with. Directed to an academic or business audience, there may be new terminology to absorb.	
Next time you **access the World Wide Web**, search for a business relevant website, and note how long it takes to access the information you want.	Some searches take a long time; you might have to use a number of different search engines to get what you want; you may want to download files – the speed of this depends on your internet connections. You are encouraged to use the Internet in the Research and Analysis Project.	
Next time you set up a spreadsheet model at work or at home, time yourself – make the model reasonably complex, containing formulae and a graph.	The topic you have chosen may well require you to set up a spreadsheet and use it to model or manipulate data and present it an alternative form.	
Next time you **write a long letter or email** to someone, or a detailed report at work, time yourself and count the words. Note when you started and when you finished to account for distractions. Make sure that this is **word processed**.	Writing the Research Project will take a **lot** longer than this, as you will have to think about what you must do. If you **word process** a report, you may be surprised at the time you might spend formatting, printing out, editing what you have written and so on.	
In the **next meeting** you attend with your boss to discuss a substantive issue, time how long you spent: • Preparing for the meeting • In the meeting • Writing up any notes about what was said and decided	Note that guidance is given for meetings with your mentor but you may be meeting other people in the course of your project.	

We have chosen the activities above, because reading, surfing the net, spreadsheets, note taking, writing and meetings are typical activities you will do in the course of the Research and Analysis Project.

When you have identified the tasks you have to do, you might **classify** them as:

- Reading
- Web-searching
- Writing and word processing
- Data manipulation
- Spreadsheets
- Meetings: preparation, the meeting itself, notes afterwards

3.2 Combining tasks

In Section 2, we suggested breaking down each task to get a realistic idea of what you have to do and the time available – so you know precisely what is involved.

Clearly, however, some jobs are best done in a **sequence or grouped together** in a batch.

(a)   For example **attending a meeting** and **writing up your notes afterwards** are two different tasks. It does make sense, however, to write up your notes as soon as you can after the meeting, while it is fresh in your mind.

(b)   **Sending out questionnaires**

   (i)   Response rates are typically low – 15% to 20%
   (ii)   So, to get resources you need to send over 130 questionnaires

If you are unlucky, you will have to photocopy, address and mail these yourself. Get it over in one hit, so you don't miss any out and you have a better idea as to when you should chase them.

Other jobs are best done uninterrupted or where concentration is needed. Creating a spreadsheet model of any sophistication is one of those jobs, given the need for formulae even in relatively simple models.

4 Building up a schedule

The Research and Analysis Project is a project with an end in view, a degree. You may have heard of people – perhaps friends (or friends of friends) from university – who have stayed on to do a further research qualification, such as a PhD, and whose research programme has drifted off.

Furthermore, unlike someone doing an undergraduate degree, you will almost certainly have to do your Research and Analysis Project work around your job and other social commitments – but you should already have experience of this in doing your ACCA exams to date.

4.1 Deadlines

Your deadlines and schedules are basically up to you. Again, you need a different mind-set to what you are used to for your normal ACCA exams. Studying for your ACCA exams, you made a decision to attend a particular exam sitting and then, perhaps, worked backwards from this, identifying that you had so many available hours to study for those papers

For the Research and Analysis Project, rather than working backwards from an exam date, you may be better advised to work **forwards** from a start date. This is because the Research and Analysis Project will involve work you are unfamiliar with. You will not know precisely the result you will come up with; you do not know exactly what the ramifications of the research will be.

Step 1   **Decide on a start date**

Simple? Yes, but have you briefed your partner, friends, family, and work colleagues that you are engaged on a final step to getting a degree from one of the UK's universities? They will support you if they know how important it is to you, and it will help them to be understanding – we hope – of long hours spent in the library, or even temporary increases in paper costs as a result of printing out the results of your Internet research.

Your mentor will need to know too.

Step 2   **Review your programme of work**

The next section and chapters will describe in brief some of the typical tasks you will encounter in the Research and Analysis Project. You may already have some idea as to the number of hours needed.

Step 3   **Identify the learning resources you will need and when available**

Unlike ACCA studies, where you may have used the BPP Study Text, Practice & Revision Kits, and Passcards as your principal learning tools, the Research and Analysis Project requires you to hunt around and discover things. It may simply not be possible to do everything in the evenings – you might need to do some of this work during the week.

4.2 Resources

(a)   **Library**. How far do you have to travel? Opening and closing times? Are there days when it is closed? Do you need a library pass? How will you get there? Walking distance? Bus and train times?

(b)   **Local ACCA student society or centre**. You could enquire if there are facilities for you to use.

(c)   **Computing power**. Do you have access to a PC? If you do not have one at home, you may be able to use your office PC after hours or at weekends, for spreadsheet work and word processing your report. If you have to go into the office for this, this again affects the time you have available.

(d)   **Internet**. If you have Internet access at home, all you need worry about is timing and maybe the cost. (Some useful hints and tips for Internet use in your research are given in Chapter 6.) Otherwise consider:

   (i)   Are you close to a cyber-café? When is it busy or cheap? Can you print from it?

   (ii)   Does a friend have net access?

   (iii)   Could you obtain permission to use facilities at work to research via the net – always ask first!

Step 4   **Identify when the people you need to consult are available**

People

(a)   Clearly, you need to find out when your **mentor** is available for the **three** mentor meetings you have to report on and other advice.

   (i)   At work, you should be able to find out from your mentor when he/she is on holiday or is busy. Try to avoid busy periods – for example, if you mentor is the Financial Controller, it would be advisable to avoid the time between the year end cut-off and audit clearance.

   (ii)   If your mentor is a tutor at an academic institution, you will have to take into account teaching and marking commitments, and the fact that they may be unavailable in the holiday periods.

(iii)   If your mentor is a member of the ACCA, in practice say, you will have to find out when he/she is free – it is wise to check and reconfirm meetings, as the urgent needs of a client will almost certainly come before the needs of your Research and Analysis Project.

Step 5   **Identifying other lead times**

Oxford Brookes' University timetable

Although you are under no pressure to attend a 'sitting', you should note that Oxford Brookes will mark the Research Project and Skills and Learning Statement only at particular times of year. You need not schedule your work around this, but you might have to wait a certain amount of time before submitting your Research Project and Skills and Learning Statement.

At the moment, you may submit your Project in the four week period immediately after each set of ACCA exam results. You can do the work whenever you like, but you can only submit it at the specified times. The timetables for the next two submission periods are given in the Information Pack on page 10. Always check the final date on the ACCA website.

4.3 Lead times

Some of your research, as will be seen, may involve interviews and primary data as well as secondary data. With the possible exception of the World Wide Web, you must also build in lead times from when you ask something to when you receive it. Here are some indicative examples.

Example	
Reserving a book from the library if it is not stock	Two weeks? Perhaps longer if someone else is using it. You might have to wait until the weekend to collect it.
Ordering a book over the Internet (eg from amazon.com)	Amazon.com delivers worldwide, but a local internet book supplier might have better access to local materials. Depends on closeness to wholesalers.
Ordering a book from a bookshop	A quick phone call will establish if one is in stock.
Obtaining articles	Hopefully, your library will have relevant journals, or you have retained copies of the Students Newsletter.
Web searching	In theory, if material is downloadable you should be able to do immediately – a matter of minutes.
Postal questionnaire and other written requests for information to third parties	Remember that people are doing you a favour by filing in questionnaires. If you are unlucky, it may treated as junk mail! At certain times of year respondents may on holiday.
Meetings	Some people may be able to see you with no notice. For others, you may have to book some time in advance – weeks even.

4.4 Other planning aids

Useful planning tools are Gantt charts (or bar charts) and network analysis.

You thus need to **schedule the activities** or tasks in the most efficient way given these two factors.

(a)   The **dependency** of some activities on others. In other words, Job B may need to be done before Job C. For example, you may need to read articles before, say, designing a questionnaire.

(b) **Constraints on resources and their availability.** Some resources may not be available at the ideal time.

You will have a broad-brush time estimation for any activity. For this you need, in addition to the **duration** of each sub-unit of work:

(a) The **earliest time** work on a particular unit **can** be started

(b) The **latest time** it must be started – less of an issue unless you really are working to a deadline or around people's holidays.

4.5 Gantt charts

A simple plan for a project is based on a **bar line chart**. This is sometimes called a **Gantt chart**.

(a) It can be used as a **progress control chart** with the lower section of each bar being completed as the activity is undertaken.

(b) A delay in a particular piece of work and its 'knock on' effect on other work can be shown in a **linked bar chart**. This shows the links between an activity and preceding activities which have to be completed before this particular activity can start.

Here is an example, from a construction project for a garage. We can see the delays to the foundations can then have a knock-on effect throughout the project.

No.	DESCRIPTION OF WORK OR ACTIVITY	TIME (DAYS)													
		1	2	3	4	5	6	7	8	9	10	11	12	13	14
1	Excavate for foundations and services (drainage)														
2	Concrete foundations														
3	Build walls and soakaways for drainage														
4	Construct roof														
5	Fit garage doors														
6	Provide services (electric)														
7	Plaster														
8	Decorate														

(a) **Advantages**

(i) Easy to understand

(ii) **Flexible**: you can draw it on paper or on a spreadsheet – perhaps use colour coding for different jobs

(iii) You can add other things, such as holidays or work commitments

(iv) You can see at glance where you are, by showing 'actual' performance against plan

(b) **Disadvantages**: none, really, as far as the Research and Analysis Project is concerned, although for larger more complex projects its main drawback is that it does not specifically show how aspects of work are linked together.

4.6 Critical path analysis (CPA or network analysis)

To overcome this problem, there is a more sophisticated technique known as network analysis or critical path analysis. You are **unlikely** to need this, but you **may at work have access to project management software** and if, for some reason, you need to use it here is the underlying method.

Network analysis is a project planning technique which aims to map the activities in a particular project, and the relationship between them. CPA describes the **sequence** of activities, and how long they are going to take. These diagrams are drawn left to right.

(a)   **Events** (1 and 2) are represented by circles. Activities (eg A) connect events.

(b)   The **critical path** is represented by drawing an extra line or a thicker line between the activities on the path. It is the **minimum amount of time** that the project will take.

(c)   It is the convention to note the earliest start date of any activity in the **top** right hand corner of the circle.

(d)   We can then work **backwards** identifying the **latest** dates when activities have to start. These we insert in the bottom right quarter of the circle.

A completed network diagram would be as follows. The **critical path** is AEG. Note the **float time** of five days for Activity F. Activity F can begin any time between days 4 and 9, thus giving the project manager a degree of flexibility.

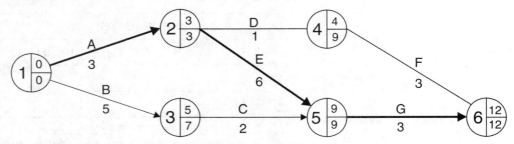

Use of network analysis in the Research and Analysis Project

(a)   Use it if **lots** of activities **depend** on others and you can do things in parallel. For example, you can develop your spreadsheet model after you have, say, sent out a questionnaire (providing you know what you are looking for).

(b)   It is less good at helping you **schedule** your Research and Analysis Project work with other areas of **your** life.

4.7 So what should my main planning aid be?

We strongly recommend that – whether on spreadsheet or paper – you draw up an overall schedule on a day-by-day basis, from the start until you intend to complete the project, analysing your time between:

(a)   Work
(b)   Weekend/holiday
(c)   The Research and Analysis Project

Submit your plans to a **reality check**.

(a)   Your partner and/or family may feel that your plans to work 12 hours on Saturday and Sunday may not be conducive to personal happiness or family life; or that your plans to rise 2 hours earlier every morning are unlikely to meet fruition if you are a notoriously late sleeper.

(b) Your **boss and work colleagues** may be able to advise you of busy times you have not already thought of, for example when you will be expected to provide cover for someone else on holiday.

(c) Your **mentor** (at the first meeting) may have experience of other projects.

(d) Lecturers at your college will have had years of experience dealing with undergraduate and postgraduate dissertations and research projects.

5 Using IT to help manage the Research and Analysis Project

Although it is not the purpose of this book to provide you with a guide to various IT software packages on the market, here are some hints and tips.

5.1 Using spreadsheets to plan your Research and Analysis Project

Although spreadsheets are designed for numerical analysis, they do offer a number of useful features that can be adapted for planning. Below is a simple example using Microsoft Excel. Let us assume that Task 1.1 is library research; you intend to spend 12 hours on this and you commence it on 8 April.

	A	B	C	D	E	F	G	H	I	J	K	L	M	N	O	P	Q	R	S
1			Plan	Actual		Week beginning													
2			(hrs)	(hrs)		08-Apr							15-Apr						
3						Mon	Tues	Wed	Thurs	Fri	Sat	Sun	Mon	Tues	Wed	Thurs	Fri	Sat	Sun
4	No. of hours																		
5	Work						8	8	8	8			8	8	8	8	8		
6	Holiday					8													
7	Shopping										2								
8	Cousin's wedding											6							
9																			
10																			
11	Research & Analysis																		
12	Project																		
13																			
14	Task ref																		
15																			
16	1.1	Library	12			5					5	2							
17				12		3					3	0						6	
18																			
19	1.2	Etc																	

5.2 Dates

You can easily **format cells** to show the **dates**, and you can do this automatically by using the **drag** command. If you are doing a Gantt chart, you can therefore set up the dates very easily. You could use the top cell of each column to signify dates.

5.3 Research and Analysis Project tasks and other commitments: time available

You can input your commitments down the side – as you see we have shown your work commitments at the top, as well as other calls on your time, and have given an hourly approximation.

You can use a **formula** to add up the total hours you plan to spend, and, in the row below, how many hours you have actually spent. You can use the Format/Cell/Pattern command to add colour or shades to each row of cells. You can see that you were over-optimistic in planning to do two hours work on the day of your cousin's wedding.

With time for experimentation and practice, you can do a lot more than this, for example flagging up if some tasks are overdue – but you will need to try this out for yourself.

5.4 Scheduling and diary software

If your office operates a network system, such as **Microsoft Outlook** or Lotus Notes, it is quite possible to use this to plan your work.

(a)   Microsoft Outlook has a **calendar** facility. You can book time in your calendar by clicking on the date and booking the time as 'busy' or 'tentative' for your project work. You can print off your calendar by day, week or month.

(b)   When you are planning a meeting or activity, you can book **reminders** to yourself that something needs to be done.

(c)   Microsoft Outlook also has a 'task' list – this has the advantage of identifying automatically when something is overdue by turning it red.

Note that Microsoft Outlook is not designed to manage a project – but it can be a big help in managing your working life into which the Research and Analysis Project must fit.

5.5 Project management software

Specialised software is available to help you manage projects, for example Microsoft Project. This is almost certainly far too sophisticated and complex for the Research and Analysis Project, but if you are familiar with it anyhow, and, for example, it is available at work, you could use this to plan.

Here are some overall guidelines on using IT in planning and managing the Research and Analysis Project.

Subject	Comment
Garbage in, garbage out	No IT application is better than the data you put into it. If you do not think about **what** you have to do and **how long** it will take, and if your plan is fundamentally **flawed**, no amount of tinkering with IT will help you.
IT is a servant not master	If you feel that the project is taking shape in a different way from how you had planned, then you will need to change your plan; it will have to be flexible.
IT can waste time as well as save it	If your model is more complex or too sophisticated, and the stages in your project are quite simple, then maintaining the model may eat up time which you could more usefully spend on the project content.

6 Setting up your project file

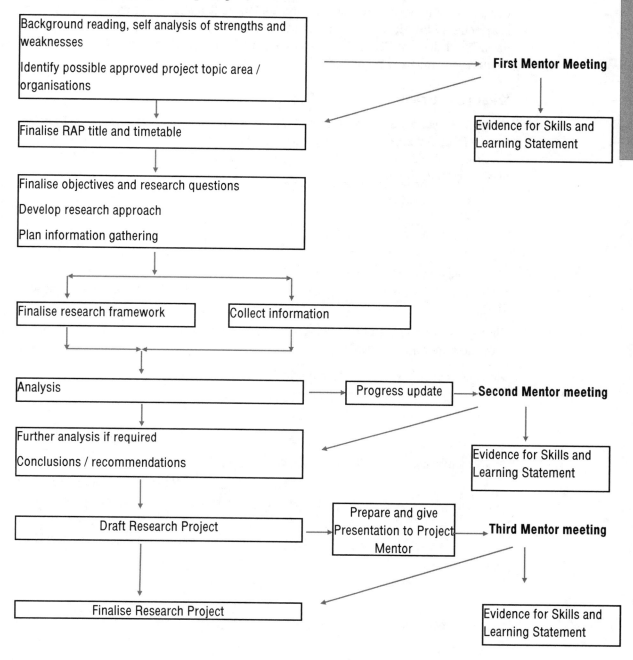

If you go back to the Information Pack, you will note that Oxford Brookes University has already suggested a way of planning your project.

This is a useful framework for the Research and Analysis Project, but you do not have to adopt it of course. If you do, however, we strongly suggest that you break down the work into a work breakdown structure.

6.1 Setting up your file

One important planning task is **setting up a file for you to manage your data**. You may need two or more but if you start to order and record your paperwork from the outset, this will help you control and keep track. The abilities the Research and Analysis Project seeks to test are not only the content and thought but how you **organised** the process.

What you've read

Furthermore, you MUST keep a record of where you obtained your data as you MUST reference it in your Research Project. So, if you read an article about the logistics industry in the *Economist*, say, or the business section of the *Middle Eastern Economic Digest* or the *Straits Times*, and if you have used this, then always note down:

- Article source
- Date
- Author, if attributed
- Page references

This is **evidence** of what you have done – as important for this Research and Analysis Project as your other work – DON'T RELY ON MEMORY. DON'T FORGET TO NOTE REFERENCES DOWN AS YOU USE THEM.

We suggest you obtain an A4 ring binder with twice as many file dividers as you think you can possibly need. Here are some subdivisions.

Planning section	Your schedules
	Meeting dates
	Any related correspondence
	Printouts of any emails regarding meetings
Project topic choice	Notes of why you chose the topic
	Copies of any articles you read to turn your topic into an objective: you may need this when writing your Research Project and discussing it with your mentor
	Notes with references: who wrote the article, who published it, when was it published, what journal published it
Notes of mentor meeting 1	Details of preparation, notes of meeting; everything you will need for the Skills and Learning Statement
Details of research	Research design
	What you did
	Notes and references
Analytical frameworks	Where you got them from
	Why you obtained them
Evidence	What data you decided to collect
	Rationale – why
	How you collected it (eg interview, questionnaire)
	You may need subsections for detailed working papers, questionnaires received
	Include copies of any authorisations you have had to reproduce material not in the public domain

Analysis	What you did
	What tools you used
	Spreadsheet models you drew up – show the model first, and the formulae underneath it, so that you meet Oxford Brookes University's requirements.
Notes for mentor meeting 2	
...and so on	

7 Planning issues for each stage of the Research and Analysis Project

Step 1   **Choose a topic**

We have covered this in Chapter 4. The only **planning** issues are these, as discussed.

(a)   A **reality check** to ensure that your choice of topic and the project objective are internally consistent and feasible. You may find, as you plan in detail what you want to do that you had not really appreciated the work involved. Creating a project plan will help you, here.

(b)   Your first mentor meeting – see Chapter 9 for details.

Step 2   **Read around the subject matter**

Unlike a fully fledged undergraduate dissertation, you are not required to complete a formal literature review; however, reading round the subject will help define the project objective. Planning issues are:

- Do only what you need to do to create a coherent project objective.

- Take notes of what you have read, as you may need to cite these in your Research Project and make sure you have kept a note of the source, so that it can be **referenced**.

- If possible, collect copies in your file.

Step 3   **Define aims and objectives; choose analytical frameworks**

The main planning issue is to make sure that your choice is feasible and sensible.

Step 4   **Information gathering: getting permission**

Getting permission

We must now highlight a key point. IF YOU ARE IN ANY DOUBT AS TO WHETHER YOU CAN REPRODUCE MATERIAL, GET PERMISSION TO DO SO.

Furthermore, if you work in an audit department, **unauthorised** use of client data is a BREACH OF PROFESSIONAL ETHICS.

You might therefore need to obtain permission **as part of the planning process**.

Obtaining permission is something you must do at the start. Failure to do so may mean you will have to reconsider the whole project.

(a)   If you are **an auditor,** you have access to client data on a confidential basis.

   (i)   The client is paying for the work to be done and may, quite reasonably and correctly, be concerned about breach of commercial confidentiality. Many clients might also object, as a matter of principle, that you are getting a benefit that the client has paid for.

   (ii)   On the other hand, some audit clients may welcome a project on a matter of commercial concern to them.

   (iii)   Do not assume that using the data and changing the name will be good enough.

   DO NOT approach the client directly. Instead speak to the **audit partner**.

(b)   If you are using data from your **own** employer, ask permission from your boss (or your mentor), who may have to get further clearance.

(c)   Finally, obtain these **permissions in writing**. Be quite precise in what you are asking.

Getting data

Data gathering is the area in which your planning and scheduling skills will come to the fore. We have already discussed the work breakdown structure, estimation and scheduling.

7.1 Example

Assume that you are to do **Project Topic 13: The relationship between an organisation's human resources activities and business objectives**. You are fortunate in that you have received permission from the human resources department of your own employer, X plc, to assess the personnel requirements of the sales administration, inventory control, fulfilment (despatch) following the introduction of an online ordering system enabling customers to order directly via the web.

What to collect

You have decided that you want to gather data from all these departments covering:

- What managers perceive the human resources needs to be
- What employees consider the human resources needs are
- How they came to those views

To gather the information, you might plan to interview the managers and conduct a written anonymous survey of employees.

How to collect the data

- Design a list of questions to cover with managers in the interview – will have to be done outside of working hours

- Design a questionnaire for employees to answer

- Ask human resources to agree to the questionnaire. Bearing in mind the sensitivity of the issues, this could take a few days.

- Set meeting dates with managers – this may have to be during working hours

- Distribute questionnaire

During this time, you could also be expanding your awareness by reading how other firms coped with technological change and motivation theory.

You may find, therefore, that you have to do some tasks in parallel with others, and that you have different types of data collection exercise taking place at the same time.

Step 5   Analyse information

Order your work in a methodical way and, more importantly, the allow yourself the time to be thorough. We strongly suggest that you do not carry out this stage only in a succession of lunch breaks. Use up some holiday and devote a weekend to it.

Above all, record the work you have done.

Steps 6/7   Report findings and conclusions

We cover how to plan the mentor meetings, the Research Project and the Skills and Learning Statement in Parts C, D and E of this text.

Chapter roundup

- This chapter has covered some of the basic planning issues.

- You will have to dovetail your work in line with the job and other commitments.

- There will be varying lead times according to the tasks you will do.

- Be realistic about your ability to set deadlines. Other people's needs also should be considered.

chapter 6

Carrying out research

INTRODUCTION

This chapter covers the main area of the research part of the Research and Analysis Project. This determines what data you obtain and the procedures you have to go through to find it. Although the content of the Research and Analysis Project might seem very different from, say, researching the behaviour of sub-atomic particles or researching into changing social attitudes, it is still **research**.

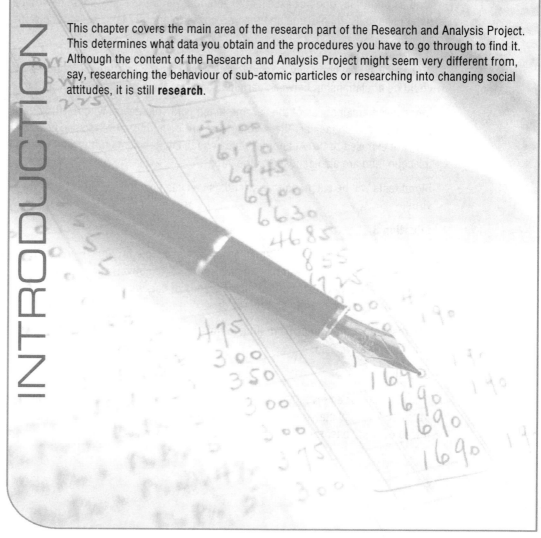

1 Types of research methods: a short practical guide

Before launching into the practical detail, you might be as well to consider the **assumptions** upon which your choice of research methods is based. If you have certain prejudices as to what matters, then this might affect your review of the data or indeed the type of research you do.

There are a variety of different approaches to research. A number of contrasting approaches are shown below to illustrate some of the key issues.

Exercise 1

What would you say are the key differences between the research methods below?

Situation 1

You have just been into a new fast food outlet. After your meal, a uniformed member of staff approaches you and says 'I am carrying out a survey into how customers view the quality and service we supply. By collecting a representative view of our customers' needs, we will be able to improve our service. The results will be fed into a database and anonymity is guaranteed'. You are then asked a series of pre-scripted questions, to which you must choose an option for an answer. (For example, 'would you rate our food as poor, fair, good or excellent?') After answering the questions, the interviewer takes some of your personal details, thanks you and then proceeds to another table asking the same questions.

Situation 2

A pharmaceutical company is researching a new type of vaccine for influenza. Its scientists believe there could be a relationship between certain aspects of the virus's chemistry and the immune system.

It has given small doses of the vaccine to ten paid volunteers, who for the duration of the test are living in a special research facility. These volunteers are being monitored to see how the vaccine affects them when they are exposed to flu. At another research facility, the same number of volunteers is being given a 'placebo' and are also exposed to the virus.

Blood tests will be taken, so that scientists can see how the vaccine affects the body's response to the flu virus.

Situation 3

You have been asked to join a small group of five people for an evening to do some 'focus group research' on makes of car. The researcher introduces topics of conversation and asks people what they feel about motoring, what they feel about different brands of car, what their motoring habits are, and what frustrates them most about motoring and motor cars.

The researcher intervenes from time to time to steer the conversation to topics of interest or to clarify what people have said.

Situation 4

A researcher for an investment banking firm is reviewing companies engaged in e-commerce. She has obtained financial statements of twenty firms, and also details of movements in their respective share prices over the past four years. From this she compares data and compiles a report.

Answer

Situation 1

Seeks to find out **objective** facts that have some statistical relevance, from which inferences can be drawn. This sort of research is **quantitative** in that it aims to obtain a sample of data and generalise responses from it. It is **descriptive in that is describes the current state of affairs.** It might also seek to examine the relationships between two variables: rating of food and age of customer. Does a person's age correlate with their appreciation of the food?

Situation 2

Seeks to draw out **objective** facts, and is **testing a hypothesis** against empirical data (data derived from observation or experience). Of course, a small sample of ten may not be enough to get a general view, but it is strong evidence that further research could be useful.

Situation 3

Features quite often in the early stage of market research and, indeed, in other areas of research. It is called qualitative research.

Clearly the researcher is not trying to prove anything, nor is the researcher trying to find out objective facts from which statistical inferences can be made – the sample is obviously not meaningful and the questioning is not controlled. The researcher is trying to tease out ideas from what people say they feel about the situation.

What the researcher is probably doing is trying to come up with **ideas** for further research, no more. If, say, one of the people in the group was to say that 'car designers have no appreciation of the needs of parents carrying heavy shopping and looking after children', this would give them a lot to think about.

Situation 4

The data is easily obtained, and it is not new knowledge. The main purpose of the research is, however, to analyse and draw relationships between different areas of the data, to see if there might be common features which all the sample of companies share.

To summarise, here are some key words describing the type of research encountered in the situations.

Situation	Key words	Summary
1 Market research	Statistical Objective Descriptive Quantitative	Describing facts and relationships
2 Research into a vaccine	Objective Experimental Testing hypotheses Scientific	Testing hypotheses
3 Focus group	Qualitative Non-statistical Relationships Generate ideas	Exploring ideas
4 Investment banker	Relationships Analysis Factual	Analysis

Each of these types of research approach is legitimate in its own right, and you may use a combination of them in the Research and Analysis Project.

1.1 Example

For example, let us take **Project Topic 3: The impact of an aspect of impending legislation on the operations and financial position of an organisation**.

Let us assume that the organisation is your employer and the legislation relates to the relationships businesses have with their suppliers. One aspect of this is a proposal by the government to make it much easier for suppliers to sue for interest on bills that are paid late. Here are some research tasks.

1   **Exploring ideas** – are the people in the purchasing department aware? Do they care or know about the small print? What about the sales ledger department? Does the firm want to charge its own customers for late payment?

2   **Analysis** – review payables and receivables ledger for payment periods. What is the maximum potential loss if this change is implemented? If the firm paid early, would it run up bank overdraft fees? If creditors are a source of finance, how expensive are they?

3   **Experimentation** – not really possible in this case.

4   **Describing facts** – if the firm has a large sales force, you may – if allowed – send a questionnaire to a sample (which can include all of them!) asking them if they know about the change and the terms and conditions they currently offer. The same could be sent to a buying department.

Clearly a lot of the work is going to be analysis.

Below is how BPP Learning Media would classify the project topics according to the main focus of the research – **however, your own choice of project objective will indicate the approach you should take**.

These are **only hints** – your own project objective may lead you on a quite different path.

Project topics	Main type of research activity?
1 An organisation's budgetary control system and its links with performance management and decision making	Analysis Describing Exploring
2 How the introduction of a new technology can assist an organisation in achieving its business objectives	Exploring Analysis Testing
3 The impact of an aspect of impending legislation on the operations and financial position of an organisation	Exploring Analysis
4 The impact of e-business on an organisation	Exploring Analysis Describing
5 The effects of globalisation on an organisation	Exploring Describing
6 The key factors or indicators in the motivation of employees in an organisation	Exploring Describing Testing

Project topics	Main type of research activity?
7 The restructuring of an organisation's operational activities and the effect on the organisation's financial performance	Analysis Describing Exploring
8 The business and financial performance of an organisation over a three year period	Analysis Exploring
9 The planning and implementation of an information system in an organisation	Exploring Describing
10 The effectiveness of the use of costing techniques within an organisation	Analysis Exploring
11 The financial and operational costs and benefits of the internal audit/internal review activities within an organisation	Analysis Exploring
12 The possible effects of a proposed accounting standard on the financial statements and business activities of an organisation	Analysis Testing
13 The relationship between an organisation's human resources activities and its business objectives	Exploring Analysis Describing
14 The business and financial objectives of a strategic investment decision made by an organisation and its impact on key stakeholders	Exploring Analysis Describing
15 The management of an organisation's working capital over a three year period and its impact on the organisation's funding strategies	Analysis Describing
16 The financial and operational risk management within an organisation	Analysis Describing Exploring
17 The quality of the corporate governance within an organisation and the impact on an organisation's key stakeholders	Analysis Testing Exploring
18 The marketing strategy of an organisation and its effectiveness	Analysis Describing
19 The financial and operational consequences of a merger between two organisations or of the acquisition of one organisation by another	Analysis Exploring
20 An organisation's corporate social responsibility, including business ethics, and their impact on business practice and key stakeholders	Analysis Describing Exploring

This table only gives **tentative hints**.

(a) **Testing** appears rarely – you are not conducting a scientific experiment. The very fact that you – with management's endorsement – are asking questions, can make you a participant as well as an observer of the company you are researching. If you interview people, people may welcome the attention, and tell you what they think you – or senior managers – want to hear.

(b) **Exploring** appears everywhere. This is not to say that you should set up focus groups, but that you cannot dismiss the less certain, more tentative aspects of the enquiry.

(c) **Analysis appears in most topics.**

2 Primary and secondary research

What sort of research do I have to do?

As you read through the notes below, it will help if you keep the following in mind.

	Secondary data	Primary data
What it is	Data neither collected directly by the user nor specifically for the user, often under conditions unknown to the user – in other words, data collected not by YOU but by someone else for their own purposes or for general use	Data that is collected specifically by or for the user, at source, in other words by YOU during the Research and Analysis Project.
Quantitative, 'factual' or 'objective' example	Government reports – in the UK a good example is Social Trends, which contains government statistics about British society, employment in different industries, attitudes and so on. Such a report might be relevant to **Topic 13: The relationship between an organisation's human resources activities and its business objectives**. A company's **published financial statements** summarise and interpret company transactions data for the benefit of **shareholders**, not the needs of the Research and Analysis project.	A survey you conduct with a questionnaire you have designed, with regard to a sample. You aim to get a statistically significant result. Scientific experiment
Qualitative example	An article in the ACCA *Student Accountant* magazine or in a book about theories of motivation.	A focus group you have conducted (in the manner of Situation 3 in Exercise 1 above) to talk about motivation.
Role in Research and Analysis Project	You must make some use of secondary data.	Useful – perhaps even essential given some research objectives, but not compulsory for the Research and Analysis Project.

Below is an example from an unpublished undergraduate dissertation. It should be familiar to you, because it featured in Chapter 5! Identify areas of primary and secondary research.

2.1 Example

1   Initially the work I carried out on the project was extremely informal in that whenever I met a salesman or spoke to a manager I would ask them about their feelings towards the present pay scheme or the method by which targets were allocated. When salesmen complained about errors in their commission payment due to faults in the payment scheme I was in an ideal position to suggest to managers changes and refinements in the pay scheme.

2　　Following this initial exploration I decided to familiarise myself with the theory behind targeting specifically and, more generally, how information and control system influence behaviour. At the same time as this I spoke to people outside Q Ltd both from academic backgrounds, so as to develop ideas, and in other selling companies, so as to compare Q Ltd with other selling firms.

3　　Once I felt well briefed about the problem I sought permission from the Southern Sales Director (Mr X) to interview his sales managers. He requested a questionnaire which I forwarded to him. Mr X made minor adjustments to this in form rather than content. For example, one question I asked was, 'Why do you think Q Ltd has higher turnover of salesmen than other similar companies?', this was changed to: 'Do you think Q Ltd has a higher turnover of salesmen than other similar companies? If so, why? (See appendix 1).

4　　I developed the questionnaire with the background knowledge I had acquired and discussed some of the questions with Mr A, the Statistics and Finance Manager, my immediate superior.

5　　Over a period of about a month I interviewed five sales managers, each interview lasting about one hour. I felt the questionnaire was a little restrictive, therefore I chose to approach the interviews informally using the questionnaire as a check that I had covered most of the points. This was specifically important as I felt that the psychological atmosphere of the interview would be at least as important as the mechanics of the interview. I realised that this would require me to be flexible, however, I didn't realise how flexible I would have to be. I organised one interview and found that this manager shared his room with another manager so I spent much of the interview making notes on discussion between the two of them, myself acting as a catalyst when discussion wained. This particular interview was especially useful since it uncovered issues such as the education and training of management that would otherwise have been overlooked. I decided to make written notes rather than a tape-recording because I though this might be offputting to the managers.

6　　During the interviewing and recording process I tried to avoid personal bias and judgement and when incorporating findings into this text I tried to avoid jumping to simplistic conclusions without considering their implications.

Comment

The vast majority of this is primary research both quantitative and exploratory. Secondary research is only referred to in paragraph 2.

2.2 How much research do I have to do?

This is the crux of the matter. The project is testing skills in **Research and Analysis** and so you may want to know how much you should do.

READ THIS!	
A minimalist approach	Yes, but ....
In theory, you could only cite four sources which could be, for example:	• This will not be enough for any project.
• An article in *Student Accountant*	• For all project topics you will have to read around the subject.
• A book – technical background from your BPP Study Text	
• Evidence of a website visit	
• A set of financial statements	
FEW SOURCES = HIGHER RISK OF FAILING	

3 Identifying the information you need in the light of the project objectives

You have a choice of twenty topics, but each has to be whittled down to a project objective, as described in Chapter 4. Once you have done so, you will have a fair idea of what you want. Here are two questions you might ask to clarify your thinking.

1   What am I trying to prove or disprove?
2   What am I trying to show?

	Implication	Example
1 What am I trying to prove or disprove?	Weighing up a statement in the light of collected evidence	**Project Topic 6: The key factors or indicators in the motivation of employees in an organisation** **Example objective**: to demonstrate that the white collar employees of XX2 Ltd are motivated principally by salary levels. **What am I trying to prove?** That salary is the main motivating factor for this group of employees and that they are not influenced by other factors. **Information that could disprove this** You actually find that a sizeable minority of the employees are not motivated primarily by salary. On closer analysis you find that these are the older members of staff, and further analysis of the results of your questionnaire indicate that they are motivated more by working conditions and job satisfaction.
2 What am I trying to show?	Reveal the results of your discoveries in a particular area. You are not trying to prove or disprove a point but come to some conclusions from certain types of data.	**Project Topic 7: The restructuring of an organisation's operational activities and the effect on the organisation's financial performance** **Example objective**: B Partners is a consultancy firm with offices worldwide. Its senior partners have decided to incorporate its overseas branches as separate limited companies. The information you need to illustrate this: • Tax and profit figures under the old scheme • Effect of the new scheme • Attempt to isolate effect of change of status at other times • Profit implications – not only reported profits, but changes in attitude to risk

In practice, your research is likely to involve both sorts of question. It is not our job here to give a detailed blow-by-blow breakdown of what you should do. **Each project has to be unique.**

3.1 Generating information requirements

Here you really need the detailed project objective and you have to work logically and ruthlessly from this. You need to define – and report – the following.

- Scope
- Focus
- Contexts

Define scope

Scope of your enquiries – the boundaries of what you are doing.

(a) **Over time** – a time period for your data.

  (i) **Frequency**. Review of financial statements – these are produced annually.

  (ii) **Start and end dates of the event you are describing**, for example when was it decided to buy a new information system (Project Topic 9).

  (iii) **Sensible time period for the subject in question**, for example, the costs and benefits of internal audit (Project Topic 11) need a reasonably long time horizon – two or three years, not just one month – to be assessed.

(b) **Geography** – global, international, regional, local businesses, industries or environment

(c) **Industry** etc

(d) **Size of a transaction** – for example, auditors look at 'material' or representative items, not everything.

You **may need to justify your scope** in your report – for example, if you have chosen an unusual time period, there may be a good reason (eg before and after adoption of International Accounting Standards).

Define focus

Focus of analysis – what are you collecting data about? **Here are some examples**.

- Individuals, for example on a project dealing with motivation issues
- Groups of people (eg a department, such as 'the sales force', suppliers)
- Procedures and processes within an organisation, for example how investment decisions are made
- Events, actions or decisions, for example the adoption of an International Accounting Standard, or the decision to buy a subsidiary
- Inputs (eg material, informational) or outputs
- An organisation as a whole

You may, of course, collect data about a number of the above.

Define contexts

By context, we mean factors in the **immediate environment** of the Research and Analysis Project, such as the unique characteristics of the company, which will affect:

- The data collection methods employed, perhaps
- The content of what you need to define

For example, **motivational issues** for managers in a company that has just been **taken over** and, perhaps, has seen a round of redundancies and dismissals, may be quite different from a successful firm which is taking people on and needs to integrate them into the organisation.

3.2 Example

		Information
Project objective	**Project Topic 14: The business and financial objectives of a strategic investment decision made by an organisation and its impact on key stakeholders** **Example objective**: Assess how managers in X plc invest in projects according to strictly rational, financial criteria.	What evidence do I need to show of background reading to ensure I make sensible judgements?
To prove	Investment decisions are made strictly as a result of rational criteria and follow what would be suggested by capital rationing techniques.	
Scope • Time period? • Organisational	18 months to January 20X8. X plc – compare practice in offices in London and Malaysia office	Self explanatory
Focus	Capital expenditure decisions over £20,000/RM100,000	But how big is this sample? You may have to reduce this scope.
Context	X plc is decentralised company with two main offices, in London, UK and in Kuala Lumpur, Malaysia. In the late 1990s, the Malaysian government introduced control on the import and export of foreign currency.	Each office may have different formal procedures and authorisation limits. Obtain procedures manuals from both offices. Ask accounts department to give you details of capex decisions, eg a list for you to review. You may take a sample.

We suggest that in your **project file** you set up a separate section for this issue. You may need to use a number of free flowing techniques to define the information you need, perhaps in a tree diagram.

3.3 Define what each item of information is for

Once you have decided what information you need, we advise you to keep a record of why you collected it. Here is an example. You could have a set up such as this, with even a brief summary as to the eventual usefulness of the data – the 'result'.

Information source	**Reasons**	**Result**
Procedures manual for capex of Kuala Lumpur office	• To identify formal systems for approving capital expenditure • To compare with actual decisions taken • To see whether capital rationing is mentioned in procedural criteria	Obtained Procedures manual only describes procedures for authorisation, rather than the business decision underlying it
Conversation – phone or email with relevant managers	• To ask how capex decisions are taken • To ask permission for recent examples (**Note.** Follow up in writing)	

3.4 Detailed advice

Detailed advice on primary and secondary data is given in the next sections of this chapter.

4 Secondary data, including the Internet

The following is a guide to the use of secondary data. It can only be couched in the most general terms, as each project is unique and has its own data requirements.

4.1 Where should you look

As this is a Research and Analysis Project, you are expected to think for yourself in this respect – we have already given some hints as to possible sources in the 'Thought points' section of Chapter 4, 'Choosing and defining your project'.

4.2 Internal sources of secondary data

Your employer probably has large amounts of information, not designed for your research, but useful to you, and this will be held on a departmental basis. Do not limit your interest to the accounts department! Monthly management accounts are only part of what is available for your research. And remember, the accounts department is rarely the **driver** of a business.

Accounts department

- Procedures manual
- Management accounts – balance sheets
- Financial data
- Accounting policies
- Tax details
- Working capital

Sales and marketing department

- Sales reports by region
- Sales by customer
- Sales by product
- Competitor intelligence
- Market prospects and reports
- Customer complaints
- Marketing research reports
- Brand strategy and values
- Distribution chains

Production and operations

- Operations data
- Efficiency and capacity detail
- Process flow charts
- Detailed product costings
- Input prices
- Supply chain

Human resources

- Number of employees
- Recruitment procedures
- Training programmes
- Staff turnover details
- Details of pay

4.3 External secondary data

It is hard to give detailed rules about where you should look, except that you should search for **relevant** data, and try to make use of the Internet. Clearly, the use of **secondary** data is going to be more crucial for some topics than others – such as **Project Topic 5: The effects of globalisation on an organisation**.

Books

You need to take care here. For the technical knowledge covered by the other syllabuses in the ACCA qualification, you might consult (in addition to the BPP Learning Media Study Text) the other books on the **ACCA's reading list** if they are relevant to your project.

Articles in the ACCA's *Student Accountant* magazine often refer to books that have been published recently – if there is an article relevant to your project than it might have **references**. (This is also true of other journals.)

Your college or public library. Even if you do not know what you are looking for, you may find some time spent browsing is quite useful. Many libraries use the Dewey Decimal System – there is no need to go into this here, but this is a well-established means of classifying books.

Bookshops which sell over the Internet (or a site such as Amazon.com) sometimes enable you to type in a key word, which might generate some titles about a topic – even if you do not buy them, you may find them in your local library.

Journals and articles

Your obvious first choice should be the ACCA's *Student Accountant*. This contains a wealth of articles relevant to the ACCA qualification. Otherwise, no list can be prescriptive.

A college library is likely to have other **academic journals**, such as the *Harvard Business Review*. Again, rather than list them here, you may be able to find a list from your own college library of what is published – perhaps an article may be obtained or copied for you.

Other business or current affairs journals and newspapers, such as the *Economist*, *Straits Times*, *Asian Wall Street Journal* etc, may have surveys relevant to different business areas.

Trade journals are also useful – most countries have journals produced by relevant trade bodies, detailing developments in the industry. You can use the Internet to access the websites of **trade associations**. Increasingly, businesses in an industry are setting up electronic markets.

4.4 Example

The UK has a large and developed printing and publishing industry. The trade body, PIRA, aims to promote best practice and has an extensive publication programme. Two examples – of many industry publications – are:

- *The Bookseller* – for the retail book trade
- *PrintWeek* – for the printing industry

The **Internet** is an excellent source of secondary data if used with care.

(a) For example, you can use a **search engine** which will bring up websites of interest. Some websites will allow you to download articles. Some of these websites – the *Economist Intelligence Unit* is one – offer articles for download. Another is www.ft.com, (the Financial Times). Many of these will be in PDF (portable document file) format. You will need to download **Adobe Acrobat Reader** for this – fortunately Acrobat Reader is **free** and it is possible that the site will have a link to Adobe to enable you to download the software yourself.

(b) Your Internet service provider may also refer you to magazines and online newspapers.

Government ministries and agencies

Government agencies are good sources of economic and other statistical information. Most countries have an agency that provides national statistics. This varies significantly from country to country in terms of what is produced and the format, but you should be able to find:

(a) Economic data (eg UK Annual Abstract of Statistics)
(b) Social data (eg on population size and structure)
(c) Market data (eg export promotion)

A lot of government statistics previously only available in print, such as Social Trends, Economic Trends and Regional Trends, are now available free online in PDF format at www.statistics.gov.uk, the website of the Office of National Statistics (ONS). However, it is not always easy to find them direct from the ONS home page. Searching for (eg) Social Trends on a site such as www.google.co.uk can be a quicker way of getting to the relevant part of the ONS website.

Regulatory bodies and industry associations

There are many quasi-government and other public sector bodies which can provide data on a particular industry sector.

Other sources

There are some sources of data which you may not be able to access in a personal capacity, but which your employer might have access to, by virtue of being in a particular industry or dealing with clients from a particular industry. These include:

- A business directory (eg Kompass)
- Market research data (eg Nielson consumer surveys)

5 Using secondary data

Secondary data is used in many business situations, not just in academic research. Secondary data:

- Can provide a backdrop to primary research
- Can act as a substitute for field research
- Can be used as a technique in itself

Backdrop to primary research

Secondary data may also be used to set the **parameters** for primary research. In an **unfamiliar field**, it is natural that the researcher will carry out some **basic research** in the area, using journals, existing reports, the press and any contacts with relevant knowledge. Such investigations will provide guidance on a number of areas.

- Possible data sources
- Data collection
- Methods of collection (relevant populations, sampling methods and so on)

Substitute for primary research

The (often substantial) **cost** of primary research **might be avoided** should existing secondary data be sufficient. Given the low response rate available for questionnaires, secondary research might do the job just as well. There are some situations however, in which secondary data is bound to be **insufficient**.

A technique in itself

Some types of information can **only be acquired through secondary data**, in particular **trends** over time. The **historical data** published on, say, trends in the behaviour of an industry over time, cannot realistically be replaced by a one-off study.

How reliable is secondary data?

The quality of the secondary data

(a) Preparers may have an axe to grind; trade associations may not include data which runs counter to the interest of its members.

(b) Why was **the data** being collected in the first place? Random samples with a poor response rate are particularly questionable). Government statistics and information based on them are often relatively dated, though information technology has speeded up the process).

(c) **How were parameters defined**? This is directly related to **'focus'** in 3.1 above. What do you mean by **'employees'**?

Advantages arising from the use of secondary data.

(a) Secondary data may solve the problem **without** the need for any primary research: **time and money is thereby saved**.

(b) Secondary data sources are a great deal **cheaper** than those for primary research.

(c) Secondary data, while not necessarily fulfilling your information needs, can be of great use by:

    (i) **Setting the parameters**, defining a hypothesis, highlighting variables, in other words, helping to focus on the central problem

    (ii) **Providing guidance**, by showing past methods of research and so on, for primary data collection

    (iii) **Helping to assimilate the primary research** with past research, highlighting trends and the like

(d) **You have to use this data source for the Research and Analysis Project.**

Issues to bear in mind regarding secondary data

Topic	Comment
Relevance	The data may not be relevant to the research objectives in terms of the data content itself, classifications used or units of measurement.
Cost	Although secondary data is usually cheaper than primary data, some specialist reports can cost large amounts of money.
Availability	Secondary data may not exist in the specific product or market area.
Bias	The secondary data may be biased, depending on who originally carried it out and for what purpose. Attempts should be made to obtain the most original source of the data, to assess it for such bias.
Topic	Comment
Statistical accuracy	Was the sample representative?
	Was the questionnaire or other measurement instrument(s) properly constructed?
	Were possible biases in response or in non-response dealt with and accounted for?
	Was the data properly analysed using appropriate statistical techniques?
	Was a sufficiently large sample used?
	Does the report include the raw data?
	In addition, was any raw data omitted from the final report, and why?
Sufficiency	Even after fulfilling all the above criteria, the secondary data may be insufficient and primary research would therefore be necessary.

The golden rule when using secondary data is **use only meaningful data**.

(a)   **Begin with internal sources** and a firm with a good management information system should be able to provide a great deal of data.

(b)   External information should be consulted in order of ease and speed of access: directories, catalogues and indexes before books, abstracts and periodicals.

(c)   **Do not accept it at face value. The Internet, for example, is a mine of misinformation**.

For the Research and Analysis Project, follow the **key rules** below to keep control of your use of secondary data.

KEY RULES
Reference
Record
Review
Relate

We suggest that for each item of secondary data you use, you prepare a **sheet** as follows.

Data item	Fill in
Reference • Source • Author • When and how obtained • Citation details: Note down all you need to do to reference according to the Harvard system	
Record Attach photocopy/ print out or take notes – see Reference above if you want to rely on them	
Review What is the data saying?	
Relate • How does this tie in with the project objectives? • How does it relate to other areas of the project, eg primary research? • Do I intend to use it – if so, how?	

6 Primary research

Primary research obtains the data particularly relevant to the project you have. Read the following extract from an unpublished undergraduate dissertation.

6.1 Example

The **aim** was to find out what environmental information companies make available to external parties and how useful this is. I decided that the best **method** to gather this information was to become an external party myself and write to them asking for their annual reports and any published environmental information. This way, my research would **not be subject to individual company bias** concerning what they publish, as a survey or interview may be.

Comparisons were only made on the information that I received. This may have had its limitations in that more information could exist, but this was **a representative sample of what an average external reader** would receive – the objective in question.

I **selected** seven companies to request such information from, this small number would allow a more detailed focus on issues. Companies were selected from those mentioned in past ACCA environmental reporting awards together with two randomly selected companies of my own (Dixons and Allied Domeqc).

The dimensions of performance that I concentrated my analysis on were based upon the main points that the first chapter of the literature review discovered. This would enable me to discover if what writers believed was actually being communicated and if what I found was disclosed in reality, matched.

The **annual reports** were requested, to see what **environmental disclosure** they contained and also to discover if any financial environmental information was present in anticipation of the future environmental accounting chapter.

I feel this chapter was a very effective use of primary research. However, one **weakness** was the narrow range of companies considered. A study of companies not recommended by ACCA and operating in several differing industries, may provide more issues. Although this may prove difficult if not enough environmental data is disclosed to make comparisons. To question the companies via telephone rather than an 'official' letter may result in a more relaxed attitude reaping more open responses.

Environmental questionnaire

Next, I wanted to discover how the **internal background of the firms can affect the external environmental communication** they may or may not produce.

I thought a **questionnaire** was appropriate to reach the large amount of companies that I wanted to involve. I chose 30 companies from the catalogue of annual reports at Wheatley library (see appendix 12), consciously trying to include a range of industries. Measures were implemented to increase the chances of companies replying.

- I obtained contact names by telephoning the companies beforehand.
- A stamped addressed envelope was enclosed for replies.
- Anonymity was ensured.
- The questions took a closed category format, meaning all respondents had to do was tick relevant boxes.
- Only fourteen questions were asked.

I also structured the questions to start general before getting more specific to ease respondents into the correct way of thinking. The questionnaire can be seen in appendix 11.

My approach was successful, indicated by the 73% response rate of which 18% were unwilling to take part. This left me with 18 completed questionnaires, split equally over service and manufacturing industries.

To conduct my analysis I first **identified the main categories** of environmental disclosure methods and issues that the majority of the companies portrayed. I then **formed questions** from these categories, seen in table 6.1, which I used for testing. These were answered in a basic 'yes' or 'no' manner but supplemented with detailed information within the appendices. I only based observations upon the companies I was studying and so they became each others' benchmarks for my comments.

6.2 Points to note

Some matters to note – from the words in the text highlighted in **bold**.

(a) The research had a purpose or aim.
(b) The method was developed from the aim.
(c) The author is concerned about the reliability of the data.
(d) The author described the analysis done.
(e) The questionnaire required quite a lot of work in designing and getting them completed.

Also, note that primary research can be **quantitative** and **qualitative.**

6.3 Sampling

In most practical situations the population will be too large to carry out a complete survey and only a sample will be examined. Your research project is not necessarily a statistical market research exercise but your sample should be **meaningful in terms of the project objective** – which could be to suggest further research.

The choice of a sample

If your project **does aim at statistical meaningfulness**, one of the most important requirements of sample data is that they should be **complete**. Sampling methods fall into three main groups.

- Random sampling
- Quasi-random sampling
- Non-random sampling

6.4 Random sampling

To ensure that the sample selected is free from bias, random sampling must be used. Inferences about the population being sampled can then be made validly.

A simple random sample is a sample selected in such a way that every item in the population has an equal chance of being included.

For example, if you wanted to take a random sample of library books, it would not be good enough to pick them off the shelves, even if you picked them at random. This is because the books which were out on loan would stand no chance of being chosen. You would either have to make sure that all the books were on the shelves before taking your sample, or find some other way of sampling (for example, using the library index cards).

Sampling frames

If random sampling is used then it is necessary to construct a **sampling frame**. A **sampling frame** is a numbered list of all items in a population.

Once a numbered list of all items in the population has been made, it is easy to select a random sample, simply by generating a list of random numbers.

For instance, if you wanted to select a random sample of companies in any industry, it would be useful to have a list of names:

0   Ashford
1   Da Costa
2   WM Print

...

Now the numbers 0, 1, 2 and so on can be used to select the random sample. It is normal to start the numbering at 0, so that when 0 appears in a list of random numbers it can be used.

A sampling frame should have the following characteristics.

- **Completeness**. Are all members of the population included on the list?
- **Accuracy**. Is the information correct?
- **Adequacy**. Does it cover the entire population?
- **Up to dateness**. Is the list up to date?
- **Convenience**. Is the sampling frame readily accessible?
- **Non-duplication**. Does each member of the population appear on the list only once?

Drawbacks of random sampling

(a)   Selected items are subject to the full range of variation inherent in the population.
(b)   An unrepresentative sample may result.
(c)   An adequate sampling frame might not exist.
(d)   The numbering of the population might be laborious.
(e)   It might be difficult to obtain the data if the selected items cover a wide area.
(f)   It might be costly to obtain the data if the selected items cover a wide area.

6.5 Quasi-random sampling

When it is too difficult or too costly to obtain a random sample, **quasi-random sampling** is necessary. **Quasi-random sampling** is a sampling method which provides a good approximation to random sampling. As with random sampling, it necessitates the existence of a sampling frame. The main methods of quasi-random sampling are as follows.

- Systematic sampling
- Stratified sampling
- Multistage sampling

Systematic sampling

Systematic sampling is a sampling method which works by selecting every nth item after a random start. If it were decided to select a sample of 20 from a population of 800, then every 40th (800 ÷ 20) item after a random start in the first 40 should be selected. The starting point could be found using the lottery method or random number tables. If (say) 23 was chosen, then the sample would include the 23rd, 63rd, 103rd, 143rd ... 783rd items. The gap of 40 is known as the **sampling interval**. This approach may be familiar to you from audit work, if a sample of invoices is selected for checking.

Stratified sampling

Stratified sampling is a method of sampling which involves dividing the population into strata or categories. Random samples are then taken from each stratum or category.

In many situations, stratified sampling is the best method of choosing a sample. Stratified sampling is best demonstrated by means of an example.

6.6 Example

In **Project Topic 13: The relationship between an organisation's human resources activities and its business objectives**, you are carrying out an employee attitude survey on their training needs. The firm you work for is a large retail firm with many small outlets distributed all over the country. The Human Resource Manager says that 5% of the total employees are senior executive or professional staff, 30% are managerial and supervisory staff and the remaining 65% work as sales assistants. If a sample of 200 was required:

	%
Senior executives 5% × 200	10
Managerial and supervisory 30% × 200	60
Sales assistants 65% × 200	130
	200

You would then select 10 executives at random, and so on.

The main **disadvantage** of stratification is that it requires **prior knowledge of each item in the population**.

Multistage sampling is a non-random sampling method which involves dividing the population into a number of sub-populations and then selecting a small sample of these sub-populations at random. Each sub-population is then divided further, and then a small sample is again selected at random. This process is repeated as many times as is necessary.

6.7 Example

You are doing **Project Topic 13: The relationship between an organisation's human resources activities and its business objectives.** You work for a large retail organisation with many branches.

A survey of spending habits is being planned to cover the whole of your firm.

The country is divided into a number of regions and a small sample of these is selected at random. Each of the regions selected is subdivided into smaller units. This process is repeated as many times as necessary and finally, a random sample of the relevant employees working in each of the smallest units is taken. A fair approximation to a random sample can be obtained.

Thus, we might choose a random sample of four regions, and from each of these areas, select a random sample of ten outlets. From each outlet, a random sample of five people might be selected so that the total sample size is $4 \times 10 \times 5 = 200$ people.

6.8 Non-random sampling

When a sampling frame cannot be established, **non-random sampling** is necessary. There are two main methods of non-random sampling.

- Quota sampling
- Cluster sampling

Quota sampling. In **quota sampling**, randomness is forfeited in the interests of cheapness and administrative simplicity. Investigators are told to interview all the people they meet up to a certain quota. For example you would not select a random sample but would interview the first people you came across. (The sample would not be random because not all the population in each unit has an equal chance of being selected.)

Cluster sampling is a non-random sampling method that involves selecting one definable subsection of the population as the sample, that subsection assumed to be representative of the population in question.

For example, all the employees of one region might be taken as a cluster sample of all employees in the company.

Advantages of cluster sampling

- It is a good alternative to multistage sampling if a satisfactory sampling frame does not exist.
- It is inexpensive to operate.

The main **disadvantage** of cluster sampling is the potential for considerable bias.

7 Surveys and questionnaires

The data used in a statistical survey, whether variables or attributes, can be either **primary data** or **secondary data**.

Primary and secondary data both have their advantages and limitations.

Primary data	Secondary data
Advantage	**Advantage**
The investigator knows where the data came from and is aware of any inadequacies or limitations in the data.	Cheaply available.
Disadvantage	**Disadvantages**
It is expensive to collect primary data.	The investigator did not collect the data and is therefore unaware of any inadequacies or limitations in the data.

7.1 Survey methods of collecting data

There are two basic methods of collecting primary data from individuals.

(a)   They can be asked questions.

(b)   Their behaviour can be observed.

This involves the collection of data using **surveys**, for example structured interviews, postal questionnaires or, possibly, e-mailed questionnaires.

7.2 Errors in survey methods of collecting data

There are three main types of error that can appear in survey methods of collecting data.

(a)   **Sampling error**. It is quite usual for a sample of the population to be surveyed, rather than the entire population. If the sample surveyed is **not representative** of the population from which it is drawn, a sampling error will arise.

(b)   **Response error** arises because respondents are either **unable** or **unwilling** to **respond**.

7.3 Interviews

There are basically two types of interview that can be used to collect quantitative data, the **personal (face to face) interview** and the **telephone interview**.

Advantages of personal interviews

(a)   The interviewer is able to **reduce respondent anxiety** and **allay potential embarrassment**, thereby increasing the response rate and decreasing the potential for error.

(b)   The routing ('if yes go to question 7, if no go to question 10') of questions is made easier due to the experience of the interviewer.

(c)   Interviewers can ask, within narrow limits, for a respondent's answer to be clarified.

(d)   The questions can be given in a **fixed order** with a **fixed wording** and the answers can be recorded in a **standard manner**. If there is more than one interviewer involved in the survey this will reduce variability.

(e)   **Standardised questions** and ways of recording the responses mean that less skilled interviewers may be used, thereby reducing the cost of the survey.

(f)   **Pictures, signs** and **objects** can be used.

Disadvantages of personal interviews

(a) They can be **time consuming**.

(b) They can be **costly** to complete.

(c) Questionnaires can be **difficult to design**.

(d) Questions must often be kept relatively simple, thus restricting the depth of data collected.

(e) Questions must normally be **closed** because of the difficulties of recording answers to open questions.

(f) Interviewers cannot probe vague or ambiguous replies.

7.4 Arranging interviews and meetings

(a) If the matter is at all sensitive, you may need to get authorisation from a senior member of the organisation.

(b) If you are interviewing people you do not know, give them advance warning.

(c) **Do not just turn up**. Always book a time in advance. If the interviewee works in an open plan office, you may want to **book a separate meeting room**. (You can book meetings via e-mail or use Microsoft Outlook.)

7.5 Telephone surveys

Advantages

(a) The response is **rapid**.

(b) There is a **standard sampling frame** – the **telephone directory**, which can be systematically or randomly sampled.

(c) A **wide geographical area** can be covered fairly cheaply.

(d) It may be **easier to ask sensitive or embarrassing questions**.

(e) In the Research and Analysis Project, you may need to let people know in advance that you are going to call them.

Disadvantages

(a) A **biased sample** may result from the fact that a large proportion (about 10%) of people do not have telephones (representing certain portions of the population such as old people or students) and many of those who do are ex-directory.

(b) It is **not possible to use 'showcards'** or pictures.

(c) The **refusal rate is much higher** than with face-to-face interviews, and the interview often cut short.

(d) It is **not possible to see the interviewee's expressions** or to develop the rapport that is possible with personal interviews.

(e) The interview **must be short**.

7.6 Postal surveys

We are using the term 'postal' survey to cover all methods in which the questionnaire is given to the respondent and returned to the investigator without personal contact. Such questionnaires could be posted but might also be left in pigeonholes or on desks.

Postal questionnaires have the following **advantages** over personal interviews.

(a)	The **cost per person** is likely **to be less**, so more people can be sampled, and central control is facilitated.
(b)	It is usually possible to **ask more questions** because the people completing the forms (the respondents) can do so in their own time.
(c)	**All respondents are presented with questions in the same way**. There is no opportunity for an interviewer to influence responses (interviewer bias) or to misrecord them.
(d)	It may be **easier to ask personal or embarrassing questions** in a postal questionnaire than in a personal interview.
(e)	Respondents **may need to look up information for the questionnaire**. This will be easier if the questionnaire is sent to their homes or places of work.

7.7 E-mail survey

Surveys can be done via e-mail, even though 'spamming' people with unwanted email is not likely to win you any friends.

(a)	If you are conducting an e-mail survey at work, you can **attach** a document or spreadsheet to the email, asking the respondent to open the document or spreadsheet, complete it, save it and return.
(b)	You may be able to ask your questions in the e-mail itself, asking the respondent to reply and return the e-mail.

7.8 Quantitative research questionnaire design

It is worth noting that the external examiner has commented that 'candidates who used questionnaires in their analysis generally did quite well, as they had a ready source of data for their analysis'.

Designing the questionnaire

The sampling process can be an important contributor to the quality and value of the survey process. Where survey findings are technically suspect, this is most commonly because there are **flaws in the design of the questionnaire**.

Core principles of questionnaire design

- **Decide precisely what information** you wish to obtain from each individual question
- **Ensure that the question gives you this information** as precisely as possible
- Ensure that there is **no possibility of misunderstanding or ambiguity** about the question or its answer

Common pitfalls

(a)	**Ambiguity and uncertainty about language or terminology**. Don't assume people will understand what you mean.

(b)   **Lack of clarity about the information required**. You should always stop and ask yourself some fundamental questions. Why am I asking this question? What is it intended to find out? What exactly do I want to know? **Will this question give me the information I need?** These questions are often not explicitly addressed, with the result that the wrong question (or only part of the right question) is asked. In an employee survey, for example, the questionnaire could ask:

Which of the following do you feel are barriers to your undertaking further training or development in your own time?

- Lack of spare time
- Lack of motivation
- Personal/domestic commitments
- Cost

The respondents could tick most **if not all** of these options. The survey designer really wanted to ask not **whether** these factors were seen as barriers, but **which** were the most significant barriers and **how** significant they were.

(c)   **Conflation of multiple questions into one**. In a survey, for example, respondents could be asked, 'How often does your workgroup meet to discuss performance, quality and safety issues?' The assumption behind this question – is that managers called workgroups together to discuss all three of these issues. Some workgroups may not meet at all, some may meet infrequently and some could meet relatively often but may only discuss performance issues.

(d)   **Making unjustified assumptions**. For example, 'In reviewing your performance, which of the following methods does your manager use?' The assumption here, of course, is that the manager reviews the respondent's performance at all.

7.9 Leading questions

The question may still provide misleading data if it appears to be **leading the respondent towards a particular answer**. People may still feel **uncertain** about its outcomes and they may still feel **suspicious of your motives** for conducting it. In such cases, some may feel very keen to give the 'right' answer – the answer that they believe you or the organisation would like to hear.

7.10 'Agree/disagree' and other formats

This problem occurs most commonly when respondents are asked to **indicate their level of agreement or disagreement** with a particular statement. It is prudent, therefore, to include a **mixture of positive and negative statements**, which do not suggest any intrinsic preference.

In some cases, the choice of statement can **significantly undermine the value of the information obtained**. 'The quality of work in my department is generally excellent'. If the respondent agrees with this statement the meaning was clear – that he or she thought the quality of work in the department was generally excellent. However, if the respondent **disagreed** with the statement, the meaning was less clear. Did they think the quality was moderate or even poor?

In general, the questions in a written questionnaire should be of the **multiple choice** type, so providing the basis for quantitative analysis.

Survey questions can be divided into two broad categories; those **exploring attitudes** or opinions and those **seeking some form of factual information**.

(a) In the former category would generally fall, for example, the 'agree/disagree' format, such as 'Safety is always a paramount concern for the organisation. Do you:

    (i)   Agree strongly
    (ii)   Agree slightly
    (iii) Disagree slightly
    (iv) Disagree strongly?'

(b) In the latter category might fall questions about, say, the frequency of workgroup meetings or about recent experience of training.

Respondents **are commonly reluctant to give extreme responses** and prefer to hover around the middle ground. If you have an odd number of items in your scale, you may find that respondents disproportionately opt for the neutral option. There are benefits in forcing respondents off the fence by **offering only an even number of options**, so that the respondent has to choose between, say, 'agree slightly' and 'disagree slightly'. In this way, you gain a clearer perspective on the **true direction of opinion**.

Where you are asking to identify preferences from among a number of options, you may ask respondents to **rank the options against a given criterion**, such as 'Which of the following do you think are the most important contributors to high workgroup performance? (Please rank in order of importance.)'

(a) If you use this format, you should remember to indicate **how the ranking should be applied**. Is number 1 the **most** or the **least** important factor? Ranking questions can seem **confusing** to respondents and are best used sparingly. In any cases, it is rarely worth asking respondents to rank more than the first three or four items. Beyond that, rankings usually become fairly arbitrary.

(b) A more straightforward approach is to ask respondents simply to **select one item** – 'Which of the following do you think is the single most important contributor to high workgroup performance? (Please tick one only.)' Although slightly less detailed, this question is easier both to complete and to analyse.

In collecting **factual** information, you may again wish to **use scales** where the required information lies on a continuum. For example, 'How many days have you spent training in the past 12 months? Fewer than 3 days/4 – 6 days/6 – 10 days/more than 10 days.'

Where you are exploring more discrete items of information, you may simply ask respondents to **select the most relevant items**. For example, you might ask, 'Which of the following types of training have you undertaken in the last year? (Please tick any that apply.)' In this case, you are not asking respondents to evaluate the options against one another, but simply to make a choice between those that are and those that are not significant. This format can also be applied in cases of **opinions and attitudes**.

7.11 Building the questionnaire

The overall structure of the questionnaire can take a number of forms, depending on the purpose and nature of the survey. As a general rule, when you are exploring a given topic, you should aim to be as systematic as possible in **progressing from the general to the specific**.

(a) **Context**. Typically, your initial aim should be to gain an understanding of the **broad context** within which opinions are held.

(b) You can then progress to gaining an understanding of the **nature and strength of opinion** in a given area.

(c) **Detail**. Finally, you can move, step by step, towards identifying the **detail that underpins these**.

Context

To illustrate this, let us take an example – a questionnaire designed to explore the issues of reward and recognition. The questionnaire might begin, for example, by asking a question about perceptions of reward and recognition in the organisation generally.

How satisfied are you with the level of recognition and reward you receive for your achievements at work?

- Very satisfied
- Fairly satisfied
- Fairly dissatisfied
- Very dissatisfied?

The **responses** to this question will help provide you with a **context** within which you can interpret the more detailed information you will obtain from subsequent questions.

Perceptions

Having defined the broad organisational context, you can begin to focus more precisely on the detail of the specific topic. The next question might be:

If you feel that your work achievements are recognised, what form does this recognition generally take? (Please tick any that apply.)

- Increased basic pay
- Bonus payment
- Other financial reward
- Promotion
- Verbal congratulations
- Non-financial reward
- Other (please specify)

This will provide you with an understanding of the **current perceptions of the topic** – what respondents' perceptions of the rewards they typically receive for work achievements are.

If you are researching your current employer, you may feel **tempted to omit** this kind of 'state of play' question on the basis that **you already know** enough about what happens currently in the organisation. It is easy to assume that **your** perceptions and perspective reflect those of others. But you should not assume this. Someone approaching retirement may have an entirely different view on life from someone just starting work.

Preferences

Having identified people's perceptions of the current state of play in the specific area, you can then move to the next level of detail and begin to explore, for example, their **preferences** for reward and recognition. You might ask:

Which of the following forms of recognition for work achievements do you find most motivating? (Please tick one only.)

- Increased basic pay
- Bonus payment
- Other financial reward
- Promotion
- Verbal congratulations
- Non-financial reward
- Other (please specify)

Mapping these expressed preferences against the current perceived position should indicate very clearly **if or where there is a gap between the current and the desired positions**.

Ensuring accurate responses

This general process of moving from the general to the specific is sometimes known as **'funnelling'**.

(a) It is an important device for **ensuring precision in interpretation**.

(b) It may also help you to provide a meaningful interpretation of responses that may be influenced by extraneous factors, such as **self-interest**.

(c) **The use of broad, contextual questions, however, will help you to interpret such responses** against a range of other issues and concerns. You might, for instance, ask respondents, initially, to rank areas of potential dissatisfaction in order of significance. This will then provide you with a basis on which to evaluate any specific expression of dissatisfaction with the really important issue.

Other questionnaire structures can also be used to **minimise the influence of external factors**. If you are exploring a range of issues, for example, it can be helpful to distribute questions about each respective issue throughout the questionnaire, **rather than bunching them in discrete sections**. This can help reduce what is sometimes known as the 'halo effect', which is when overall positive or negative feelings about a given issue influence responses to individual questions.

7.12 Questionnaire length and layout

There is generally a trade-off between questionnaire length and the level of response. The **longer and more detailed** the questionnaire, the **more likely** you are to encounter **resistance** from potential respondents.

Despite these caveats, the following crude guidelines for different forms of questionnaire administration may be helpful.

(a) **Cold surveys**. Where the questionnaire is being sent out with no preparation and where respondents have no particular incentive to respond, you should aim for an absolute maximum of 4 sides of paper and no more than 15 to 20 questions (including sub-questions), but in many cases, it will be preferable to aim for just 1 or 2 sides of paper and even fewer questions. The key issue here is likely to be one of presentation. You will want to suggest that the survey is easy to complete and will involve comparatively little of the respondent's time. Therefore, simple, 'user-friendly' layout is likely to be an even more significant issue than the overall length.

(b) **Postal questionnaires**. Where respondents have been briefed and prepared, but are nevertheless expected to complete the questionnaire entirely in their own time, you should generally aim for a questionnaire of some 6 to 8 sides of paper, ideally with no more than 30 to 40 questions. If potential respondents put the questionnaire to one side, the chances are that a substantial proportion will not get around to completing it at all.

(c) **Questionnaires completed in work time**. Where the **organisation** allocates some work time to completing the questionnaire, you can generally risk a rather longer questionnaire – probably up to 10 to 12 pages and 50 to 60 questions.

Some other general points about questionnaire design are also worth stressing. First, make sure that you provide **clear instructions** throughout, indicating precisely how the questionnaire should be completed. These should be simply phrased and as concise as possible. It is also a good idea to **provide some**

examples of specific question types and how they should be completed. As always, one good example is worth several dozen words of explanation.

7.13 Laying out the questionnaire

(a)   If respondents have to complete the questionnaire themselves, it must be approachable and as short as possible. Consider the use of **lines, boxes, different type faces and print sizes and small pictures**. Use plenty of space.

(b)   Consider the use of **tick boxes**. Is it clear where ticks go or how to respond in each case? For analysis, will it be easy to transfer responses from the forms to a summary sheet or a computer? Consider pre-coding the answers.

(c)   Explain the **purpose of the survey** at the beginning of the questionnaire and where possible guarantee confidentiality. Emphasise the date by which it must be returned.

(d)   At the end of the questionnaire, **thank the respondent** and make it clear what they should do with the completed questionnaire.

7.14 Pilot tests

It is vital to **pilot test questionnaires** since mistakes, ambiguities and embarrassments in a questionnaire can be expensive once the main data collection phase has been entered. Do not send any questionnaire out 'cold' without getting someone else to work through it in detail.

7.15 The Likert scale

This approach can be summarised in three steps – (a), (b) and (c).

(a)   A list of statements is prepared about the topic being researched, and a test group of respondents is asked to rate each statement on a scale from strong agreement to strong disagreement.

(b)   A numerical value is given to each response:

5   Strongly agree
4   Agree
3   Don't know
2   Disagree
1   Strongly disagree

(c)   Each respondent's scores for all the statements are added up to give a total score for the topic, which may reflect overall positive or negative attitudes: responses to individual statements can also be analysed to get more meaningful information about the pattern of responses.

Likert scales are simple to prepare and administer. You may have been asked to complete such an inventory test over the telephone, or seen one in a magazine. However, again you should be aware that scale values have no absolute meaning, and are limited in their statistical uses, on an 'interval' scale.

An example of a questionnaire using a variety of techniques can be found below.

Name	Description	Example

CLOSED-END QUESTIONS

Dichotomous — A question with two possible answers.

'In arranging this trip, did you personally phone British Airways?'

Yes ☐   No ☐

Multiple choice — A question with three or more answers.

'With whom are you travelling on this flight?'

No one	☐	Children only	☐
Spouse	☐	Business associates/ friends/relatives	☐
Spouse and children	☐	An organised tour group	☐

Likert scale — A statement with which the respondent shows the amount of agreement/ disagreement.

'Small airlines generally give better service'

Strongly disagree 1	Disagree 2	Neither agree nor disagree 3	Agree 4	Strongly agree 5
☐	☐	☐	☐	☐

Semantic differential — A scale connecting two bipolar words, where the respondent selects the point that represents his or her opinion.

British Airways

Large _ _ _ _ _ _ _ _ _ _ _ _ _ _ _ _ _ _ Small
Experienced _ _ _ _ _ _ _ _ _ _ _ _ _ Inexperienced
Modern _ _ _ _ _ _ _ _ _ _ _ _ _ _ _ Old-fashioned

Importance scale — A scale that rates the importance of some attribute.

Extremely important 1	Very important 2	Somewhat important 3	Not very important 4	Not at all important 5
☐	☐	☐	☐	☐

Rating scale — A scale that rates some attribute from 'poor' to 'excellent'.

Excellent	Very good	Good	Fair	Poor

Intention-to-buy scale — A scale that describes the respondent's intention to buy.

'If an inflight telephone was available on a long flight, I would'

Definitely buy 1	Probably buy 2	Not sure 3	Probably not buy 4	Definitely not buy 5
☐	☐	☐	☐	☐

OPEN-END QUESTIONS

Completely unstructured — A question that respondents can answer in an almost unlimited number of ways.

'What is your opinion of British Airways?'

Word association — Words are presented, one at a time, and respondents mention the first word that comes to mind.

'What is the first word that comes to mind when you hear the following'
Airline_____
British_____
Travel _____

Sentence completion — An incomplete sentence is presented and respondents complete the sentence.

'When I choose an airline, the most important consideration in my decision is _____ '

Story completion — An incomplete story is presented, and respondents are asked to complete it.

'I flew B.A. a few days ago. I noticed that the exterior and interior of the plane had bright colours. This aroused in me the following thoughts and feelings.' Now complete the story.

Picture completion — A picture of two characters is presented, with one making a statement. Respondents are asked to identify with the other and fill in the empty balloon.

The inflight entertainment's good

Thematic Apperception Test (TAT) — A picture is presented and respondents are asked to make up a story about what they think is happening or may happen in the picture.

The Semantic Differential scale

> (a) Scales are constructed on a number of **'dimensions'** – pairs of opposite attributes or qualities, expressed as adjectives – valued on a continuum from +3 to –3.

Profile of Car Model X

	+3	+2	+1	0	–1	–2	–3	
Modern								Old-fashioned
Fast								Slow
Attractive								Unattractive
Powerful								Weak
Responsive								Unresponsive
Glamorous								Ordinary

(b) Respondents are asked to **select the position of the object** being researched (in this case the car) on each continuum, according to the degree to which they think the adjective describes the object. (If the car is very powerful but not terribly responsive, say, it might rate +3 on the powerful-weak dimension, and +1 on the responsive-unresponsive scale.)

(c) A **'profile'** is thus built up by each respondent.

The main problem with Semantic Differential scales is the **subjectivity attached to language**. Words are mean different things to different people. (The word 'old-fashioned' in our car profile above may mean 'out of date' to some and 'classic' to others.)

The other problem of measuring responses to, and perceptions of, different attributes of the same thing is that **one attribute can influence our perception of other attributes** and some attributes bring clusters of other assumed attributes with them (stereotypes). Think, for example, about our Model X car: if it looks sleek and attractive, we may perceive it as a fast car – whether it is or not – and if we think of old-fashioned cars as glamorous (because of stereotypes of 'classic' cars and the people who drive them) we might distort our glamour rating.

7.16 Example

Here is an example from an unpublished undergraduate dissertation about how firms report on the environment.

ENVIRONMENTAL QUESTIONNAIRE

Environmental questionnaire

Please answer as many questions as applicable ticking the relevant boxes. All answers will be treated as anonymous.

Thank you

Q1. Is your company predominantly operating in a service or manufacturing industry?

Service ....

Manufacturing ....

Q2. What is your company's average annual turnover? £..........

Q3. (a) Does your company have a separate environmental department or manager?

        (i)   Environmental department   ....

        (ii)   Environmental manager   ....

        (iii)   Neither   ....

    (b) If you do have an environmental department or manager how long has this been operational?

        Length of time   ....

Q4. Does your company have separate environmental policy?

- Yes   ....
- No   ....

If Yes, are all employees made aware of this?

- Yes   ....
- No   ....

Some are, some are not   ....

Q5. Does your company utilise any of the following environmental initiatives? (Please tick all that are applicable.)

- Energy conservation   ....
- Control of emissions   ....
- Recycling   ....
- Reusing   ....
- Buying from environmentally friendly suppliers   ....
- Monitoring and controlling waste   ....
- Using recycled stationery   ....
- Tree planting   ....
- Other   ....

Please state...

Q6. Is your company aware of any environmental impacts it may have?

- Yes – and we are controlling them   ....
- Yes – and we are investigating them   ....
- Yes – but other organisational matters are our priority at the moment   ....
- No – we do not affect our environment   ....
- No   ....

Don't know   ....

Q7. Does your company publish any environmental information:

- Yes   ....
- No (if no go to question 12)   ....

Q8. If environmental information is published, what was the motivation behind it?

- Shareholder pressure   ....
- Government legislation   ....
- Competitive advantage   ....
- Concern for the environment   ....
- Other   ....

Please state ....

Q9.   Who is your intended audience for published environmental information?

- Shareholders ....
- Government ....
- Employees ....
- Competitors ....
- Suppliers ....
- General public ....
- Other

Please state ....

Q10.   Is this published information:

- Included in your Annual Report? ....

- Published separately but distributed at the same time as your Annual Report? ....

- Distributed at a time other than that when Annual Report is published? ....

Q11.   What form does this published information take?

- Narrative disclosure ....
- Statistical indicators ....
- Mixture of narrative and statistical ....
- Financial data ....
- Environmental achievements ....
- Environmental targets ....

Q12.   Does your company have separate environmental information that it uses for internal management decisions?

- Yes ....
- No – we use the published environmental data ....
- No – we do not incorporate environmental data in management decisions ....

Q13.   If you do have environmental information is this part of an environmental management system?

- Yes ....
- No ....

If no, are there any plans to introduce such a system?

- Yes ....
- No ....

Q14.   Does your company believe environmental impacts are going to be an increasing business issue as we approach and enter the millennium?

- Yes ....
- No ....

Thank you very much for your time and help.

Please return completed questionnaires in the stamped addressed envelope provided.

8 Qualitative research

Qualitative research is another process which aims to collect primary data. Its main methods are the open-ended interview, whether this be a depth interview (one-to-one) or a group discussion (focus group), and projective techniques. The form of the data collected is narrative rather than isolated statements reduceable to numbers. **Its main purpose is to understand people's behaviour and perceptions rather than to measure them.**

The key to qualitative research is to allow the respondents to say what they feel and think in response to flexible, 'prompting' questioning, rather than to give their responses to set questions and often set answers in a questionnaire.

8.1 Unstructured interviews

Neither interviewer or respondent is bound by the structure of a questionnaire in an **unstructured interview**. Interviewers may have a checklist of topics to cover in questioning, but they are free to word such questions as they wish. The order in which questions are covered may also be varied. This will allow the respondent to control the data flow and for the interviewer to explore more thoroughly particular views of the respondent and why they are held. Unstructured interviews are a very useful way of capturing data which is qualitative in nature. Such interviews may also provide the researcher with relevant questions which could be put to a wider audience of respondents using structured or semi-structured interview techniques, especially if quantitative data is required.

8.2 Depth interviews

Motivational research often uses the psychoanalytic method of **depth interviews**. The pattern of questioning should assist the respondent to explore deeper levels of thought. Motives and explanations of behaviour often lie well **below the surface**. It is a **time-consuming** and **expensive** process. Taped interviews and analysis of transcripts are often used. A single individual or a small team may conduct depth interviewing. Depth interviews may have fewer than ten respondents.

Advantages of depth interviews

(a) **Longitudinal information** (such as information on decision-making processes) can be gathered from one respondent at a time, thereby aiding clarity of interpretation and analysis.

(b) Intimate and **personal material** can be more easily accessed and discussed.

(c) Respondents are **less likely to confine themselves** simply to reiterating socially acceptable attitudes.

Disadvantages of depth interviews

(a) They are **time consuming** to conduct and to analyse. **Each depth interview needs to be written up shortly afterwards and reflected on.** If each interview lasts between one and two hours, a maximum of two per day is often all that is possible.

(b) They are more **costly** than group discussions.

(c) There is a temptation to begin treating depth interviews as if they were simply another form of questionnaire survey, thinking in terms of quantitative questions like 'how many' rather than qualitative issues like 'how', 'why' or 'what'.

(d) A certain amount of expertise is needed in depth interviews.

In a depth interview the key line of communication is between the interviewer and the respondent. They have an **open-ended conversation**, not constrained by a formal questionnaire, and the qualitative data are captured as narrative by means of an audio or video tape.

8.3 Focus groups

Focus groups are useful in providing the researcher with **qualitative data**. Qualitative data can often provide greater insight than quantitative data and does not lend itself to the simple application of standard statistical methods.

Focus groups usually consist of 8 to 10 respondents and an interviewer taking the role of group moderator. The group moderator introduces topics for discussion and intervenes as necessary to encourage respondents or to direct discussions if they threaten to wander too far off the point. The moderator will also need to control any powerful personalities and prevent them from dominating the group.

Group discussions may be **audio or video tape recorded** for later analysis and interpretation. The researcher must be careful not to generalise too much from such small scale qualitative research. **Group discussion is very dependent on the skill of the group moderator**. It is inexpensive to conduct, it can be done quickly and it can provide useful, timely, qualitative data.

Focus groups are often used at the early stage of research to get a feel for the subject matter under discussion and to create possibilities for more structured research. Four to eight groups may be assembled and each group interviewed for one, two or three hours.

Advantages of focus groups

(a)   The group environment with 'everybody in the same boat' can be **less intimidating** than other techniques of research which rely on one-to-one contact (such as depth interviews).

(b)   What respondents say in a group often **sparks off experiences** or ideas on the part of others.

(c)   **Differences between consumers** are highlighted, making it possible to understand a range of attitudes in a short space of time.

(d)   It is **easier to observe groups** and there is more to observe simply because of the intricate behaviour patterns within a collection of people.

(e)   Social and cultural influences are highlighted.

(f)   Groups provide a **social context** that is a 'hot-house' reflection of the real world.

(g)   Groups are **cheaper and faster** than depth interviews.

Disadvantages of focus groups

(a)   Group processes may **inhibit some people from making a full contribution** and may encourage others to become exhibitionistic.

(b)   Group processes **may stall** to the point where they cannot be retrieved by the moderator.

(c)   Some groups may **take a life of their own**, so that what is said has validity only in the short-lived context of the group.

(d)   It is not usually possible to identify **which group members said what**, unless the proceedings have been video recorded.

(e)   It is **not easy to find a common time** when all can participate.

When planning qualitative research using focus groups, a number of factors need to be considered.

Type	Comment
Type of group	A standard group is of 7–9 respondents, but other types may also be used.
Membership	Who takes part in the discussion depends on who the researcher wants to talk to (users or non-users, for instance) and whether they all need to be similar (homogenous).
Number of groups	Having more than 12 groups in a research project would be very unusual, mainly because nothing new would come out of a thirteenth one!
Recruitment	Usually on the basis of a quota sample: respondents are screened by a short questionnaire to see whether they are suitable. In order to persuade them to join in, the members are usually given an incentive plus expenses.
Discussion topics	These will be decided by the researcher with regard to the purpose of the group discussion, that is the data that are required. There should be a number of topics since the interviewer needs to be able to restart discussion once a topic has been fully discussed.
Involvement	The researcher is asking for a deep level of involvement and commitment.

9 How good is your data?

Once you have done the research you **intended** to do, you should draw your data together and take a hard look at it as a whole, the secondary data and primary data.

Remember that the Research and Analysis Project is not **deadline driven**, nor is there a syllabus. You will be marked on your ability to do some research, analysis and communication.

Ask yourself these questions.

Question	Yes/No
1 Have I done all that I set out to do?	
2 Does the data I have obtained give me a chance to conduct an analysis on the lines of the project objective?	
3 If the answer to (1) or (2) is no, have I obtained data by another adequate route?	
4 Is my use of sources sufficient to fulfil the criteria for use of references in the marking scheme for this project?	
5 Have I made sure I have referenced and recorded my data?	
6 THE ULTIMATE TEST Does the data I have collected put me on the right path for fulfilling the project objective?	

10 Cheating

We reproduce here the relevant section of the Oxford Brookes University Information Pack.

All assessments are intended to determine the skills, abilities, understanding and knowledge of each of the individual students undertaking the assessment. Cheating is defined as obtaining an unfair academic advantage and any student found using any form of cheating, attempting to cheat or assisting someone else to cheat may be subject to disciplinary action in accordance with the University's Disciplinary Procedure. The University takes this issue very seriously and students have been expelled or had their degrees withheld for cheating in assessments. If you are having difficulty with your work it is important to seek help from your tutor rather than be tempted to use unfair means to gain marks. Do not risk losing your degree and all the work you have done.

The University's regulations define a number of different forms of cheating, although any form of cheating is strictly forbidden. These are:

- **submitting other people's work as your own** – either with or without their knowledge. This includes copying in examinations; using notes or unauthorised materials in examinations

- **impersonation** – taking an assessment on behalf of or pretending to be another student, or allowing another person to take an assessment on your behalf or pretend to be you

- **plagiarism** – taking or using another person's thoughts, writings or inventions as your own. To avoid plagiarism you must make sure that quotations from whatever source must be clearly identified and attributed at the point where they occur in the text of your work by using one of the standard conventions for referencing. The Library has a leaflet about how to reference your work correctly and your tutor can also help you. It is not enough just to list sources in a bibliography at the end of your essay or dissertation if you do not acknowledge the actual quotations in the text. Neither is it acceptable to change some of the words or the order of sentences if, by failing to acknowledge the source properly, you give the impression that it is your own work

- **collusion** – except where written instructions specify that work for assessment may be produced jointly and submitted as the work of more than one student, you must not collude with others to produce a piece of work jointly, copy or share another student's work or lend your work to another student in the reasonable knowledge that some or all of it will be copied

- **duplication** – submitting work for assessment that is the same as, or broadly similar to, work submitted earlier for academic credit, without acknowledgement of the previous submission

- **falsification** – the invention of data, its alteration, its copying from any other source, or otherwise obtaining it by unfair means, or inventing quotations and/or references.

10.1 Referencing

It should be obvious from the above that you need to reference your material very thoroughly, given the requirements in the Information Pack. If you are at all uncertain as to how you should reference material, you are strongly advised to try the exercises in the Chapter 2.

Chapter roundup

- This chapter has covered research.
- The **type of research** you adopt will vary according to the project objective.
- The research you do should be **determined** by the project objective.
- There are many sources of secondary data. You may need to do some primary research also.
- Not all research is looking for statistically accurate information.

chapter 7

INTRODUCTION

Once you have obtained the data through your research programme, you will then need to analyse this in order to draw conclusions from it. The type of analysis you will do will be determined by the project objective – as we have seen some project topics are more descriptive and exploratory than others.

As the Research and Analysis Project aims to test your use of IT, it is perhaps appropriate that you use a spreadsheet in your analysis – the precise use of it will depend on what you intend to do – the spreadsheet can also be used to enhance the graphical presentation of your results.

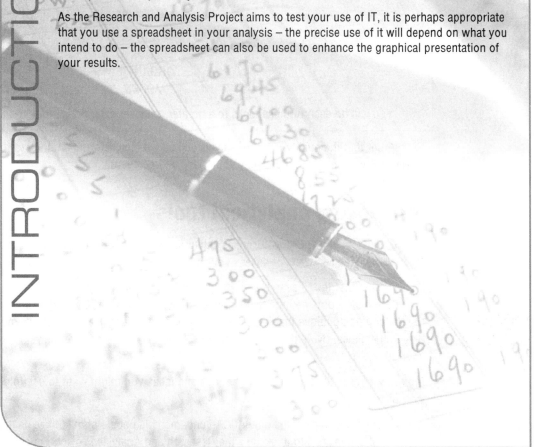

1 Analysing data in the light of the project objective

As indicated in the previous chapter, the type of information and data you obtain will be determined by the project:

- Topic
- Objective
- Scope, focus and context of your data search

You might have done a mix of quantitative and qualitative research, using a variety of methods.

(a)   You could have conducted a survey of people in an organisation by sending out a questionnaire, as we illustrated. This technique is useful even if it is not attempting to select a statistically valid sample – you may be trying to find things out for which statistical analysis is not relevant.

(b)   Interviews can be used to obtain quantitative and qualitative data.

The previous chapter suggested that you **categorise** the secondary data that you obtain. We will now go on to reviewing its content, as this will form the scope of your analysis.

1.1 The CLOM model

You are likely to succeed in your analysis task if you go about it in a systematic way. Don't just rush into creating a spreadsheet and thinking this will be enough – you may be ignoring other ways of looking at the data. We therefore propose the CLOM framework to **structure your approach to this task**.

The CLOM model

CHOOSE
LOOK
ORGANISE
MODEL

You will do each of these tasks to a greater or lesser extent depending on the project objective.

Remember that the quality of your analysis will be a major determinant in determining your Research and Analysis Project grade and possibly your class degree overall.

2 Choosing analytical tools

One of the steps in the Oxford Brookes University model suggests choosing a theoretical **framework** or ideas with which to review or assess your data.

Bear in mind that the Research and Analysis Project is testing specific research and communication skills. You should have obtained the theory while studying for your ACCA qualification. However, there is nothing to stop you going above that level, and you would be well advised to read around to demonstrate your research abilities. (Note that you can choose to do the Research and Analysis Project at various points in your studies.)

A good way of getting to know the theories and ideas you might want to use might be to **read the ACCA's syllabuses**.

ACCA students who pass the nine ACCA Fundamentals papers should have developed the necessary intellectual capabilities to undertake the Research and Analysis Project. This is reflected in the Oxford Brookes list of approved project topic areas which are linked to content of the Fundamentals syllabuses. However some ACCA students decide that they wish to complete one or more ACCA Professional examinations before completing the Oxford Brookes BSc degree. Such students will gain additional analytical skills and will be well placed to undertake a project in those project topic areas which have a greater focus on business activities.

2.1 Example

For example, you may choose **Project Topic 5: The effects of globalisation on an organisation**.

Although papers P3 and P4 contain a lot of relevant material, if you decide to do the Research and Analysis Project before you complete the professional level, you still have a lot of material to go on.

Below we have listed what we believe to be the most relevant current exam syllabuses to each of the project topics. However this depends very much on **your detailed project objective.**

Please note that the list below is indicative. The relevant papers are suggestions where you might find appropriate content and are not intended to be definitive.

	Project Topic	Current syllabus	Relevant papers in old syllabus
1	An organisation's budgetary control system and its links with performance management and decision making	P5, F5	3.3
2	How the introduction of a new technology can assist an organisation in achieving its business objectives	F1, F5, P3	1.3, 2.1, 3.5
3	The impact of an aspect of impending legislation on the operations and financial position of an organisation	F1, F4, P3	1.3, 2.2, 3.5
4	The impact of e-business on an organisation	F1, F5, P1, P3, P4	1.3, 2.1, 3.5, 3.7
5	The effects of globalisation on an organisation	F1, P3, P4	1.3, 3.5
6	The key factors or indicators in the motivation of employees in an organisation	F1, P3	1.3, 3.5
7	The restructuring of an organisation's operational activities and the effect on the organisation's financial performance	F3, F4, F6, P2, P5, P6	1.1, 2.2, 2.3, 3.2, 3.3, 3.6
8	The business and financial performance of an organisation over a three year period	F3, F7, F9, P1, P2, P4, P5	1.1, 2.4, 2.5, 3.3, 3.6, 3.7
9	The planning and implementation of an information system in an organisation	F1, F5, P3	2.1
10	The effectiveness of the use of costing techniques within an organisation	F2, F5, P1, P4, P5,	1.2, 2.4, 3.3, 3.7
11	The financial and operational costs and benefits of the internal audit/internal review activities within an organisation	F5, F8, P5	2.1, 2.6, 3.3
12	The possible effects of a proposed accounting standard on the financial statements and business activities of an organisation	F3, F7, P2	1.1, 2.5, 3.6
13	The relationship between an organisation's human resources activities and its business objectives	F1	1.3

	Project Topic	Current syllabus	Relevant papers in old syllabus
14	The business and financial objectives of a strategic investment decision made by an organisation and its impact on key stakeholders	F9, P1, P4, P5	2.4, 3.3, 3.7
15	The management of an organisation's working capital over a three year period and its impact on the organisation's funding strategies	F2, F9, P1, P4	1.2, 2.4, 3.7
16	The financial and operational risk management within an organisation	F5, F8, F9, P5, P7	2.1, 2.6, 3.1, 3.3
17	The quality of the corporate governance within an organisation and the impact on an organisation's key stakeholders	F4, P1, P4, P5	2.2, 3.3, 3.7
18	The marketing strategy of an organisation and its effectiveness	P3	3.5
19	The financial and operational consequences of a merger between two organisations or of the acquisition of one organisation by another	P1, P2, P3, P4	3.5, 3.6, 3.7
20	An organisation's corporate social responsibility policies, including business ethics, and their impact on business practice and key stakeholders	P2, P7	3.1, 3.6

2.2 Other sources

However, there is no need to restrict yourself to this. Your reading – particularly the **secondary research** you have done – may have included theoretical models and frameworks which you can use to interpret or apply to your data.

3 Looking at the data

In the Research section, you went into some detail about reviewing your data, as to whether it is suitable to satisfy the project objective. You want to take a **broad overview** of what you have found.

3.1 Secondary data

We suggest that you set up a schedule listing the data down the side with the project objective across the top and noting the analytical work you can do on each.

3.2 Example

Let us say that you are doing **Project Topic 8: The business and financial performance of an organisation over a three year period**. You have focused on the financial situation of a mobile phone company which has recently spent a significant amount of money in bidding for a licence to run 'third generation' **mobile phone** services in the UK.

Your **project objective** is a review of the financial position of X plc to assess the impact of licence expenditure on the financial position of the company.

All your information has come from the public domain – you do not have privileged access to the firm's accounts and plans. When you have contacted the firm, you have been given copies of marketing literature and press releases.

This is what you may have obtained.

Project objective: assess impact of licence expenditure on X plc's financial position.

Item	What does it tell me? How can I use it?
Published financial statements for the past three years of the firm and its competitors. You have obtained these by writing to the firms concerned (note that financial statements can also often be downloaded from the company's website).	• **Source data:** trends in financial position • **Accounts:** relevant ratios can be calculated • **Key issues** 'before and after' comparisons • **Chairman's report:** contains operational information and assumptions for the future growth and development of the business • **Segmental reporting**
Press releases by X plc and its competitors justifying the expenditure on the licence	• **Public justification** as to why investment decisions were taken; may be supported by estimates of future demand
A special supplement from the *Economist* about the mobile telecommunications industry	A general contextual study written by expert journalists. Can be used to provide a framework for X plc in the light of other companies. A useful 'reality check'.
Downloads from the company's website and that of its competitors	
Current consumer advertising material regarding wireless application protocol (WAP) phones	What is currently promised
Relevant BPP Learning Media Study Texts dealing with ratio analysis and decision making	Provide analytical tools to be applied to any company
An article from *Student Accountant* about decision making	Analytical tools to be applied to any company
A report by Oftel (the UK's regulatory body for the telecommunications industry) on Consumers' Use of Mobile Telephony, downloaded from Oftel's website.	Contextual study about the industry. Current consumer usage and concerns. Could be used to assess X plc's statements about its strategy

You need to **integrate** these items of data, a mix of quantitative and qualitative data. Hence, you can apply ratio analysis techniques in the BPP Learning Media Study Text to the financial statements. You can use the Oftel study to assess the realism of the forecasts.

You may find you need more information than that suggested above.

3.3 Example

Here is an example from an unpublished undergraduate dissertation into environmental reporting by companies, cited in the last chapter.

ANALYSIS OF COMPANY ENVIRONMENTAL INFORMATION
AVAILABLE TO EXTERNAL PARTIES

A plc

THE ENVIRONMENTAL INFORMATION AVAILABLE	
WHAT ENVIRONMENTAL INFORMATION WAS RECEIVED IN ADDITION TO THE FINANCIAL ANNUAL REPORTS AND ACCOUNTS?	A joint Health, Safety and Environment Report 1997.
THE FINANCIAL ANNUAL REPORT AND ACCOUNTS	
ANY ENVIRONMENTAL INFORMATION GIVEN IN FINANCIAL ANNUAL REPORT AND ACCOUNTS?	Environmental costs are 'considered to be an ordinary part of business and as such these amounts are not accounted for separately'. Estimates of environmental costs and liabilities are given. Notes to the accounts give policies regarding environmental expenditure recognition and measurement. Chairman's foreword; 'A group companies are increasingly working with community and environmental groups'.
THE ADDITIONAL ENVIRONMENTAL INFORMATION	
NARRATIVE ENVIRONMENTAL INFORMATION?	Detailed on environmental issues such as sustainable development and renewable resources along with sections entitled 'A's view' – although lengthy and slightly shallow.
VISUAL CHART ENVIRONMENTAL INFORMATION?	Seven pages of performance charts with both direct and relative data concerning emissions etc, together with a commentary.
ENVIRONMENTAL TARGETS?	Projections of performance are given but not specific targets.
ENVIRONMENTAL POLICY?	
ENVIRONMENTAL DATA EXTERNALLY VERIFIED?	Yes, by their independent auditors.
OTHER COMMENTS?	General commitment statements. Glossary of terms included.

3.4 Primary data

Your data collection exercise may include a survey or records of interviews or conversations. You should do a brief summary of this to cover what it should tell you, as you will want to do further analysis. (Numerical analysis is still useful even if it is not statistically perfect.)

3.5 Data health check

It is worth your while carrying out a health check on some of the data obtained, particularly secondary data.

Is the data up to date?	
Who is the data intended for?	
Why has the data been produced and what are the interests of the producer of the data?	
What does the data leave out?	

If this is **too** specific, use the following guidelines.

Guideline	Comment
Common sense	Clearly data which is 'dated', which emanates from dubious sources or which is based on unrepresentative samples should be treated with caution.
Statistical approaches	There are a variety of sampling methods for survey data as already described, which are appropriate to different situations. All of them involve some degree of risk (some probability of error). The degree of risk of statistical error can, however, be computed.
Expert judgement	The same data can be interpreted differently by different people. The following array – 98.7, 98.6, 98.6, 98.4, 98.1, 98.1 – might be regarded by a statistician as a declining trend but to a business manager the figures may represent a very steady state.
The intuitive approach	Some people have a better feel for figures than others and seem able to judge the value and validity of data intuitively. However, this requires specific knowledge and experience.
The questioning approach	Always question the origin and the basis of the data. Recognise that human errors occur when manipulating data, that bias can occur in questionnaire design: ask to see the questionnaire, check the figures. Furthermore, for information released to the public domain, bear in mind that: • Governments and political parties tend to be very selective in the data they choose to use • Many newspapers follow a 'political' line and are likely to be selective or even biased • Most journalists are not trained statisticians and may interpret data incorrectly

4 Organising the data

Once you have reviewed your data, you should now be in a position to extract information from it. This process can take a variety of forms, depending on the volume and variety of the data collected. The starting point is going to be **organisation**. Key tools are:

- Your **project file** organised in the most suitable way to structure the data to meet the project objective

- A **spreadsheet** perhaps to collect and arrange data you may have collected

- A **photocopier** so that data relevant to different areas of your Research Project can be duplicated, so that you do not have to go back and forth in your files for key results

- **Highlighter pens** to mark up key words and key points

You will need to organise your data and your analytical work in the light of the objective of the project.

(a) We have drawn on the distinction between structured and unstructured data in an earlier chapter.

(b) Structured data may be primary or secondary, but you need to incorporate it into a model for further analysis.

(c) Unstructured data needs to be organised in your mind so that you can draw lessons from it and relate it to other areas of data.

4.1 Example

The data below is taken from an unpublished undergraduate dissertation.

'My approach was successful, indicated by the 73% response rate of which 18% were unwilling to take part (see note below). This left me with 18 completed questionnaires, spilt equally over service and manufacturing industries.

I analysed the data by dividing it into three groups.

- Company's internal environmental background
- Company's environmental information available for external parties
- Environmental information used for internal management decisions

The questions asked were designed to fit these categories enabling linkages and hypotheses between them to be made in answering the original objective of the chapter.

Obviously there are certain limitations such as a lack of knowledge by the respondent or differing interpretations of the questions. This may be improved by using a telephone survey, however, this would be a lengthy process, meaning that I would have to reduce the questionnaire and so may harm data in this way.'

Note. A 73% response rate is truly amazing, but may have been achieved by detailed preparation, choice of sample, or pre-arrangement. Do not be surprised if response rates are between 15 – 20%.

A good place to start is an **example**. Here, the author has written to a number of companies and has obtained data in a **variety of formats**, but wants to extract relevant information for purposes of comparability. This is the start of a thorough review to see how companies report environmental data.

4.2 Example

Analysis of a company environmental data

COMPANIES	QUESTION							
	1	2	3	4	5	6	7	8
A plc	Y	Y	Y	Y	Y	?	N	Y
B plc	N	N	Y	–	–	–	–	–
C plc	Y	N	Y	Y	Y	Y	Y	?
D plc	Y	N	Y	Y	Y	N	N	Y
E plc	N	N	Y	–	–	–	–	–
F plc	Y	Y	N	Y	Y	Y	Y	Y
G plc	Y	Y	Y	Y	Y	Y	Y	Y

Key

About the Environmental Information Available

Question 1: Is separate environmental information published other than that included within the financial annual report and accounts?

About the Financial Annual Report and Accounts

Question 2: Is any environmental financial[1] information given?

Question 3: Is any narrative environmental information given?

About the Separately Published Environmental Information

Question 4: Is any narrative environmental information given?

Question 5: Are visual environmental performance charts given?

Question 6: Are environmental targets detailed?

Question 7: Do they give an environmental policy?

Question 8: Is the environmental data externally verified?

Y = Yes
N = No
? = To some extent
– = Not applicable

[1] Includes both figures and financial policies regarding environmental issues.

By 'organising' your data you are beginning to identify connections and relationships.

4.3 Organising structured data

In the last chapter we illustrated, in some detail, a questionnaire sent to respondents to discuss data about companies' responses to the environment. Already, part of the 'organisation' work had been done in the data design. The questionnaire is relatively structured; it may or may not produce results of statistical validity from the population from which it is drawn in total, but you will be able to do a lot of work on your sample. At the very least, this will suggest further work for you to do.

What you need to do, therefore, is **collate** the available data in a means susceptible to **manipulation**. This obviously depends on the size of your sample, but even if you have only obtained twenty interviews, you can find it quite useful to manipulate the data in a model.

4.4 Example

If you review the 14-question questionnaire in Chapter 6, you will note that the format of the required response differs from question to question.

Q1   Is your company predominantly operating in a service or manufacturing industry?

    Service ....

    Manufacturing ....

    Does your company utilise any of the following environmental initiatives? (Please tick all that are applicable.)

    Energy conservation ....

    Control of emissions ....

    Recycling ....

    Reusing ....

    Buying from environmentally friendly suppliers ....

    Monitoring and controlling waste ....

    Using recycled stationery ....

    Tree planting ....

    Other ....

    Please state...

You could prepare a spreadsheet in order to capture the data of a spreadsheet application. Spreadsheets offer a variety of tools from simple arithmetic – still very useful – to more complicated statistical analysis as revealed by the formula keys.

Remember that Oxford Brookes requires you to demonstrate reasonable evidence of having accessed online information sources and having used a spreadsheet and / or other software in preparing your Research Project. Organising your data using a spreadsheet will help you meet this requirement.

4.5 A very simple application of Excel to collect data

If you use Microsoft Excel, look at the manual or try the help keys. Even with quite simple spreadsheet operations, you can generate a lot of information. Here is an example.

(a)   **Head up the columns of the spreadsheet** with the names of the five companies. Indicate the date you received the responses, if at all. Alternatively, you might set up a separate spreadsheet schedule for this planning aspect.

(b)   Head up further columns: total, percentage and so on, for some work to do on the data.

(c)   The questions are on the rows. Each response has a row to itself.

(d)   Now, you want to turn these responses into data. Not all will be susceptible to manipulation, but for some responses you could give a YES the value of 1. By adding across you can get the total number of companies answering YES to a question and you can carry out a percentage calculation.

	A	B	C	D	E	F	G	H	I	J	K	L	M	N
1	Version 1													
2				A	B	C	D	E					Total	%
3	Is your company													
4	predominantly in													
5														
6	Services		Yes = 1	1				1					2	40%
7	Manufacturing		Yes = 1		1	1		1					3	60%
8														
9	Does your company													
10	utilise													
11	Energy conservation		Yes = 1	0	0	1	0	0					1	20%
12	Emission control		Yes = 1	0	0	1	0	0					1	20%
13	Recycling		Yes = 1	0	1	1	1	0					3	60%
14	Reuse		Yes = 1	0	1	1	0	0					2	40%
15	Eco-friendly suppliers		Yes = 1	1	1	0	0	0					2	40%
16	Waste monitoring		Yes = 1	0	1	0	0	0					1	20%
17	Recycled stationery		Yes = 1	1	1	0	1	0					3	60%
18	Tree planting		Yes = 1	0	0	0	0	0					0	0%
19	Other		Yes = 1	0	0	1	0	0					1	20%

You could organise your data further. Before you input it, you could identify which companies are in **services** and which are in **manufacturing**, thereby enabling you to calculate percentages for each. Of course, **you can use formulae and modelling tools** to do this – but if you think a key difference will be between services and manufacturing companies, simply organising your data into these columns can provide you with more information. You can see for example that whereas 60% of all the sample use recycled stationery, 100% of service companies do so.

	A	B	C	D	E	F	G	H	I	J	K	L	M	N
23				Services				Manufacturers					ALL	
24	Version 2			A	D	Total	%	C	B	E	Total	%	Total	%
25														
26	Is your company													
27	predominantly in													
28														
29	Services		Yes = 1	1	1								2	40%
30	Manufacturing		Yes = 1					1	1	1			3	60%
31														
32	Does your company													
33	utilise													
34	Energy conservation		Yes = 1	0	0	0	0%	1	0	0	1	33%	1	20%
35	Emission control		Yes = 1	0	0	0	0%	1	0	0	1	33%	1	20%
36	Recycling		Yes = 1	0	1	1	50%	1	1	0	2	67%	3	60%
37	Reuse		Yes = 1	0	0	0	0%	1	1	0	2	67%	2	40%
38	Eco-friendly suppliers		Yes = 1	1	0	1	50%	0	1	0	1	33%	2	40%
39	Waste monitoring		Yes = 1	0	0	0	0%	0	1	0	1	33%	1	20%
40	Recycled stationery		Yes = 1	1	1	2	100%	0	1	0	1	33%	3	60%
41	Tree planting		Yes = 1	0	0	0	0%	0	0	0	0	0%	0	0%
42	Other		Yes = 1	0	0	0	0%	1	0	0	1	33%	1	20%

4.6 More sophisticated uses

We will cover the use of Excel to analyse and model data in the next section. Some universities have access to a statistical package called SPSS. SPSS enables you to do a much wider variety of statistical tests then Excel, but you may not have access to it.

4.7 Organising other data in your file

The other data you have obtained may appear in a variety of formats: newspaper articles, extracts from textbooks, website download, notes you have taken of interviews. Doubtless you have read them in some detail, but you want to start thinking of the story that you are going to tell about them.

We have already suggested various different tasks in setting up your filing system.

4.8 Organising quantitative secondary data

Again, the best way of looking at this is by use of **examples**. You want to ensure that the data is organised in a form that can support your project objective.

4.9 Example

This time we will look at **Project Topic 13: The relationship between an organisation's human resources activities and its business objectives**.

For the sake of argument, your project is based around an information technology service firm. This firm, as part of its global expansion, needs to operate on a 24 hour basis to serve overseas markets, and your project is based on the personnel needs of this policy.

The firm is based in the UK, and as part of your secondary data collection you have obtained government statistics as follows (Social Trends, ONS).

(a) At the end of June 1998 there were 116,000 young people on the Modern Apprenticeship scheme, over four times more than the figure for 1996. There are considerable differences in the choice of Modern Apprenticeships undertaken by men and women. The most popular MA, with 15 per cent of all apprenticeships, was engineering manufacturing, although only 4 per cent of these were undertaken by women (chart). Men also form the majority of those taking apprenticeships in the motor industry, construction and electrical installation engineering. Women, on the other hand, predominate in business administration (the second most popular MA with 14 per cent of all apprentices), health and social care, hairdressing and retailing. Overall the ten most popular MA sectors shown in the chart account for more than three-quarters of all apprenticeships; in all there are 77 MA sectors.

Among employees, training and development in the workplace are increasingly important aspects of working life. The Investors in People (IIP) provides a national standard which helps employers to look critically at their training needs, and links investment in training directly to the achievement of their business goals.

People in training on Modern Apprenticeships: by sector and gender, 1998[1]

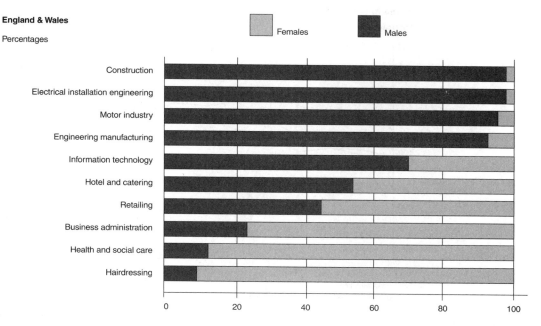

England & Wales

Percentages

1 At 30 June 1998

Source: Department for Education and Employment

(b)　In Spring 1998, around half of all UK employees in temporary jobs were on fixed period contracts, around one in five were engaged in casual work, and one in seven worked for agencies. Gender differences were apparent when employees gave reasons for taking on temporary work. A higher proportion of women than men stated that they did not want a permanent job, whereas a higher proportion of men than women stated that they could not find a permanent job.

The number of people holding second jobs rose steadily from 1992, reaching a highpoint in 1995 and 1996 (chart 4.11). More women than men have second jobs. Almost half of those with a second job worked part time in their main job. In Spring 1998 the average actual weekly hours worked by full-time employees with a second job was 47, compared with an average of 39 hours a week worked by full-time employees without a second job.

People in employment with a second job[1]: by gender

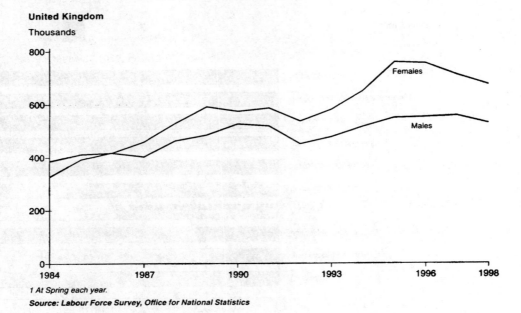

1 At Spring each year.
Source: Labour Force Survey, Office for National Statistics

Time at work

In Spring 1998 more than 5 million people, around a fifth of all those in work in the United Kingdom, usually worked more than 48 hours a week in their main job (Chart 4.12). About a quarter of those working more than 48 hours a week were self-employed. About 30 per cent of men worked more than 48 hours a week compared with 7 per cent of all women.

Total usual weekly hours of work[1]: by gender, Spring 1998

1 At Spring for all of working age in employment: males aged 16 to 64; females aged 16 to 59.

Source: Labour Force Survey, Office for National Statistics

What is each piece of data telling you?

Problems with the data are that it is more impressionistic than you might like, and you will have to make some effort to glean out what you want.

Item (a) tells you about training needs in general and the balance between the sexes. You could **file this under the 'employee development'** as it addresses training and modern apprenticeships. You could also **file this under 'recruitment'** if, for example, you want to relate this to catchment groups of employees.

Item (b) provides you with details of the working population. Combined with (a) you could surmise that employing part time workers is going to mean employing more women; however, fewer of them do Modern Apprenticeships in IT, which can **suggest** possible problems in obtaining people with the right skills.

As well as filing data physically (taking two copies if necessary) you may need to transfer or recast the data to a spreadsheet model, if such statistics can be applied for modelling purposes. For example, in dealing with conditions of change, you might show that – in your 24 hour internet operation, you might expect a certain percentage of your shift workforce to be women working part time.

4.10 Dealing with organising qualitative data

The key in any project file is to be practical – so that you know where the data is when you want to find it.

(a)   If you have taken notes of interviews, say, you should summarise them on a front sheet.

(b)   If an item of data such as an article is relevant to more than one area, make copies.

(c)   By **organising your data**, you are, in a way, **taking a decision** about how to use it.

(d)   If data is unstructured and awaiting further analysis you might leave it in a separate 'unprocessed' section.

5 Modelling the data

In a **model**, you are, effectively, seeking to set up relationships to allow further analysis. You can do this in a number of ways.

(a)   Spreadsheet modelling. As well as using a spreadsheet as a glorified calculator, it does offer a variety of statistical tools – not as good as SPSS, but sufficient for the Research and Analysis Project.

(b)   There are various techniques of modelling and analysing **qualitative** data.

5.1 Spreadsheet models – an example

In Section 4.5, we described the use of a spreadsheet as a means of capturing and organising data in a very simple way.

Constructing a spreadsheet model is something you might do as a matter of course in your work, in preparing budgets or analysing performance. We do not intend to provide a guide to working with spreadsheets but here is a possible application.

Any spreadsheet model is constructed using formulae. You will find a simple guide in the **help facility** of your spreadsheet package – print this out, if you want a manual record. Here are examples.

(a)   =C4*5. This formula **multiplies** the value in C4 by 5. The result will appear in the cell holding the formula.

(b)   =C4*B10. This **multiplies** the value in C4 by the value in B10. In general this is better than option (a). Why? Because the result is in a separate cell and if '5' is a variable that can change, you can first enter the new number to the cell.

(c) =C4/E5. This **divides** the value in C4 by the value in E5. (Note that * means multiply and / means divide by.)

(d) =(C4*B10)−D1. This **multiplies** the value in C4 by that in B10 and then subtracts the value in D1 from the result. Note that generally the computer will perform multiplication and division before addition or subtraction.

(e) =C4*117.5%. This **adds** 17.5% to the value in C4. It could be used to calculate a price including 17.5% VAT. When you enter 17.5%, it may be displayed on screen as 0.175, depending on how the spreadsheet is set up.

(f) =(C4+C5+C6)/3. This, in effect, calculates the **average** of the values in C4, C5 and C6. Note that the brackets tell the computer to perform the addition first. Without the brackets the computer would first divide the value in C6 by 3 and then add the result to the total of the values in C4 and C5.

(g) = 2^2 gives you 2 **to the power** of 2, in other words 2^2. Likewise = 2^3 gives you 2 cubed and so on.

(h) = 4^ (1/2) gives you the **square root** of 4. Likewise 27^(1/3) gives you the cube root of 27 and so on. Do not forget the brackets.

To **display all the underlying formulae** in your spreadsheet, instead of the numbers, click on Tools, then on Options, then on View and put an X in the box next to Formulas to display them or remove it to display numbers. You could usefully do this to display a sample of your formulae for your spreadsheet, as suggested by Oxford Brookes. Include the sample as one of your appendices.

5.2 Example

The following four insurance salesmen each earn a basic salary of £14,000 pa. They also earn a commission of 2% of sales. The following spreadsheet has been created to process their commission and total earnings.

	A	B	C	D	E
1	*Sales team salaries and commissions - 19XX*				
2	Name	Sales	Salary	Commission	Total earnings
3		£	£	£	£
4	Northington	284,000	14,000	5,680	19,680
5	Souther	193,000	14,000	3,860	17,860
6	Weston	12,000	14,000	240	14,240
7	Easterman	152,000	14,000	3,040	17,040
8					
9	Total	641,000	56,000	12,820	68,820
10					
11					
12	*Variables*				
13	Basic Salary	14,000			
14	Commission rate	0.02			
15					
16					
17					
18					
19					
20					

Possible formulae are as follows.

(a)   =B4*B14, for cell D4.

(b)   =C6+D6, for cell E6.

(c)   =SUM(D4:D7), for cell D9.

(d)   For cell E9, there is a **variety of possibilities** here, depending on whether you set the cell as the total of the earnings of each salesman (cells E4 to E7) or as the total of the different elements of remuneration (cells C9 and D9). Of course, it would be nice to **know that the calculation works in both directions.** This would give added assurance that there are no errors. A suitable formulae for this purpose would be:

=IF(SUM(E4:E7)=SUM(C9:D9),SUM(E4:E7),"ERROR")

You may want to compare actual results with budgets or targets to see how far it has exceeded, or fallen short of, its expectations. It is useful to express **variations as a percentage of the original budget**, for example sales may be 10% higher than predicted.

5.3 Conditions in formulae

Suppose the company employing the salesmen in the above example awards a bonus (in addition to the commission) to those salesmen who exceed their target by more than £1,000. It is possible to **get the spreadsheet to work out who is entitled to the bonus.** (In our example you can see this for yourself easily enough, but if there were 100 salesmen it would be tedious to have to look down a long list.)

Look at the first section of the spreadsheet. We are trying to determine whether Northington would be shown as entitled to a bonus. The formula used may vary slightly from one spreadsheet program to the next. We will enter the following:

=IF(B4>1000,"BONUS"," ").

The formula could be entered in column F.

This formula has three parts inside the brackets.

IF (**condition**, result if **true**, result if **false**).

The **inverted commas** (") mean that **text** is to appear in the cell. Here the text will either be the word '**bonus**' or, if the target was not exceeded, a **blank space**. The contents of the cell could equally well be a number.

Note the following symbols which can be used in formulae with conditions:

<	less than
<=	less than or equal to
=	equal to
>=	greater than or equal to
>	greater than
<>	not equal to

There is nothing very difficult about conditions in formulae, but great care must be taken to put **brackets** and **commas** in the right places.

5.4 Examples of formulae with conditions

Discounts

A company offers a discount of 5% to customers who order more than £1,000 worth of goods. A spreadsheet showing what customers will pay might look like this.

	A	B	C	D	E	F
1	**Discount Traders Ltd**					
2	*Sales analysis - April 19XX*					
3	Customer	Sales	5% discount	Sales (net)		
4		£	£	£		
5	Arthur	956.00	0.00	956.00		
6	Dent	1423.00	71.15	1351.85		
7	Ford	2894.00	144.70	2749.30		
8	Prefect	842.00	0.00	842.00		
9						
10						

The formula in cell C5 is: =IF(B5>1,000,(0.05*B5),0). This means, if the value in B5 is greater than £1,000 multiply it by 0.05, otherwise the discount will be zero. Cell D5 will calculate the amount net of discount, using the formula: =B5-C5. The same conditional formula with the cell references changed will be found in cells C6, C7 and C8. **Strictly**, the variables £1,000 and 5% should be entered in a **different part** of the spreadsheet.

Examination results

Suppose the pass mark for an examination is 50% and you want to see easily from a long list who has passed and who has failed. If a candidate's score is in cell B2, an appropriate formula for cell C2 would be: =IF(B2<50,"FAILED","PASSED").

As you may have noticed from an earlier example, the placing of text in inverted commas in a conditional function will cause the text to be printed out or displayed as appropriate.

Oxford Brookes strongly recommend that if possible you include a sample printout of the formulae for part of the spreadsheet as evidence of your IT skills.

5.5 Graphics

It is usually possible to convert tabulated data in a spreadsheet into a variety of bar chart or graphical formats. We will look again at the Discount Traders Ltd example from paragraph 5.4.

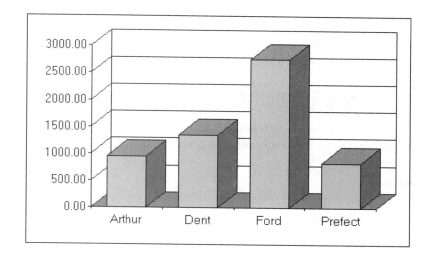

Other spreadsheet features

Excel offers many more facilities for analysing data.

(a) If you go to the **formula bar** in Excel, and click on the = sign you will get a list of options such as SUM, AND and so on, including Averages and NPV analysis, correlation and regression and so on.

(b) The help facility also lists everything you can do.

5.6 Avoiding over-complex models

When building a spreadsheet model to analyse your data, be sure to remember the following key points.

(a) **Do not make your spreadsheet more complex** than it needs to be – for some calculations, a pocket calculator will be just as good.

(b) Use **the auditing tool to check your formulae are correct**.

(c) Check your formulae are correct by doing some manual calculations

(d) Do a trial run. If you are not quite sure what you want to do, experiment with a small number of data items before applying them wholesale.

Here are examples as to how you could use Excel in the Research and Analysis Project.

5.7 Examples

Project Topic 8: The business and financial performance of an organisation over a three year period

Ratio Analysis

Project Topic 12: The possible effects of a proposed accounting standard on the financial statements and business activities of an organisation

You could model the effect, say, of differences in the treatment of taxation or pension benefits on the financial statements. You could even go further by using the spreadsheet to help you re-cast the financial statements drawn up under the proposed standard.

Project Topic 15: The management of an organisation's working capital over a three year period and its impact on the organisation's funding strategies

You could use what if? analysis to assess the impact of different payment periods and means of finance.

Project Topic 4: The impact of e-business on an organisation

This is less obvious as the spreadsheet would depend very much on the data collected but if you wanted to use the graphic facilities to interpret data collected you could do so.

5.8 Analysing qualitative data – some hints and tips

This requires you to take a more creative approach. The technique you adopt will depend on the type of data you have collected and **we cannot be prescriptive**.

Précis

If you are using an article, the most important thing you must do is **read it carefully**. For some articles, we can suggest that you do a **précis**. This forces you to read it thoroughly and gut it for the key points.

5.9 Example

Here is some data from a newspaper. Précis it into 100 words.

Financial Times	Précis
Halifax, the mortgage bank, yesterday agreed to pay £760m for a controlling stake in St James's Place Capital (SJPC), the holding company for J Rothschild Assurance, in a deal designed to pull the upmarket life assurer into the internet age.	
Halifax bought 17 per cent of the company from Prudential late on Tuesday at 300p a share, a premium of 70p to Tuesday's closing price. It will now extend the offer to up to 60 per cent of the shares, leaving SJPC with a separate listing.	
The bid is the latest move in Halifax's aggressive internet strategy, begun earlier this year when it poached Jim Spowart from Standard Life bank to set up Intelligent Finance (IF), an online bank due to launch this summer.	
It hopes to add £5bn of assets to IF by selling a St James's-branded private banking service, run by IF, through SJPC's 1,000-strong salesforce.	
'This is an absolutely cracking business,' said James Crosby, Halifax chief executive. 'It increases the scale of our distribution operation in long-term savings and will assist our drive for diversification (away from mortgages).'	

Financial Times	Précis
Sir Mark Weinberg, chairman of SJPC, said the company had decided last year to seek a strategic partner to help it use the internet to extend its product range, and began talks with Prudential, which then owned 29 per cent of the shares. 'It became clear that their vision and our vision were not parallel to the extent that there wasn't the opportunity for a value-creating partnership,' he said.	
Analysts said the deal, which is expected to be earnings-enhancing in the first year, would help IF as long as the product, still under wraps, is as exciting as the bank claims.	
The SJPC salesforce own about 8 per cent of the company and have options on another 8 per cent.	

Helping hand

Financial Times	Précis
Halifax, the mortgage bank, yesterday agreed to pay £760m for a controlling stake in St James's Place Capital, the holding company for J Rothschild Assurance, in a deal designed to pull the upmarket life assurer into the internet age.	Halifax, the mortgage bank, has spent £760m to control St James's Place Capital (SJPC), a life assurer with internet potential.
Halifax bought 17 per cent of the company from Prudential late on Tuesday at 300p a share, a premium of 70p to Tuesday's closing price. It will now extend the offer to up to 60 per cent of the shares, leaving SJPC with a separate listing.	Halifax acquired the controlling stake from Prudential Insurance in two stages.
The bid is the latest move in Halifax's aggressive internet strategy, begun earlier this year when it poached Jim Spowart from Standard Life bank to set up Intelligent Finance (IF), an online bank due to launch this summer.	The bid forms part of Halifax's strategy to develop internet businesses, such as Intelligent Finance (IF) an online bank.
It hopes to add £5bn of assets to IF by selling a St James's-branded private banking service, run by IF, through SJPC's 1,000-strong salesforce.	In addition, there will be cross-selling opportunities.
'This is an absolutely cracking business,' said James Crosby, Halifax chief executive. 'It increases the scale of our distribution operation in long-term savings and will assist our drive for diversification (away from mortgages).'	There are economies of scale in distribution and opportunities for diversification.

Financial Times	Précis
Sir Mark Weinberg, chairman of SJPC, said the company had decided last year to seek a strategic partner to help it use the internet to extend its product range, and began talks with Prudential, which then owned 29 per cent of the shares. 'It became clear that their vision and our vision were not parallel to the extent that there wasn't the opportunity for a value-creating partnership,' he said.	SJPC had been looking for a partner to develop its internet business for some time.
Analysts said the deal, which is expected to be earnings-enhancing in the first year, would help IF as long as the product, still under wraps, is as exciting as the bank claims.	The deal will help IF and it is expected to increase earnings
The SJPC salesforce own about 8 per cent of the company and have options on another 8 per cent.	

Précis (1)

Halifax, the mortgage bank, has paid £760m to Prudential Insurance to control St James's Place Capital (SJPC) a life assurer with internet potential. The bid forms part of Halifax's strategy to develop internet businesses, such as Intelligent Finance, an online bank. In addition, there will be cross selling opportunities, economies of scale in distribution and opportunities for diversification. SJPC had been looking for a partner to develop its internet business for some time. The deal will help IF as it will increase earnings.

What do you think? Could it be improved? It appears a bit unstructured.

Précis (2)

1   Halifax has paid £760m to Prudential to acquire St James's Place Capital.

2   Rationale

    (a)   Halifax and SJPC both want to develop an internet business and felt they would make good partners.

    (b)   Other benefits include cross selling opportunities, economies of scale in distribution, and diversification, and increased earnings.

Précis 2 is probably too concise. It misses out the fact that Halifax is to launch an online bank, a key area of its strategy. However, it is clearer in terms of structure, because it adopts report format and has a heading.

Why is this technique useful?

    (a)   It **forces you to read** the material thoroughly.

    (b)   It forces you to **understand** the material – you have to understand it before you can summarise it.

5.10 Key words, phrases, themes and concepts

If you need to be more rigorous, instead of summarising each paragraph, as you go down the side, you can identify which **concepts apply**. Give each paragraph a number and note down in a short phrase what concepts are being discussed – based on your research questions and the project objective.

Step 1   Photocopy the article or type the transcript so that you have a **large** space in the margins either side.

Step 2   You may want to allocate simple **codes** for each theme or item relevant to the project topic.

Step 3   When this theme appears in a sentence, mark down the relevant code in the margin, at the same level.

You may decide that it is worthwhile **highlighting key words** or ideas with a colour highlighter pen – but this will make it harder if the same item can relate to two themes.

5.11 Example

Let us say that you have transcripts of tape recordings of interviews with sales personnel in an effort to understand how well they are motivated. You want to reach sensible conclusions on what the data says.

Say that you want to ask certain questions of the data.

(1)   You can **search for key words** – ie the same word repeated as indication of certain topics being covered. This is perhaps a bit mechanistic but is used by some researchers in an attempt to convert qualitative into quantitative data.

(2)   You could use a **highlighter pen to colour code** areas dealing with each of the questions you are interested in. This also encourages close reading but it is less mechanistic. An area colour coded pink, for example, could deal with salary, areas coloured yellow could deal with salespeople's feelings about the job.

However some items of data could relate to two themes, so you would be better off with the **coding approach** in Step 2 above.

5.12 Organisation

We have already suggested that you collect and organise your data in a way that is appropriate to how you intend to use it – don't just file things in chronological or alphabetical order. By filing it in the order of how you intend to use it, you are, in effect, making a decision about its importance or use.

5.13 Visual aids

An aid you could use is a mind map or tree diagram – a visual aid. The advantages of this are that you are using the spatial relationships on paper to illustrate the connections between different concepts. The example below employs this approach.

5.14 Example

As part of **Project Topic 5: The effects of globalisation on an organisation**, you have chosen an aircraft manufacturer and have done widespread reading. You have obtained the following information about Airbus.

Airbus has recently launched a super-jumbo, seating between 550 and 650 people, challenging the Boeing 747. Development costs were originally estimated at $12bn, but exceeded that. Although the first deliveries were scheduled for 2005, the first operational aircraft was not delivered to a customer until late

2007, and the order book is running very late, with many airlines having to wait an additional two or three years for deliveries of their orders.

The UK government offered launch aid of £530m to get it started. This is a large plane, to be marketed at the major airlines. Airbus has promised a 15% to 20% fall in aircraft operating costs. The terms of the launch aid remain secret. (Many years ago, the EU and US agreed on a formula for assessing state aid to their relative industries. American aircraft makers enjoyed indirect support thanks to the demands of the arms industry. The US government is concerned that the launch aid breaches this agreement.)

There are relatively few aircraft makers in the world. Airbus's main competitor is Boeing. At time of writing Airbus is not a normal company. Each participant (Aerospatiale of France, BAe of the UK, DA of Germany and Casa of Spain) has the right to make part of the plane. Governments have a great interest in the aerospace manufacturing industry for defence reasons, and Aerospatiale is part owned by the French government. Aircraft engines are supplied by Rolls Royce, Pratt and Whitney and GE. Boeing is a principal competitor.

Below are some environmental factors, taken at random.

(a)   Classify them as of high, medium, low importance to Airbus.

(b)   Draw a mindmap of the general and competitive environment.

Factor

1   Better video and web conferencing
2   More working at home
3   Greater demand in rich countries for tailor-made holidays
4   Genetically modified food
5   EU-US disputes at the World Trade Organisation
6   Deregulation in air markets (in terms of destination served)
7   Ageing population in western world
8   Political instability in Asia (N Korea)
9   Air traffic is projected to rise 5% pa to 2030
10   Stricter asylum and immigration laws applied over Europe
11   Continued expansion of high speed train networks in Europe

Answer

(a)   **Classification of importance**

You may well disagree with these – but you need a rationale.

High

5. May well affect financing of the project and Airbus's status as a company.

6. Firms can compete on different routes. This may restrain demand for jumbo jets: but this might be overridden by overall growth.

9. A huge increase. Airports cannot expand fast enough and there is only so much space: bigger aircraft are one solution.

11. High speed trains compete with aircraft for speed and are often more convenient; more relevant to short haul flights than long distance flights.

Medium

1. May reduce demand for business travel.

3. Affects destinations people want to fly to, and the market for scheduled and chartered flights: perhaps people will prefer smaller planes.

8. May slow demand for air traffic, or increase economic problems in the region.

Low

2. Affects other transport firms but not airlines, as this affects normal commuting not business trips.

4. Nothing to do with Airbus at all!

7. Demand can come from elsewhere; population is getting wealthier.

10. Affects airline operations but not overall demand.

(b)

If you have sat paper P3, you will recognise that this diagram incorporates facts – about Airbus – and two theoretical models (PEST analysis and Porter's Five Forces Analysis) and shows how they are linked together. It both summarises and explains the interconnections between issues.

Chapter roundup

- Data has to be reviewed in the light of the project objective, regarding the scope, forms and context of the project.

- BPP Learning Media suggests: Choose analytical tools, Look at the data, Organise the data, and Model the data.

- The ACCA's syllabus provides plenty of ideas as to the analytical frameworks you can adopt.

- Once you have collected data, you need to review it to ensure that it meets the project objective.

- Data should be organised in your file so that it supports the project objective.

- There are a number of techniques for modelling data, including spreadsheets, graphical approaches and textual analysis.

chapter 8

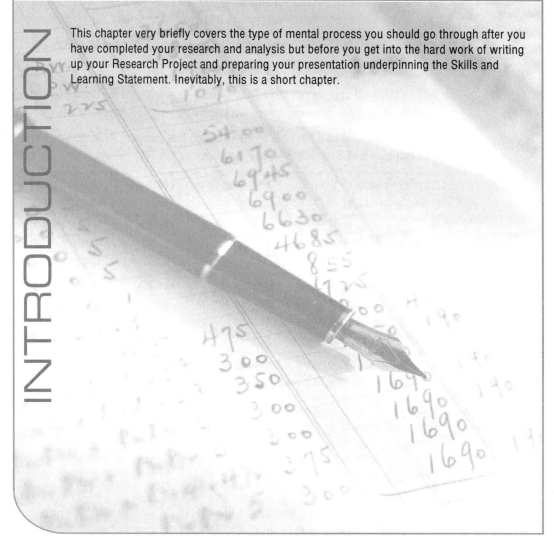

Synthesis

INTRODUCTION

This chapter very briefly covers the type of mental process you should go through after you have completed your research and analysis but before you get into the hard work of writing up your Research Project and preparing your presentation underpinning the Skills and Learning Statement. Inevitably, this is a short chapter.

1 Concluding your work

1.1 How do you know you have finished?

Many research projects are open ended and take time to complete, simply because of the size and range of the subject matter. This is particularly true of postgraduate research in the UK, where a PhD requires original research and an original contribution to knowledge. Three years' full time work is often given as an example.

At undergraduate level, this does not hold. The advantage of deadlines – whether at university or in doing ACCA exams – is that you are forced to come to a halt. With the Research and Analysis Project you can choose your own deadline.

But your Research and Analysis Project is in a different category of course. You do not face the deadline pressure of an undergraduate student, but there is a limit to the extent of your work, caused by the project objective.

If you have followed the advice of the earlier chapters you will have:

- Identified a precise project objective

- From the project objective, you will have identified the research and analytical work you need to do to find enough information to satisfy the project objective

Arguably, if this is what you have done and you have carried out your plans, you need go no further.

In practice, life might not be that simple.

(a)   If you are unused to undergraduate work, you may lack **confidence** in what you have done.

(b)   You may be unhappy with the work you have done, or feel that you need to do more.

Here is a checklist as a possible guide to taking this decision. How do you know you've finished? See if you can give a YES to **most** of these questions.

1	Have I done all the research and analysis activities I planned to do?	Yes/No	1	If yes, a good enough start – check with your mentor.
2	Do I already have ideas about what I want to say in my Research Project from the work I have done?	Yes/No	2	If yes, write them down – this suggests you are drawing conclusions and can support them.
3	Although I'd really like to know more about the subject as it interests me, I don't think this is necessary for the Research Project.	Yes/No	3	If yes, you are brimming with enthusiasm but you have a clear head. Of course some extra reading might help and may add extra points.
4	The project has proved to be much harder than I thought, but I have not given up.	Yes/No	4	You have not cut corners – if your planning was good enough, and your research and analysis work covers the project objective, this indicates you have done enough.
5	I was unable to complete some of the research and analysis tasks that I had planned to do. However, I reviewed the project objective and found there were other ways of finding the same information and pursued these.	Yes/No	5	If yes, this implies you have kept sight of what you have tried to prove, although the road has been rockier than you thought.

| 6 | Do the results of my research support the conclusions I expected to find? | **Don't answer!** | 6 | If you **expected** an outcome and the results proved your original hunch as to what you'd find to be **incorrect**, so what? You have still researched and analysed data and drawn conclusions from it. |

Even if you still do not know what you are going to say, if you've answered YES to most of the questions above, you are perhaps ready to start tying all the threads together.

2 Conclusions and the project objective

2.1 What if you still do not know what to conclude? Second mentor meeting

Your second mentor meeting is for you to discuss briefly how you have done, perhaps with a summary outline of what you are going to put in your Research Project. Your second mentor meeting should cover your conclusions and initial plans for your report.

However, you may not feel ready or able to discuss this with your mentor, but you need to marshall your thoughts.

(a)   Some people are able to keep everything in their heads, and plan what they are going to write before they start.

(b)   Other people **think** as they write or speak. Often, the easiest way to start something is to talk to a friend, summarising in a brief sentence what you think your research and analysis has covered and what you think about it.

2.2 Help yourself come to conclusions

Step 1   Answer the questions in the project objective

Earlier on we suggested that two ways of looking at your research are to ask:

(a)   What am I trying to prove or disprove?
(b)   What am I trying to show?

In your own mind, can you begin to answer these questions?

2.3 Example

You have done **Project Topic 13: The relationship between an organisation's human resources activities and its business objectives**.

Your project objective has been to review and describe the effect of a company merger on the finance departments of the two merged companies.

If you ask 'What am I trying to show?' and can **describe** the following, you are in good position to draw a conclusion.

(a)   Some theories of change management

(b)   The effects of mergers on other companies, including problems such as systems incompatibility etc

(c)   The training that staff felt they needed and what they actually received

(d)   Managers' plans for the change, and how they responded to the new situation

(e)   Details of human resource plans and procedures

(f)   Operational and systems problems

(g)   Notes from discussions

Your conclusion might be that the change was not properly prepared for. The firms' HRM planning systems were not effective in that there was mismatch between training delivered and actual needs, and that issues of productivity arising from the merger had not been dealt with effectively.

2.4 Example

Assume you are asking 'What am I trying to prove or disprove' and you have chosen **Project Topic 11: The financial and operational costs and benefits of the internal audit/internal review activities within an organisation**.

Your project **objective** has been to prove that strengthening the internal audit department of Z Bank is of benefit. If you have the data below you should be able to come to conclusions, either way.

(a)   Annual budget of internal audit department
(b)   External audit fees
(c)   Reliance placed by external auditors on internal audit
(d)   Errors detected which would have been picked up by the department
(e)   Background information about two major bank failures
(f)   New controls introduced
(g)   A new approach to risk management on internal audit advice

2.5 Still having difficulty?

If you are still having difficulty, we suggest you try to structure your thinking as below.

Force yourself to rewrite your findings and conclusions in terms of the project objective.

2.6 Example

For example, take **Project Topic 14: The business and financial objectives of a strategic investment decision made by an organisation and its impact on key stakeholders**.

Your project is an analysis of the sources of capital used by Philibee Sdn Bhd, a Malaysian-owned fast food company, as it opens outlets over south east Asia, including the Philippines, Thailand and Singapore. The **project objective** seeks to address whether and why Philibee adopted different sources of capital for each market as opposed to the most theoretically efficient method overall.

Findings	Re-wording	Project objective
1 Franchising is used in Thailand, owing to the difficulty of obtaining bank credit. The operation in Thailand has grown rapidly, but the local partner shares in the profits.	A spreadsheet analysis would suggest that, ideally, the cheapest source of capital would have been debt issuance overall.	Sources of capital for each market as opposed to the most efficient method overall.
2 Philibee invested its own money in Singapore with no local partner	In Thailand, Philbee expanded in the local market via franchise arrangements. This means of sourcing capital for expansion costs more and hence is less efficient than other sources overall.	
3 You did a spreadsheet model which identified how much Philibee had spent, and the return expected by shareholders and bondholders in Kuala Lumpur.		

2.7 Try again

Another way is to work **backwards from the project objective**, in a hierarchy.

Step 1   Start with the project objective.

Step 2   Identify key questions to be answered or points demonstrated.

Step 3   Slot in your points raised from your analysis in the 'boxes' identified in two.

2.8 Example

An unpublished undergraduate dissertation came to the conclusions below.

(1)   Demands for 'green' information from companies, are increasing. However, the way in which companies meet this demand is varied. Through an analysis of published environmental data and questionnaires it was found that this disclosure ranges in depth, format and distribution times and places. This is heightened because few environmental disclosure regulations are in existence. Differing information makes it hard for comparisons to be made between companies, which hinders decision making regarding environmental issues.

(2)   The varying standards of environmental information raise questions as to who the intended audiences are and what are the companies' motivations for disclosing? An overwhelming hypothesis was that it is being treated only for publicity and corporate benefit purposes. A wider accountability and, therefore, the stakeholder view, is not high in companies' thoughts. This is all linked to the internal approach a company takes to environmental issues. The more dedication and resources applied internally, the better foundation for external reporting.

(3)   **No standard methodology** is in place for environmental disclosure and, therefore, **no verification procedures**. This has questioned the credibility of this disclosure. **Environmental cost accounting** and **environmental reporting** both offer **solutions** to achieving standardisation. However, complex procedures, information requirements and audience readability make them not entirely fault-free. Equally, there is no common framework on how to interpret results.

Main findings

(4)   How and why companies are disclosing environmental information is extremely varied at the current time. This is causing problems for both comparability purposes and the level of seriousness the business world is taking these issues.

(5)   **Activity based costing** would increase accountability by correctly allocating environmental costs. However, the process is long, information requirements are high and understandability may be hindered for those with little accounting knowledge. Additionally, interpretation of environmental costs is perceived differently by individuals.

Recommendations

(6)   Clearly a form of standard methodology concerning disclosure of environmental data is required. This would then focus businesses on the seriousness of the issue and the audiences they need to aim at. It would also enable verification procedures to be put in place providing credibility to environmental information across the business world and enabling environmental issues to be incorporated within business decisions.

(7)   A mixture of ABC and EPIs would aid communication, providing a balance of complexity and giving an even picture of environmental issues in both annual and environmental reports. However, environmental communication will never achieve all its objectives until a common framework for interpreting environmental figures is achieved.

The subject matter

(8)   Environmental issues are becoming increasingly important as more natural resources are depleted. Companies can wait no longer to show accountability for their use of earth's gifts. Environmental disclosure is a way of expressing this to external parties whilst making their internal procedures aware of such matters. Within this field of writing the common census of opinion is that standard procedures need to be agreed upon. Guidelines, although voluntary, are in place but no regulations are available indicating that this topic is not as straightforward as may first appear.

(9)   The benefits are clear, now it is time for more research to be carried out on disclosure methods. I have offered a combination. However, this has its limitations. Perhaps other formats with more testing for ease of use over different industries need to be carried out. This would offer a range of methods from which the simplest and most effective could implemented.

Comment

Paragraphs (1) and (2) briefly summarise the work done and some difficulties interpreting it.

Paragraph (2) continues a wider context, linked to an earlier chapter discussing how companies managed environmental issues.

Paragraphs (3) and (4) should refer to work done earlier, largely summarising.

Findings of research and analysis of data. See paragraph (9) on the need for more research on disclosure methods.

3 Unexpected results vs project failure

3.1 Unexpected results

If you take the example in 2.6 above (Philibee), you might have found that your results did not answer your question either way. Let's see how the story develops.

3.2 Example

You had expected, for example, that the availability of sources of finance should make no difference to expansion plans in individual countries, but instead found wide variations. Area managers were under instructions to build the brand, and they chose the easiest ways to do so, such as franchising, rather than the most profitable.

You have come to the conclusion that in this case the sources of finance are not relevant to investment decisions, and capital rationing is not even thought of in Philibee.

Even if this is not the result you wanted, it is still a valid conclusion from the research you have done. You have carried out your investigation, and your result is clear. You may have wanted to prove that investment decisions were finely calibrated and that local managers calculated the best proportion of debt/equity, with allowance for risk.

3.3 What if I have identified areas for further research?

If your project identifies areas for further research, this is **not an unsuccessful** project. It is a statement of the limitations of scope and focus – nothing to be ashamed of.

3.4 Project failure

A failed project is different. This means that you are unable to come to any conclusion, that your research has proved impossible, to that you are unable to answer any of the questions you set yourself.

Effectively, you cannot even say – 'these are my findings, more work is needed'.

4 Before you start your report

Remember the mentor meeting? You should prepare an outline on two sheets of A4 paper. This is a good opportunity to plan your report and summarise your main themes. This is covered in the next chapter.

5 Frequently asked questions

Refer to the ACCA website where frequently asked questions may be posted.

Chapter roundup

- This chapter has covered how to draw conclusions from your data.

- Sometimes, the conclusions will be blindingly obvious.

- In other times you will have to force yourself to answer the questions suggested.

- An unexpected result does not necessarily indicate a failed project.

Part C:

The project mentor meetings

chapter 9

Mentor meetings

INTRODUCTION

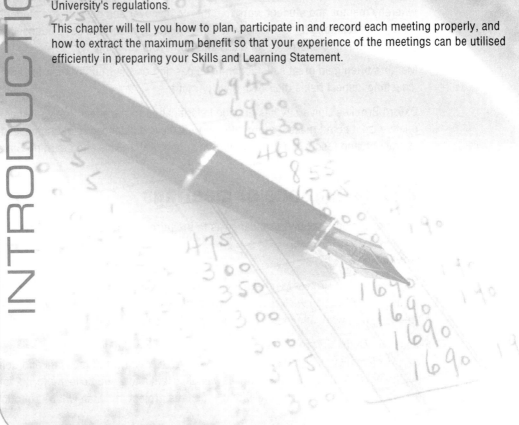

It has already been explained that the role of your mentor is to monitor your progress throughout the Research and Analysis Project. He or she will be asked to verify your participation in the three meetings that are compulsory within the module. Your mentor will also be asked to confirm that your project has been carried out in accordance with the University's regulations.

This chapter will tell you how to plan, participate in and record each meeting properly, and how to extract the maximum benefit so that your experience of the meetings can be utilised efficiently in preparing your Skills and Learning Statement.

1 The role of the mentor

It is important that you recognise and understand the role of the mentor and bear it in mind while you are planning your meetings. The Information Pack set out in Chapter 1 should help. You should remind yourself of this now.

Your mentor will also be required to sign a form declaring that to the best of their knowledge your work is entirely your own.

> **Mentor Information Pack guidelines**
>
> You will have three meetings with your Project Mentor. These meetings provide your Project Mentor with the opportunity to guide your RAP work and provide feedback to you. The meetings also provide you with the opportunity to develop your personal skills including questioning, listening and giving a presentation. You will reflect on this graduate skills development in your Skill and Learning Statement.
>
> Your Project Mentor is not expected to have specialist knowledge within your project topic area or of academic research methods. Your Project Mentor does not play any part in the assessment of your RAP beyond the certification provided to Oxford Brookes. You should not have to ask your Project Mentor what you have to do to pass – this is given in the assessment criteria for the RAP. You should not expect your Project Mentor to give you detailed advice on the structure and content of your Research Project or to write any of your RAP for you. Those decisions and actions are solely your own responsibility.

The mentor, therefore, will be taking an overview of your Research Project, rather than becoming embroiled in the fine detail and technical content.

Some business texts deal with the role of the mentor. One authority regarded mentoring as a process whereby mentor and student work together to discover and develop the student's latent abilities (Shea, 1992). The relationship is one in which the mentor is described as '...counsellor, friend and foil...' enabling you the student to sharpen your skills and hone your thinking.

Mentors often gain great satisfaction from passing on the fruits of their experience, and can find that the 'coaching' aspect helps their own development.

Oxford Brookes University has provided clarification to the effect that your mentor should not be a close relative, as it could make it more difficult to achieve a balanced relationship leading to the appropriate interaction and feedback required for completion of the Skills and Learning Statement.

2 The sequence of meetings

The Information Pack gives guidance as to the purpose of the meetings. The guidance is set out here.

> **Meeting 1**
>
> Before your first Project Mentor meeting you should identify possible project topic areas and / or the organisation that you wish to study. You should also think about the way in which you plan to undertake your research work and prepare a draft RAP timetable.
>
> You can use the first meeting to discuss your possible choices of topic area and project objectives with your Project Mentor. It is very important to have a clear idea of the aims and objectives of your RAP at the beginning of your research work. This will determine how you collect information and how you evaluate data. Getting a robust structure within which the project research will be conducted is crucial to your success.

Meeting 2

The second meeting is the opportunity for you to get feedback from your Project Mentor on the indicative findings of your Research Project. Before the second meeting you should have gathered your information and data and done some evaluation to give you some insight into how well you are meeting your Research Project aims and objectives.

You should provide an update on your progress to your Project Mentor. This could include a word-processed document with the structure of your finished Research Project. This draft report could include the early chapters covering aims and objectives, why you have chosen to apply particular accounting or business techniques and how you have chosen to undertake the project research. Your findings may be provisional at this point but such a document will give your Project Mentor a very clear idea of your progress.

Meeting 3

By the time you get to the third meeting, you should have completed your research and nearly finished writing your Research Project. You should provide a copy of your draft Research Project to your Mentor before the third meeting. This meeting includes a 15 minute presentation that you give to your Mentor and perhaps also to other students who have undertaken their own RAP.

You will need to investigate how to prepare an effective presentation, using PowerPoint or overhead slides. A copy of your presentation must be submitted as part of your Skills and Learning Statement. You will also gain experience of giving a presentation to an audience and responding to questions.

The Information Pack also supplies a process model, which is a diagram showing the interaction of work stages and meetings. You have already seen this in the Information Pack (in full) and a summarised one based on the former on page 62.

Although the Information Pack guidelines require three compulsory meetings, following a set format, there may well be scope for other meetings with your mentor. This may hinge on:

(a)   The topic you have chosen
(b)   Your relationship with your mentor
(c)   The number of other students involved.

The examiner has said that additional meetings with your mentor are to be positively encouraged. They are likely to happen if you are encountering problems or you just feel that you need to chat something through. They will demonstrate that you are taking the project very seriously. If you do have additional meetings with your mentor, you should **plan** for them, **record** them and then **reflect** upon them in the same way as for the three 'formal' meetings. In fact it would be advisable to treat any additional meetings as being a formal part of your project structure and refer to them in your Skills and Learning Statement. Therefore you should arrange an appointment with your mentor for an additional meeting and ensure that both of you document it.

Do not ask your mentor questions in passing, on a 'by the way' basis when you happen to see him or her, as you may then lose track of what has been said and what advice offered. Results obtained in a casual *ad hoc* way will be of less value in the construction of your Research Project and Skills and Learning Statement.

2.1 The advantages of meetings

At the start of your Project work, you may wonder why you have to go through such a clearly defined structure of meetings and give a presentation. You may think that it would be more straightforward for you to submit your Research Project and Skills and Learning Statement, and that you are capable of doing that without having to undergo any consultation process.

It is important that you appreciate that the Research and Analysis Project as a whole, and specifically the production of the Skills and Learning Statement, is an exercise in communication. Your meetings with your mentor are the vehicle by which you demonstrate your ability to communicate.

2.2 Face to face discussion

Face to face discussion is particularly effective as it:

(a) Allows **non-verbal cues**, both **audible and visual**, to be used to enhance understanding and persuasion.

(b) Allows immediate **exchange and feedback**.

(c) Allows communication **between** or with a number of people.

(d) Humanises the **context** of communication by opening the parties to each other's direct scrutiny and to personality factors.

These qualities make it particularly suitable for the following **applications**.

(a) Generating and **developing new ideas**, since each party may be encouraged and prompted by the others.

(b) **Feedback, constructive criticism and exchanges of views**, where necessary to resolve problems or conflicts.

(c) **Decision-making**, since each party may contribute a necessary viewpoint or piece of information.

(d) Using **personal charisma and logic** (especially with the opportunity to invite and answer questions) to persuade.

(e) Encouraging **co-operation**, information-sharing and sensitivity to others.

(f) Dealing with difficult or **personal issues** (such as discipline, grievance, counselling, bad news etc) honestly and sensitively.

(g) Encouraging **honest, open and spontaneous** communication – since it is much more difficult to give a dishonest or prepared answer or opinion face-to-face than in writing or on the phone.

Due to the fact that face to face discussion is perceived as being particularly effective, Oxford Brookes have clarified that it is not acceptable for you to hold meetings with your mentor by video-conferencing. Additionally, all meetings with your mentor, and the project itself, must be in English.

3 The first mentor meeting

The objective of this meeting is to reach a final decision on your choice of topic, and to have clearly identified your research method and the draft aims and objectives for your Research Project.

Before the first meeting, you should establish some basic 'terms of reference':

3.1 Location

It is most likely that the meeting will be held in the mentor's office at work or at your college. You should consider whether you are happy with this, or whether you would prefer to meet on neutral ground or indeed your own 'home territory'.

Given that your relationship with your mentor should be amicable and supportive, you are unlikely to feel that the mentor's office is a hostile environment, but it is a factor worth considering.

3.2 Date, time and likely duration

The date and time must be agreed with the mentor in advance. Make sure that you will have enough time before the meeting to do the basic groundwork and preliminary investigations and give sufficient thought to your likely topic and how you will work on your Research Project.

The Information Pack guidelines suggest that each meeting will be about half an hour long, although you should appreciate that this is just a guideline. Bear in mind, however, whether you will be able to cover the matters you want to discuss in half an hour, and ensure that you do not have to rush off elsewhere should the meeting exceed half an hour.

3.3 Outline agenda

It would be helpful to send this to your mentor in advance, so that he or she can be adequately prepared for the meeting too. If you have supplied your proposed title, or even a list of possible topics to the mentor, they will be far better placed to use the time in the meeting constructively.

An outline agenda for the first mentor meeting could look something like this.

3.4 Example

OXFORD BROOKES RESEARCH AND ANALYSIS PROJECT

MENTOR MEETING 1

15 January 20X8

Offices of A, B, C & Co., Chartered Certified Accountants

Student: Paul Smith

Mentor: Rosie Barker

AGENDA

1   Proposed topic: The impact of e-business on the XYZ Bank

2   Methods of research: primary and secondary

3   Potential problems with finding information

4   Proposed timetable:

- Mentor Meeting 2
- Mentor meeting 3 (and presentation)
- Submission of Project

From this, the mentor knows the likely topic, the fact that you want to discuss finding information and that you will probably suggest dates.

3.5 Likely questions

The discussion will in reality consist of a series of questions and answers, probably starting with your mentor asking how you are getting on.

To this end, the Information Pack guidelines set out some example questions which may be asked by the student or the mentor. You may want to use these to start to structure your first meeting, and to anticipate what your mentor is likely to ask you. Remember, **planning and anticipation** are the two key tools for making a meeting effective.

These are the examples of questions to be asked at the first meeting:

MENTOR	STUDENT
Have you a clear view of what you want to do?	I have considered the following alternatives; can I talk them through with you?
Are your project ideas realistic given your previous learning?	This is my plan; what do you think? Is my approach appropriate? Is my timescale realistic?
Do you know how you will undertake your research?	These are my thoughts on my personal skills.
Is your information gathering approach robust?	
How will you demonstrate your analytical and evaluative skills?	
Is your RAP timetable realistic?	

There are also some examples of questions which the student should not expect the mentor to answer. These relate to any of the three meetings, not just the first one.

Examples of such questions may include the following:

> What do I have to do to pass?
>
> What do I do next?
>
> What shall I read on this topic?
>
> What do you know about this topic?
>
> Will you structure my project for me?

This is an extract from a first meeting between mentor and student. Do you think that the meeting is being conducted within the spirit of the Information Pack guidelines?

 Exercise 1

M: So, S, have you had any thoughts about the topic for your Research and Analysis Project?

S: No, not really. I read through the list of suggestions supplied by Oxford Brookes, but none of them appealed to me. I thought I might do something about the brewing industry. What do you think?

M: I think that you need to be more specific. Firstly you need a specific organisation not a general industry. So perhaps you should narrow the list down to those, for example the effects of globalisation on the industry, the impact of e-business, the motivation of employees, and so on. You could select a specific brewer you know about and build the Research Project around that.

S: Yes, maybe. But can't I choose a topic I want to do?

M: You can, but only in exceptional cases. You have to put details in writing to Oxford Brookes and ask them to confirm whether it is acceptable. You must give them 10 days to reply, and there's no point in starting work until you've received confirmation. That means you've wasted 10 days if you want to submit by the April deadline, and it also means that this meeting is a bit of a non-event.

S: OK, let's forget about that: I'll do the effect of globalisation on a brewing company. So what shall I do next? Can you suggest some good web sites I can get information from?

M: I don't really have much knowledge of brewing, and in any event you should be doing this basic research for yourself as a forerunner to the detailed research you will need to do later. I think that you need to go away and do some basic research into sources of information, the type of research you are going to do and the basic structure of your Research Project, and then we should have another initial meeting to establish these facts before you go on. But you need to think seriously whether you will be able to submit by April: it might be wiser to submit in October, which will give you more time to really get to grips with the work involved.

Answer

In this example, S has not done anything approaching the necessary amount of basic research, and the meeting is really a waste of everybody's time. S is trying to get M to tell him what to do, and the Information Pack guidelines make it clear that the mentor is not a tutor or supervisor in this context.

S would have done better to have chosen the project topic prior to the meeting, or at least to have identified a short list. That would have given focus and structure to the meeting. Additionally, S clearly has not researched the necessary timing issues. On balance, a poor start, and this would not demonstrate the skills of communication and business acumen which are expected.

4 The second mentor meeting

The second mentor meeting should take place mid way through the production of the Research Project (although you will not necessarily have started writing yet). You should have completed the gathering of information, and should be en route to reaching some initial conclusions.

You should present to your mentor a word-processed interim update on progress achieved to date, and this will then form the basis for your discussion. The Information Pack guidelines do not specify how long this should be. Rather than word counting, you should take the view that this should contain adequate information so that the reader knows where you have got to. If your mentor agrees, you may want to supply this in advance of the meeting, so that your mentor has good background knowledge. It will also then provide the structure for your meeting.

Again the meeting should take about half an hour.

4.1 The interim report

Your interim report should be structured around a number of headings. This will effectively create the plan for the meeting. Here are some suggestions.

(a) Summary of the title and objectives of the Research Project (so you can assess whether you are achieving them)

(b) Background reading carried out (in general terms)

(c) Primary research done: list what you have read

(d) Problems encountered, for example in accessing source material, and impact on the Research Project

(e) Initial conclusions reached

(f) Further work to do and likely impact on conclusions

As well as these subjects, you are likely to discuss

(a) How you are managing to stick to your timetable
(b) Any potential word processing problems, such as tricky diagrams or tables of statistics
(c) Generally how you are feeling about the Research Project as a whole.

4.2 Likely questions

The Information Pack guidelines contain some examples of the questions which might be asked by the student and the mentor at the second meeting.

MENTOR	STUDENT
Does your written work contribute towards meeting your aims and objectives?	I have had this problem; could you offer some advice?
Does your written work meet the Research Project assessment criteria?	
Have you been able to do everything you planned?	
If you have had to change your approach, is it still consistent with your objectives?	
Is your evaluation of information and data in sufficient depth?	
What further work do you still have to undertake?	
Are you still confident that you will meet your RAP deadline?	

You should notice that these questions are **constructive**, and their terminology implies that the student and the mentor between them will try to resolve the issues. For example, the mentor asks how a problem can be resolved, and the student has the opportunity to ask for advice as to how to solve the problem.

The potential need to reschedule can be raised and discussed, and the mentor would be in a good position to recognise whether the student is now setting too tight a deadline.

It is this second stage which highlights the benefits of the mentor-student relationship.

As in the first stage, however, the mentor is not expected to tell the student what to do next or to write the Research Project for them. He or she must still stay one step removed from the process of producing the Research Project.

If you and the mentor are to schedule additional meetings, they could well occur between the second and third meetings. This is likely to be the case if the second meeting did not go very well or you had not completed the information gathering stage.

Such meetings should be **planned for and documented** just like the three scheduled meetings. The most appropriate method of planning for an additional meeting would be to produce another interim report, focusing on the headings listed earlier.

5 The third mentor meeting

The third meeting should be held towards completion of your Research Project. It is the most formal and arguably the most nerve wracking of the three meetings, as you are required to give a presentation, fifteen minutes, to your mentor and also, if appropriate, to your peer group.

Your peer group consists of any other students with whom your mentor is working. This is most likely to be the case where your mentor is your college tutor or your employer in a location where there are other students studying for the ACCA qualification.

As well as giving the presentation, you should also be prepared to answer questions and provide explanations when requested.

5.1 Timing

The process model shown in Section 2 of this chapter shows Meeting 3 at the end of the Research Project production process, at the stage when you are drawing your conclusions. You should certainly not plan to hold the third meeting prior to that, as you will not have completed the necessary thought and writing processes. Since you are expected to answer questions and explain your comments and findings, you must have all the necessary information when preparing your presentation.

If you are working alone, and your mentor has no other students, you will probably be able to set the date of the third meeting to suit you. You should bear in mind, however, that Oxford Brookes envisages two Research and Analysis Project assessment periods each year, with the two deadlines in April and October. If you miss the deadline you are aiming for, your Project will be held over for another six months, until the next assessment period.

If you have a peer group, the date of the third meeting will be less flexible, as it is likely that the students in the peer group will all give their presentations at the same session.

5.2 Likely questions

The procedure for planning and giving the presentation will be discussed in detail in the next chapter. There will be some opportunity at the third meeting for a discussion between you and your mentor, as well as the open forum of discussion after your presentation.

Here are some examples of the questions your mentor may ask you when reviewing your project.

- Is the content of the presentation consistent with the Research Project findings?

- How effective was the presentation? Did it make sense?

- Are there satisfactory links between the different parts of the project, from objectives through to findings and conclusions?

- Is the quality of the analysis and evaluation sufficient to meet the required standard?

- If you were to do the RAP again, what might you do differently?

- Given the feedback and questions, will you make any changes to your Research Project before it is submitted to Oxford Brookes?

As you can see, these are very broad and general questions, reflecting the **summarising and concluding** nature of the third meeting with your mentor. At this stage you should not be discussing the fine detail of the contents of your Research Project and the research you undertook, but should be considering **wider issues such as the conclusion reached and whether or not your Research Project can be regarded as a success.**

This is reflected in the fact that the Information Pack guidelines do not suggest any examples of questions which you might ask your mentor at the third meeting: the assumption is that you have virtually finished.

6 Questioning

Questioning and listening are the elements that the three mentor meetings have in common. The mentor will be asking you about the progress you are making at each stage, and you are able to ask the mentor for a limited amount of help and advice.

The principal questioner, however, will be the mentor, and it is your answers, and the discussions which ensue, which will enable the mentor to confirm to Oxford Brookes that the correct procedures have been observed.

In any questioning situations, there is a simple recipe for the right procedure:

(a)   **Ask** the right questions.

(b)   **Listen** to the answers.

Questions should be paced and put carefully. The mentor should not be trying to confuse the student, plunging immediately into demanding questions or picking on isolated points. Nor, however, should the mentor allow the student to digress, or gloss over important points. The mentor must **retain control** over the information-gathering process.

A variety of **questioning styles** may be used to achieve different purposes.

6.1 Open questions

These are open-ended questions of the type 'Who...? What...? Where...? When...? Why...?'.

(a)   They force you to put together responses in **complete sentences**.

(b)   They **encourage** you to talk.

(c)   They keep the interview **flowing**.

(d)   They are much more **revealing** than allowing the student to 'get away with' 'yes' or 'no' answers.

For example: 'Why do you want to write about CVP analysis?' is more effective than 'So you want to write about CVP analysis, do you?'

6.2 Closed questions

These only offer a **choice** of responses, such as 'yes' or 'no'. They have several drawbacks, compared to the open question.

(a)   They elicit answers only to the **question asked** by the mentor: there may be other questions and issues that he has not anticipated – but will emerge if the student is given the chance to express himself freely.

(b)   They do not allow the student to **express** his personality so that interaction can take place on a deeper level.

(c)   They make it easier for students to **conceal** things ('You never *asked* me....').

(d)   They make the mentor **work** very hard to get information.

However, a closed question can be useful for **pinning down** an item of information that the student seems reluctant to give, or is being long-winded about. 'Will you finish the work on 1 April?' will get the required information more quickly than 'How long will it take you to finish?'

6.3 Probing questions

These are similar to open questions in their phrasing but aim to discover the **deeper significance** of an answer. ('But what was it about **the motor industry** that particularly appealed to you?')

Such questions provide a **clearer focus** to too short or too generalised answers. Some mentors too often let a general and fairly uninformative answer pass without a probe, simply because they are working through a list of prepared open questions.

6.4 Multiple questions

These are just that: two or more questions asked at once. ('Tell me about your topic. How did your knowledge of Just In Time procedures help you there, and do you think you are up-to-date or will you need to spend time researching?')

This type of question can be used to encourage the student to talk at some **length, without straying** too far from the point. It might also test the student's ability to listen and handle large amounts of information, but should be used judiciously in this case: it can be rather intimidating and that is not the purpose of the Research and Analysis Project.

6.5 Leading questions

These suggest a certain reply to the student, for example 'Don't you agree that...?'. 'Surely...?')

The danger with this type of question is that the student will simply give the answer that **he thinks** the mentor **wants to hear**. It might, however, be used to deal with a highly reticent or nervous student, simply to encourage him to talk, or to test a student's ability to stand up for his own views.

Exercise 2

Identify the type of question used in these examples, and consider the effect they might have on you if you are the student who is responding to them.

1   'So you're interested in researching the effect of conditions of change on future personnel requirements, are you, Mark?'

2   Surely you're not interested in personnel issues, Mark?'

3   'How about doing something really interesting, like the impact of changing conditions on personnel requirements, Mark? Would you consider researching that?'

4   'Why are you interested in personnel issues, Mark?'

5   'Why particularly personnel issues, Mark?'

Answer

1   A closed question: it expects a yes or no answer, and would not give the student enough scope for expanding the discussion.

2   This is a leading question expressed in negative terms. The student could be intimidated into immediately dropping the idea of researching personnel issues.

3   This is another form of leading question, although this time it is couched in positive terms. The questioner is inviting the student to agree with the questioner's view of personnel as a research topic, and the implication is that the questioner will disapprove should the student disagree.

4   This is an open question which enables the student to expand the discussion and put forward his own viewpoint. It would enable the student to demonstrate the thought processes behind the decision.

5   This is also an open question but rather more specific. It invites the student to home in on the precise topic under discussion and explain why other alternatives were discarded.

7 Feedback

One of the most useful features of each of the three meetings with your mentor is the feedback you will receive. At the third meeting you may also receive feedback from your peer group, if applicable, but this will be on your presentation and Research Project as a whole.

At the two earlier meetings, you will receive valuable feedback from your mentor on the progress of your work. Receiving feedback is a recognised skill, and using it constructively can improve your prospects of success.

Useful guidelines on feedback

(a)   listen carefully to what is said: active listening skills are covered in the next section.

(b)   be appreciative of the feedback: the giver will then probably give you more feedback, which may be useful, if he is confident that you appreciate it.

(c)   ask for clarification if you don't understand the point that is being made.

(d)   don't take criticism too personally: negative feedback does not mean that the giver does not like you. It just means that one aspect or idea can be improved.

(e)   try to take positive steps to improve on the basis of feedback received.

8 Listening

During your meetings with your mentor you will be **talking**, but also, just as importantly, **listening**. This is often regarded as a passive activity, but you will find that if you engage in 'active listening' it will pay dividends in terms of what you gain.

The Research and Analysis Project tests your communication skills, and the ability to listen, along with the ability to talk and question, provide the basis of communication.

Listening is about decoding and receiving information. Effective listening helps

(a)   The sender of the message to **listen effectively** in turn to the receiver's reply

(b)   Reduce the effect of **'noise'**

(c)   **Resolve problems** by encouraging understanding from someone else's viewpoint.

If someone is talking to you, no matter how clearly and lucidly, but you are not listening properly, the communication process will fail.

Definition of listening

The assumption tends to be that listening is not so much an ability or skill as a physical attribute of human beings: we all have ears, so we can all listen – barring a physical hearing deficiency. Listening is simply equated with **hearing**. However, tests show that the average person remembers only half of what he has heard immediately afterwards.

By consciously engaging in the process of active listening, we can improve the effectiveness of our listening, and develop listening skills.

8.1 Why is it important to listen effectively?

Many benefits are available from effective listening.

(a)   It is a **quick**, **direct** source of information, which you may be interested in, or need in order to make decisions.

(b)   It offers the opportunity to use the speaker's **tone** of voice, to help you interpret underlying messages.

(c)   It is **interactive** and flexible, so you can:

   (i)   Make sure the information is **adapted** to your needs and that you understand it

   (ii)   **Add** information of your own, to stimulate new ideas and solve problems.

(d)   It builds **relationships**, encourages understanding of the other person's feelings and point of view, and establishes a personal element to the discussion.

(e)   It encourages **further** and more spontaneous communication, which deepens relationships. It also encourages honesty because the speaker has less time to plan ahead, is less likely to withhold information, and will find it more difficult to disguise his feelings.

Try the following exercise.

Exercise 3

Applying these benefits to the business context, why do you think listening might be particularly useful for a marketer or salesperson?

Answer

(a)   **It is a quick, direct source of information** – say, for getting an initial feel for customers' receptivity to a new product.

(b)   **It is interactive and flexible**. The marketer can ensure that he has got and understood the information he requires. If creative thinking is required, active listening can stimulate ideas. Active listening is vital for handling and overcoming customers' objections.

(c)   **It contributes to relationships**.

   (i)   A salesperson who listens shows respect for his customers' expertise, experience and opinions in a more direct and personal way than one who asks for written feedback.

   (ii)   Listening also allows the salesperson to use his personality: say, for greater effectiveness in making the customer feel important.

   (iii)   Human relationships are a prime factor in customer satisfaction (or dissatisfaction): customer loyalty may be enhanced by a communication style based on interpersonal communication and a degree of informality.

(d)   **It encourages communication**. The perception that the salesperson is interested and willing to listen motivates customers to offer information and ideas which may be commercially useful for the organisation. Writing down ideas can be time consuming (or even intimidating for those who are not confident about their writing skills): the opportunity to speak informally to a sales rep is both more convenient and encouraging.

8.2 Ways of listening

Like reading, listening may have a number of purposes, which should be borne in mind as you listen.

8.3 Listening for content

If you trust the source of the message to be correct and objective, or you only want to know what the source's viewpoint is (in which case it doesn't matter if it is incorrect or subjective), listening for content will be a straightforward receiving activity – but still requires skilful listening in order to:

(a)   **Receive** physically as much as possible of what is said (ensuring that it is audible, and that your attention doesn't wander).

(b)   **Interpret** as much as possible of what is said, in the way the speaker intends (understanding the message).

(c)   Give appropriate **feedback** to achieve both of the above (asking for repetition or louder delivery, asking questions, encouraging the speaker to continue and so on).

In addition, you may want to make an effort to **remember** the content of the message. The surest way is to write down the important points, but the way you listen – noticing key words, for example, or listening just as hard to repetitions and summaries – will make recall easier.

8.4 Critical listening

If you require an objective viewpoint or accurate information, and you do not have absolute confidence that the source is able and intending to give it to you, you will need to listen critically. This is essentially like evaluating a piece of writing.

(a)   Be **alert** to things you know to be factually false, and reappraise the source's credibility.

(b)   Appraise the speaker's **vocabulary** and way of speaking for attempts to distract or persuade you. Tone of voice and **body-language** – if you can see the speaker – will be an additional source of guidance in this.

(c)   Question the speaker's **assumptions** and logic (if only to yourself). Consider whether an illogical argument is the product of muddled thinking or an attempt at manipulation – and whether the conclusion is therefore invalid, or may still be true.

(d)   Look for **balance** – or bias – in the argument. It may or may not be conveniently signalled verbally ('On the one hand ... On the other hand ...').

(e)   Appraise the **supporting evidence** given, if any.

(f)   Consider the source's **credibility** and purpose in communicating.

(g)   Bear in mind your own biased **perceptions** as you respond critically to the message and to the speaker: don't dismiss the message because you dislike the voice!

Listening to the tone of voice of the speaker adds an extra dimension to the process of interpreting (is he being ironic, for example, or serious?) and evaluating (is he carried away by emotion, or trying to be persuasive?).

8.5 Empathetic listening

'**Empathy**' is defined as 'the power of understanding and imaginatively entering into another person's feelings'.

Empathetic listening is a highly active form of listening, which goes a step beyond critical listening in the attempt fully to understand the message and what lies behind it. In effect, the listener must engage with the speaker, interpreting in the content and style of the message both the surface and underlying meanings and the feelings and motives which prompted them: a third, unspoken 'message' in its own right. Questions to ask yourself when listening empathetically include the following.

(a)   **What** do the speaker's vocabulary, tone, manner and selection of content say over and above the surface message?

(b)   **Why** is the speaker saying this, and in this way (vocabulary/tone of voice)?

(c)   How does the speaker **feel** about this – whether or not it is actually said?

(d)   How would **I** feel in the same situation?

(e)   How might this idea/information **apply to me**, to my life?

(f)   What **feedback** can I give that would be helpful to the speaker, both to improve and encourage communication (say, asking a question) and to meet the underlying motives and needs (for encouragement, respect, friendliness, comfort or whatever)?

8.6 Attentive listening

Here are some brief hints to being a good listener, whether it be in one-to-one discussions, lectures, meetings or telephone conversations. In the context of your Research and Analysis Project, you will listen mainly to your mentor and your peer group.

(a)   **Be ready**. Get your attitude right at the start, and decide to listen. You should have done some background research for the meeting or discussion so that you have established a context for the message you intend to receive.

(b)   **Be interested**. Don't try to soak up a message like a sponge, and then complain that you found it dull. Make it interesting for yourself by asking questions: how is this information relevant to me and how can I use it?

(c)   **Be patient**. Try to hold yourself back from interrupting if you disagree with someone, and don't compete to get your view in before the previous speaker has properly finished. Wait until a suitable opening (while your point is still relevant to the immediate discussion, but not while the speaker is just drawing a breath between phrases). Don't be so preoccupied with how you're going to respond that you forget to listen to what is said in the meantime.

(d)   **Keep your mind open**. Be aware of your negative reactions to the speaker's message, delivery or appearance. Control them, and don't jump to conclusions: you may miss something.

(e)   **Keep your mind going**. Being open-minded does not mean accepting everything blindly. Use your critical faculties: test the speaker's assumptions, logic and evidence. Also test your own interpretation of words and ideas, making sure they make sense in their context.

(f)   **Keep your mind on the job**. Concentrate. It is very easy to switch off as attention wanders or you get tired. Don't be distracted by details of the speaker or the room. Don't get side-tracked by irrelevancies in the message: co-operate with the speaker in getting to the point of what he is trying to say. Listen for main points, and the summary or conclusion.

(g) **Give feedback**. You can encourage the speaker and ensure your own understanding by sending feedback signals, particularly during pauses in the speech or message. For example, try an interested and attentive look, a nod, a murmur of agreement or query ('Yes... Really?'). If there are opportunities, use some verbal means of checking that you have understood the message correctly. Ask questions, referring to the speaker's words in a way that demonstrates your interpretation of them ('You said earlier that...' 'You implied that..'): the speaker can then correct you if you have missed or misinterpreted something. Remember, you're not trying to score points for cleverness or clairvoyancy: co-operate with the speaker, and if you don't understand something, or you think you've got something wrong, say so.

(h) **Use non-verbal cues (if available)**. Be aware of the messages given by gestures, factual expression, tone of voice and so on.

(i) **Avoid interruptions**. If you interrupt it will disturb the speaker's flow, and can cause the conversation to go right off the rails. There are different reasons for interruptions:

(i)   boredom
(ii)   failure to understand
(iii)   a burning desire to state your own case and not hear out the other person

but they can all cause communication to break down completely.

(j) **Allow silence**. Many people are embarrassed by silence and think that it is a sign of weakness or conversation drying up. In a complex, technical conversation, however, nothing could be further from the truth. Participants must have time to formulate their thoughts, mentally come to a conclusion and prepare what they are going to say, and this cannot happen instantaneously.

Try to indicate that you are happy with silence when it does occur, by looking relaxed and not pre-empting the speaker's next remarks.

Exercise 4

James, a mentor, and Pat, a student, are about to conduct the second meeting to discuss the progress of Pat's Research and Analysis Project on the financial position of Barclays Bank. Pat is quite nervous about the meeting and lacking self-confidence, as he feels that things are not progressing very well. He is wondering how to extract the maximum benefit from the meeting.

J: So, Pat, how have you been getting on?

P: Well, not too badly, but I've...

J: Sorry, I completely forgot to offer you a coffee. Would you like one?

P: Yes, thank you, that would be lovely. I've got to the stage where I've done the basic background reading and quite a lot of information gathering, but I seem to have come to a bit of a grinding halt.

J: I see. Milk and sugar?

P: Milk, please, no sugar.

James gets up, goes out of the room and reappears five minutes later with the coffee. While James is out of the room, Pat can hear him chatting in the corridor outside

J: There we are. So, you've done the background reading and finished the information gathering, have you? Well that's excellent progress. You are doing well. I must congratulate you.

P: Well, yes, thank you, I have done those stages, I suppose, but I don't think it's going all that well.

J: Oh come on, don't do yourself down: it sounds as though you're bang on schedule.

P: It's just that whenever I start to try to plan the Research Project itself I can't ......

Pat's mobile phone, buried in the depths of his briefcase, starts to play the Star Wars theme tune

P: Sorry, do you mind if I get that, it might be about my holiday flights. I'm expecting the travel agent to ring me.

      Hello. Yes, that's fine. So you'll charge my credit card today? Thanks. Bye.

J: Where are you going? Somewhere nice?

P: Just Majorca. I can't wait though. I love the sunshine.

J: So where were we? Oh yes, you can't get down to work and write the Research Project. Well I suggest we look at the headings you've got.....

Can you identify the features within this conversation which indicate that poor listening skills are being displayed? What rules do you think you could set for yourself to avoid these pitfalls?

Answer

(a)   Immediately after the key question 'how are you getting on?' James **interrupts** Pat's response. Had James been listening, he would have heard the 'but' at the end of Pat's opening phrase, which should have alerted him to potential problems.

Rule: don't interrupt straight after a key question.

Rule: listen out for words like 'but', 'and' and 'because' tailing off at the end of a sentence. They can be indicative of the other person having a problem.

(b)   James puts a stop on the conversation completely by **changing the subject** (and Pat's thought processes) to coffee.

Rule: arrange the social aspects of the meeting (drinks, who sits where, take coats etc.) before you start. Then you can focus on listening.

(c)   James goes out of the room to make the coffee and obviously **holds another conversation.** This means that he is less likely to retain the previous conversation in his head.

Rule: concentrate on the conversation in hand and don't start another one.

(d)   When James resumes the conversation, he **summarises inaccurately**. He has obviously not listened to Pat's comment that he has come to a grinding halt. James has heard what he wants to hear, that is that the Project is going well. When Pat tries to tone down James' praise, James brushes Pat's protests aside.

Rule: when you summarise a conversation inaccurately, let the other person correct you.

(e)   Pat's mobile phone rings just as Pat is trying to express his concerns. The fact that Pat is expecting a call means that he could have been half waiting for the phone to ring, rather than concentrating on the conversation.

Rule: turn off mobile phones and pagers completely before any situation where you are required to listen carefully. Even if you just turn it off instead of answering, it will interrupt your train of thought. Do not engage in a complex or more interesting conversation until you have finished the first one.

(f)   James tries to get the conversation back on track, but again summarises inaccurately, and suggests an inappropriate course of action.

Rule: if you have been interrupted in a conversation and are not exactly sure what has been said, ask the other person to summarise and see how well their memory of the conversation matches yours.

9 Recording the meeting

The Information Pack guidelines, on meetings with your mentor, suggest that

> If you make a note after each meeting or keep a personal diary of reflections then you will have developed some content for possible later use in your Skills and Learning Statement.

This is valuable advice, as the meetings are likely to take place over a period of some months and you could easily forget, or even misinterpret, what has been said. We cannot stress enough the importance of making notes at your meetings. It is almost impossible to remember what was said at a meeting which happened months ago.

9.1 Means of recording

The Information Pack guidelines suggest a personal diary, but there are various ways of recording the meetings.

Tape recorder

This will provide a totally accurate record, but you should request permission from your mentor before you tape your conversations. Some people do not like having their conversations recorded as it detracts from the spontaneity and means that the discussion is less likely to be free-ranging. You may also find that having a verbatim recording makes it more difficult to reflect on the conversations, as you may be tempted just to write down what is said rather than think about it.

However, recording the meetings means that you need not worry about missing or forgetting anything, and it means that you can concentrate on listening to and participating in the conversation, only writing key points down.

Minutes

You would take minutes during the course of the meetings and then write them up afterwards. You could ask your mentor to read the minutes and confirm whether your understanding of proceedings is correct. The mentor may find this helpful as he or she has to provide confirmation to Oxford Brookes that the meetings have happened in accordance with the Information Pack guidelines, and a structured set of minutes could serve as useful evidence.

The drawback is that you might become so engrossed in taking minutes at the meeting that you don't participate fully in the discussions and miss the opportunity to raise important points.

Brief notes

Where a critical point is made during the meeting, or some piece of factual information is passed on by your mentor, you would just jot it down in the course of the meeting. It would then be sensible to write up the notes immediately after the meeting, so that you do not lose the thought processes while they are fresh.

You must make the time to write up the notes, or at the very least to write a comprehensive summary of the conversation held. Some authorities say that for a traditional lecture, you should spend at least twice the time again as the lecture time in writing up and ensuring that you understand your notes. This may be slightly over the top for writing up the notes of a meeting, but you should think in terms of at least spending as much time again as the time of the meeting.

10 Reflecting on the meeting

Notice that the Information Pack guidelines use the word 'reflections'. One definition of the verb 'to reflect' is **'to meditate, to consider attentively'**, while a reflection can also be described as a **thought which generates further thinking.**

Your reflections will be discussed in your Skills and Learning Statement. This contains much self-analysis and should contain examples taken from your discussions. You need to consider how **successful and relevant** your discussions were, and how they could have been more **effective.**

Comparison of meeting process with meeting outcome

The Information Pack guidelines provide you with detailed guidance of the objective and probable subject matter of each mentor meeting. They can be summarised like this:

Meeting 1	•	Finalise the topic
	•	Agree the research method
	•	Set out draft aims and objectives
Meeting 2	•	Report that information gathering is complete
	•	Formulate initial view of findings
	•	Present interim report
Meeting 3	•	Give presentation to mentor and peer group
	•	Review completion of Research Project

If you regard those as a checklist of what should be achieved at each meeting, you can then consider whether they have been achieved and tick them off once done.

If at the end of a meeting you think that the objectives have not been achieved, try to identify why that is the case, and think what you would have done differently. This will tell you whether the meeting has been successful or not, and you should be realistic in your assessment of this in the Skills and Learning Statement.

10.1 Documenting your thoughts

You must document (or record) your thoughts so that they provide an adequate framework for the self-reflection which is a critical part of the Skills and Learning Statement.

Since you will be writing up your Skills and Learning Statement some time after the event, the notes must contain sufficient detail for you to remember what you felt at the time. It might be helpful to structure your notes for each meeting around these headings.

(a) **Title of meeting**

1, 2, 3 or an additional meeting?

(b) **Planning**

(i)   Was a plan prepared?
(ii)   Did the meeting follow the plan?
(iii)   If not, how did it diverge from the plan?
(iv)   What could I have done to keep to the plan?
(v)   Should I concentrate more on the plan for the next meeting?

(c)   **Questions**

    (i)   Were they open or closed?

    (ii)   Did they generate further discussion?

    (iii) Could the mentor and I answer them?

    (iv)   Could any questions have been phrased better (by either student or mentor)?

    (v)   Were any key questions left out?

    (vi)   Did I think after the meeting 'I wish I'd asked X'?

(d)   **Listening**

    (i)   Achieved satisfactorily?

    (ii)   Conscious attempt to use listening techniques/avoid interruptions etc.?

    (iii) Any errors/distortions/noise?

(e)   **Interaction**

Consider a model of communication (eg in Chapter 12)

Mentor meetings:

    (i)   Was it a two-way conversation with participation from both?

    (ii)   Did I extract the most from the discussion?

    (iii) Did I act upon suggestions made by the mentor?

    (iv)   Do I need to do anything specific before the next meeting as a result of the mentor's comments?

    (v)   Does the mentor think that I am doing OK?

    (vi)   What shall I do with the feedback?

Peer group presentation:

    (i)   Was their reaction positive or negative?

    (ii)   Did I respond well to questions?

    (iii) Was I sufficiently well prepared?

(f)   **Presentation**

    (i)   Could I have done the presentation better?

    (ii)   Was I sufficiently well-prepared?

    (iii) What general comments emerge from the feedback?

    (iv)   What will I do about those comments?

    (v)   Did I feel confident?

    (vi)   Did I learn anything from the other presentations I saw?

(g)   **Overall**

    (i)   Was the meeting useful?

    (ii)   Did it achieve its objectives?

    (iii) Did it contribute to the production of my Project?

When you are formulating and answering these questions, you must be scrupulously honest. In the Skills and Learning Statement you are expected to recognise your strengths and your weaknesses, and identify ways in which you can improve.

11 The mentor's certification

A student's project mentor is required to complete the mentor certification section of the project submission form, which can be downloaded from the BSc degree pages on the ACCA website.

After each project submission period Oxford Brookes contacts individual project mentors to confirm that the information provided in the mentor's certificate is correct. A number of students have been subject to disciplinary action by the University as a result of this Oxford Brookes audit work which identified discrepancies in the project submission forms.

Chapter roundup

- The mentor is the person who will monitor the progress of your work through the Project but they will not be regarded as your tutor.

- The three meetings with your mentor are a fundamental part of the project.

- The Skills and Learning Statement requires you to reflect upon your meetings with your mentor and consider ways in which they could have been more effective.

- Questioning, feedback and listening are essential elements in every meeting with your mentor.

- It is important that you record the events at your mentor meetings adequately.

chapter 10

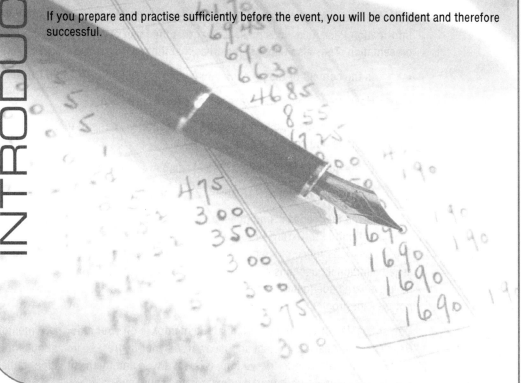

Delivering your presentation

INTRODUCTION

This chapter is devoted to the presentation which you must make to your mentor, and probably also to your peer group, in the third meeting.

You may find this prospect, especially if you are presenting to a group, absolutely terrifying. You need not feel this. The cardinal rule when preparing for a presentation is:

PREPARATION
PREPARATION
PREPARATION

If you prepare and practise sufficiently before the event, you will be confident and therefore successful.

1 The requirement for a presentation

You are required to prepare and deliver a fifteen minute presentation on your Research Project to your mentor, and if applicable your peer group. You should use appropriate presentation techniques (PowerPoint or overhead slides) in conjunction with your talk. You should be prepared to answer questions and provide explanations when requested.

The presentation is one of the topics which must be specifically incorporated into the Skills and Learning Statement. In meeting the Skills and Learning Statement requirements you will reflect on the preparation and delivery of your presentation to your Project Mentor.

You must submit a copy of your PowerPoint presentation or overhead slides as evidence of skills development.

You can deduce from these requirements that Oxford Brookes University attaches great importance to the presentation, and it is a critical part of the assessment procedure which will grant your degree.

2 Presenting to your mentor

If you are a student working alone (ie not in a college environment) or your mentor does not act in that capacity to other students, you will deliver your presentation solely to your mentor. This may feel like a slightly artificial situation, as in many ways it is more difficult to present formally to one person than it is to a large group.

2.1 Preparation

If you are delivering your presentation just to your mentor, you should prepare for it in exactly the same way as you would if presenting to a group, as covered in detail in later sections of this chapter. You should be standing, treat the mentor as if he or she were an 'audience' and use PowerPoint or overhead slides.

You may find it easier to pre-empt the questions you will have to field after your presentation. The Information Pack guidelines make it clear that the main purpose of the third mentor meeting is the presentation. They also suggest the areas that the mentor is likely to focus on.

- Is the content of the presentation consistent with the Research Project findings?

- How effective was the presentation? Did it make sense?

- Are there satisfactory links between the different parts of the project, from objectives through to findings and conclusions?

- Is the quality of the analysis and evaluation sufficient to meet the required standard?

- If you were to do the RAP again, what might you do differently?

- Given the feedback and questions, will you make any changes to your Research Project before it is submitted to Oxford Brookes?

These questions reflect the fact that this is the **review stage**. Of course, it is highly likely that you will be asked additional questions on some aspects of the technical content of your Research Project, but if you have prepared adequately and covered your material in an appropriate way, as discussed later, this should not present problems.

One critical factor to remember is that the mentor **is on your side**. Your mentor wants you to pass the Research and Analysis Project and be awarded your degree, so you should not regard him or her as a hostile audience trying to trip you up. It is not an 'us and them' situation' rather it is an 'us and us' situation, as you are both working towards the same end.

3 Presenting to your peer group

Your peer group may consist of only one or two other students, or there may be a large number, depending on the other responsibilities of your mentor. You may never have met any of them before, or you may know them all well from studying for the ACCA exams together.

A peer group is exactly as its name implies: it is a group of your peers, or equals. They will be at various different stages in their ACCA studies, as some will have done the minimum number of exams necessary prior to submitting the Research and Analysis Project, while others may have completed the ACCA qualification. The common feature is that you are all at the point of submitting the Project, so you will have almost written the Research Project, and be embarking on the Skills and Learning Statement.

You may find that being part of a group provides a refreshing change. If you have been working alone on your Research and Analysis Project, and have only discussed it with your mentor, the comments and views of other people could be enlightening.

Many authorities believe that learning in a group is beneficial, and most degree courses adopt it to some extent, usually by means of seminars and discussion groups.

Discussion helps you:

(a)   To think
(b)   To develop your ideas
(c)   To see things from a different perspective
(d)   To unravel problems where previously you had met a dead end
(e)   To realise you are not the only person with the problems you have

An advantage of presenting to a peer group is that you will see other people's presentations and be able to participate in question and answer sessions yourself. This may help you in putting the final touches to your Research Project and in preparing to write your Skills and Learning Statement.

4 Planning your presentation

The aspects of planning considered here are relevant for a presentation both to your mentor or to your peer group.

There are three key elements to consider when planning a presentation:

(a)   The audience
(b)   The logistic arrangements
(c)   The content

In later sections of this chapter we will look at communication aids, dealing with questions and coping with feedback.

4.1 The audience

In the case of this presentation, you will be faced with a captive audience, in that they are there because the mentor is hearing all the presentations at the same time. They are likely to be a receptive and responsive audience, because they will know that they can learn from the experience.

You should consider these points:

(a)   **Will they be interested in the topic of the presentation?**

The audience may have a general expectation that they will learn something new, interesting, or useful on a topic that they are pre-disposed to **gather information** about: it is up to the speaker to hold their attention by satisfying the desire for relevant information.

They may also have some **prior knowledge**, on which the speaker can build: there will be a fine line to tread between boring the audience by telling them what they already know, and losing them by assuming more knowledge than they possess.

(b) **Do they need specific information from the presentation**?

An audience which is deliberately seeking information, and intending to use it to further their own objectives, is highly motivated. If their objectives match the speaker's (which should certainly be the case among the peer group: you all want to pass the Research and Analysis Project), this motivation aids the speaker. It is therefore important to gauge, as far as possible, what this highly-motivated group **want** to hear from you, and **why**.

Taking into account audience needs and expectations, your message needs to have the following qualities.

(a) **Interest**. It should be lively/entertaining/varied or relevant to the audience's needs and interests, or preferably both.

(b) **Congeniality**. This usually means positive, supportive or helpful in some way (eg in making a difficult decision easier, or satisfying a need). Avoid:

   (i) **Sensitive** comments on which your listeners may have strong beliefs or feelings contrary to your own.

   (ii) Language or suggestions that might be **offensive**, threatening or detrimental to their interests (involving competition, cost, danger, risk and so on).

(c) **Credibility**. It should be **consistent** in itself, and with known **facts**; apparently **objective**; and from a source perceived to be **trustworthy**.

(d) **Accessibility**. This means both:

   (i) **Audible/visible**. (Do you need to be closer to the audience? Do you need a microphone? Enlarged visual aids? Clearer articulation and projection?)

   (ii) **Understandable**. (What is the audience's level of knowledge/education/experience in general and of the topic at hand? What technical terms or **jargon** will need to be avoided or explained? What concepts or ideas will need to be explained?)

4.2 The logistics

At the planning stage, you might also consider **physical factors** which will affect the audience's concentration: their ability and willingness to **keep** listening **attentively and positively** to your message. Some of the these may not be in your control, as you will probably not have any choice over the location but as far as possible, give attention to the following.

(a) **Listening conditions**. Try and **cut out background noise** – conversations outside the room, traffic or loud air conditioning, say. (There may be a trade-off between peace and quiet, and good ventilation, also required for alertness: be sensible about the need to open a door or window or switch on a fan.)

(b) **Freedom from interruption and distraction**. Do not let the **focus shift** from you and your message to outside views of people passing by and so on. Arrange not to be disturbed by others entering the room. Announce that questions and comments will be invited at the end of the session.

(c) **Ventilation, heating and lighting**. A room that is too stuffy, or draughty, too hot or cold, too bright or too dim to see properly, can create physical malaise, and shifts attention from the speaker and his message to the listener and his discomfort.

(d) **Seating and desking**. Excessive comfort can impair alertness – but uncomfortable seating is a distraction. Combined with inadequate arrangements for writing (since many people may wish or need to take notes), it can cause severe strain over a lengthy talk.

(e) **Audibility and visibility**. Inadequate speaking volume or amplification is a distraction and a strain, even if it does not render the message completely inaccessible. Excessive volume and electronic noise is equally irritating. Visibility requires planning not just of effective visual aids (clear projection in suitable light, adequately enlarged etc) but also of seating plans, allowing unobstructed 'sight lines' for each participant.

(f) **Seating layout**. Depending on the purpose and style of your presentation, you may choose formal classroom-like rows of seating, with the speaker in front behind a podium, or informal group seating in a circle or cluster in which the speaker is included. The formal layout enhances the speaker's credibility, and may encourage attention to information, while the informal layout may be more congenial, encouraging involvement and input from the whole group. You may have little choice about this.

(g) **Time**. Listeners get tired over time – however interesting the presentation: their **concentration span is limited**, and they will not be able to listen effectively for a long period without a break. Although your presentation is only 15 minutes long, the cumulative effect of a number of presentations may make the audience tired when it comes to you. Bear in mind, too, that the **time of day** will affect your listeners' concentration, even if your presentation is a brief one: you will have to work harder if your talk is first thing in the morning, late in the day (or week), or approaching lunch-time.

(h) **The speaker's appearance**. We will talk more about this under **delivery**, below – but it should already be obvious that the appearance of the speaker may sabotage his efforts if it is uncongenial or unappealing, lacks credibility or the authority expected by the audience, is distracting in some way, and so on.

4.3 Planning the structure

Structure is all-important in a presentation. If your presentation is not well-structured and your audience loses the thread, it can be difficult to continue to hold their interest. This in turn means that you can feel vulnerable, if you feel that the presentation is not going well, so your performance deteriorates.

Remember that a presentation differs from private reading. If you are reading a book or an article and do not understand something, you can go back and read through it again or take a break and go back to it later. The audience at a presentation does not have that luxury, so you the speaker must get it right first time.

The classic advice on delivering a presentation is:

(a) Tell them what you are going to say
(b) Say it
(c) Tell them what you've said

This means that your presentation can be split into three broad sections:

(a) The introduction
(b) The presentation itself, and
(c) The conclusion

Armed with your clearly-stated objectives and audience profile, you can plan the **content** of your presentation. This can be quite a daunting prospect as you need to remember the information, put it in the right order and state it clearly, all in one fluid movement.

One approach which may help to clarify your thinking is as follows.

(a) **Make a mindmap (or brainstorm)**. Write down all the thoughts and points that come to you on the subject in hand. Do not worry at this stage about the **order or relevance** of the ideas – just keep them coming, until your brain 'dries up' on the subject.

(b) **Prioritise**. Using the techniques of **classifying/clustering ideas** or the hierarchy of objectives approach, select the **key points** of the subject, and a **storyline** or theme that gives your argument a unified sense of 'direction'.

The **fewer** points you make (with the most emphasis) and the clearer the **direction** in which your thoughts are heading, the easier it will be for the audience to grasp and retain your message. Discard – or de-emphasise – all points which do not further your simple design.

(c) **Structure**. Make notes for your presentation which show your selected main points and how they **link** to each other. In other words, **illustrate** simply the **logical order** or pattern of your speech as a whole. Ideally this will follow the structure of your Research Project.

(d) **Outline**. Following your structured notes, **flesh out** your message. The outline should include an **introduction**; **supporting evidence, examples and illustrations**; **notes** of where (and what) **visual aids** will be required; signals of **logical progressions** and a **conclusion**. These points are developed later.

(e) **Practise**. Learn the **basic outline**, or sequence of ideas, rather than a word-for-word 'script': if you repeat a speech by rote, it can sound stilted, unspontaneous and mechanical. Practice runs, or rehearsals, will help you to remember your storyline, and will give you confidence that you **can** find the words to put it across, once you get going. (You may, however, choose to polish and learn by heart certain important elements of the outline: introduction, supporting facts/quotes/anecdotes, and conclusion, say.)

Your **rehearsals** should **indicate** difficult logical leaps, dull patches, unexplained terms and other potential barriers to understanding, which you can then eliminate or minimise by adjusting your outline or style. They will also help you gauge and adjust the **length** of your presentation. You should attempt **at least** one full, timed 'dress' rehearsal. You may choose to rehearse in front of a mirror, to a mock audience of family/friends, or on audio or video-tape, in order to assess the full effect. This will also help you get the timing right.

(f) **Cue**. Your outline may be ideal for rehearsal, but may be too unwieldy to act as a cue or **aide-memoire** for the talk itself. You should be now be fairly familiar with your material: memory 'joggers' are all you require, and help you to avoid the tendency, when nervous, of trying to read word-for-word from a script, instead of getting involved in communicating spontaneously and directly with the audience.

Small cards, which fit into the palm of the hand, are ideal. (If you are using overhead slides, they may be used in a similar fashion to guide you – and also the audience.) They should contain very brief, clear notes (verbal or pictorial – whatever works for you), which give you:

(i) **Key words** for each topic, and the logical links between them

(ii) Reminders for when to use **visual aids**

(iii) The **full text** of any detailed information you need to quote

Exercise 1

Planning for a presentation

You have been asked by your manager to give a brief talk to the junior staff on the subject of: 'The tidy office: efficiency, safety and image'.

You know this issue is a bit sensitive at the moment, having recently had to tell people off about the state of the Sales Administration Department offices. The staff are on the defensive, and have been complaining loudly about the cleaning lady. However, several files have been mislaid, others turning up in wastepaper bins or marked by rings from the bottom of coffee cups. It seems as if, every time a visitor is due in the Department, you have to make people interrupt their duties to have a swift 'spring clean': they sulk. Unfortunately you do not always get enough warning of visits – and morale suffers again, because the staff are as aware of the mess as you are. Most recently, you have lost two of your assistants through illness, one suffering asthmatic attacks caused by dust (which you know *is* the cleaning lady's fault), and another having strained his back picking up a stack of loose files which he had accidentally knocked off the edge of his desk.

You are going to have to do something about the tidiness problem. The staff's habits will have to be corrected firmly – but tactfully, because of the atmosphere of hostility that is creeping into the issue. Stress positive aspects of a tidy office, in line with the title of your talk. Make *helpful* notes for your talk.

Answer

TIDY OFFICE

Efficiency	Safety	Image
Files etc easily traced and secure	Dust etc – x's asthma	Coffee-stained, crumpled files
[*NB – don't criticise specific ...*]	[NB = 'appreciate = not down to *you*', but ... *all* responsible for safety ...]	Impression to visitors
Easier use of desk surface	Accidents; tripping over, knocking things off desk	
Easier movement round office		
No interruptions for spring cleaning!		

CO-OPERATION

We've all been
guilty of lapses

We all hate the:
inconvenience; danger;
embarrassment

Together – let's make this a

TIDY OFFICE: FOR EFFICIENCY, SAFETY + IMAGE

5 Planning the content

Some authorities think that the best approach is to plan the introduction and the conclusion more or less together (tell them what you're going to say and tell them what you've said) and then plan for the chunk that goes in the middle. This is not compulsory, however, and you may prefer to plan just by going through the structure of your Research Project.

5.1 Introduction

This is a **vital part** of your presentation, because if you do not establish your credibility and gain the audience's interest at this stage, when their concentration is at its peak, it will be very difficult to win them back later. It is also useful for the audience to get an overview of the **shape** of your presentation, to guide them through it: a bit like the scanning process in reading. The **introduction** should therefore do the following.

(a) Make an **initial impact** which focuses the audience's attention on your presentation. Establish – quickly – the **relevance** of the topic to the audience: set up the problem they need solved, the question they need answered, the threat or opportunity facing them. Use curiosity, or surprise.

(b) Establish the **speaker's (that means your!) credibility** (and congeniality, if appropriate). Establish – quickly – your authority to speak on the subject, the clarity of your thinking and the supporting evidence you have available. Establish a rapport with the audience – through anecdote, humour or identification with them (in solving the problem, facing the threat etc).

(c) Give them a **taste** of the subject and the **style** in which you intend to address it, to arouse their curiosity or interest, and **focus** their thoughts on the matter in hand.

(d) **Prepare** the audience for the content and structure of your presentation.

5.2 The conclusion

Again, this is an important stage of the talk, because people tend to rally their concentration when they realise the end of a talk is approaching. The **conclusion** should be used to accomplish the following.

(a) **Clarify and draw together** the points you have made into the single main idea or **story**: use an example, or anecdote, review, summary or conclusion – but do **not** introduce any new ideas at this stage.

(b) **State, reinforce or imply** what you want/expect your audience to do (or know, believe, feel, agree to etc) following your presentation. As in a letter, leave the audience with the seed of response or action in their minds, particularly if your purpose is persuasive.

(c) **Reinforce** the audience's recall of the content of your talk, and the response they are expected to make as a result. Again, you may use repetition, or something more theatrical (a joke or anecdote, quotation or surprising statistic) to make your main message **memorable**.

5.3 Title

This may be devised after you have planned your talk, to reflect its content and style, or may be given to you. The title is **part of the message**, and – as a first impression – an important part. It should be:

(a) **Brief**

(b) **Meaningful** – preferably a clear indication of what your talk is about

(c) **Interesting**, curiosity-arousing (though not obscure), motivating to the audience

(d) **Honest**, so that the audience do not feel cheated when they hear the talk itself. (Do not title your talk 'How to make a million pounds' if you are not going to tell the audience how ....)

For example:

(i) An analysis of the financial situation of Microsoft
(ii) Implementation of information systems: avoiding the pitfalls
(iii) Internal audit for X plc: What are the costs and benefits?

Clarifying the message

Your structured notes and outline should contain cues which clarify the **logical order**, shape or progression of your information or argument. This is helpful for you, because it keeps you 'on track', but it is primarily intended to guide your audience, in order to:

(a) Maintain a **sense of purpose**, which keeps up their motivation to listen

(b) Help them to **follow you** at each stage of your argument, so that they arrive with you at the conclusion

Logical cues indicate the **links** between one topic or statement and the next. Here are some examples.

(a) You can simply begin each point with **linking words or phrases** like:

This has led to ...
Therefore ...
So ...   [conclusion, result or effect, arising from previous point]
As a result ...

However ...
But ...   [contradiction or alternative to previous point]
On the other hand ...

Similarly ...   [confirmation or additional example of previous point]
Again ...

Moreover ...   [building on the previous point]

(b) You can set up a **framework** for the whole argument, giving the audience an overview and then filling in the detail. For example:

'There are three main reasons why ... Firstly ... Secondly ... Thirdly ... .'

'So what's the answer? You could take two sides, here. On the one hand .... On the other hand ... .'

'Let's trace how this came about. On Monday 17th ... . Then on Tuesday ... .'

'Of course, this isn't a perfect solution. It has the advantages of ... . But there are also disadvantages, in that ... .'

'You might like to think of communication in terms of the 5 C's. That's: concise, clear, correct, complete, courteous. Let's look at each of these in turn'.

(c) You can use more elaborate devices which **summarise** or repeat the previous point and lead the audience to the next. These also have the advantage of giving you, and the listener, a 'breather' in which to gather your thoughts. They are particularly effective in **persuasive** communication, since they can set up a logical progression, or contrast, in a dramatic way.

'So we've seen some of the effects of poor communication in the banking industry. We probably agree that they are something! So what can we do? How can we improve our communications? Let's look at some ideas ... .'

'As we've seen, the competition's Brand X has the advantage of price, and a popular brand image. It looks good, doesn't it? They're reaching a lot of people with a clear message: Brand X is cheaper. But – does Brand X represent *value* for money? Let's look at the facts...'

Other ways in which **content** can be used to **clarify** the message include the following.

(a) **Examples** and illustrations – showing how an idea works in practice.

(b) **Anecdotes** – inviting the audience to relate an idea to a real-life situation.

(c) **Questions** – rhetorical, or requiring the audience to answer, raising particular points that may need clarification.

(d) **Explanation** – showing how or why something has happened or is so, to help the audience understand the principles behind your point.

(e) **Description** – helping the audience to visualise the person, object or setting you are describing.

(f) **Definition** – explaining the precise meaning of terms that may not be shared or understood by the audience.

(g) The use of **facts**, quotations or statistics – to 'prove' your point.

Your **vocabulary and style** in general should contribute to the clarity of the message. Remember to use short, simple sentences and non-technical words (unless the audience is sure to know them): **avoid** jargon, clichés, unexplained acronyms, colloquialisms, double meanings and vague expressions (like 'rather', 'good'). Remember, too, that this is **oral** communication, not written: use words and grammatical forms that you would normally use in speaking to someone – bearing in mind the audience's ability to understand you, the formality of the occasion and so on.

Visual aids will also be an important aspect of content used to clarify meaning. We discuss them specifically later in this chapter.

5.4 Adding emphasis

Emphasis is the 'weight', importance or impact given to particular words or ideas. This can largely be achieved through **delivery** – the tone and volume of your voice, strong eye contact, emphatic gestures and so on – but can be **reinforced** in the content and wording of your speech. Emphasis can be achieved by a number of means.

(a) **Repetition:** 'If value for money is what the market wants, then value for money is what this company must deliver.'

'One in five customers has had a quality complaint. That's right: one in five.'

(b) **Rhetorical questions:** 'Do you know how many of the customers had a quality complaint? One in five. Do you think that's acceptable?'

(c) **Quotation:** '"Product quality is the number one issue in customer care in the early 21 century." That's the conclusion of our survey report.'

(d) **Statistical evidence:** 'One in five of our customers this year have had a quality complaint: that's 10% more complaints than last year. If the trend continues, we will have one complaint for every two satisfied customers – next year!'

(e)   **Exaggeration:** 'We have to look at the quality control system of X Ltd. Because if the current trend continues, the company will end up without any customers at all.'

5.5 Adding interest

Simple, clear information often **lacks impact**, and will only be interesting to those already motivated by the desire for the information you will need to **balance** the need for your clarity with the need to make his message vivid, attention-grabbing and memorable. All the devices discussed so far can be used for impact.

Here are some further suggestions.

(a)   **Analogy, metaphor, simile** etc – **comparing** something to something else which is in itself more colourful or interesting.

'Customer relations is like planting a seed. You may not see anything happening for a while. But you keep watering the soil. And one day – without your having done anything special – there's a shoot there, with deep roots. And that plant will keep growing and – with a bit more care – bear lots of fruit.'

(b)   **Anecdote or narrative** – telling a **story** which illustrates or makes the point, using suspense, humour or a more human context.

(c)   **Curiosity or surprise** – from incongruity, anticlimax or controversy.

'I'm going to tell you how you can read twice as fast, *and* understand more – not less – of what you've read.'

'If you put all the widgets we've sold this year end to end, they would stretch twice around the equator.'

'Improving communication is a complete waste of time ... Is that what you think?'

6 Communication aids

The Information Pack states that you should use overhead slides or PowerPoint in your presentation and that a copy must be submitted as part of your Skills and Learning Statement. We will now look at how such visual aids can be introduced into presentations.

They act as an aid to communication. This may seem obvious, but it is important to remember that visual aids are not supposed to be impressive or clever for their own sake, but to support the message and speaker in achieving their purpose. They should 'add value' to some extent to what you are saying.

6.1 Overhead projector

An **overhead projector** allows the presenter to place sheets of clear film, on which any form of message can be drawn or printed, on a light box which projects the image onto a screen behind and above the presenter. This is commonly used as a tuition medium in lecture halls.

The films or **acetates** can be pre-prepared, by hand or printing or using a photocopier or PC (see below), or can be written on by the presenter during the presentation. They are versatile, therefore, for text or line drawings, in black or colour. Use of the photocopier allows copies of documents to be shown much more cheaply than by photographing onto slide format; the same is true of professionally-prepared text which can be generated on a computer or word processor and printed out on acetate. Because the acetates themselves are clear, this medium is particularly useful for **building up** images and diagrams, adding extra layers for each new stage, or degree of complexity, or to demonstrate similarities of line and layout.

Disadvantages of overhead projection are mainly due to the need for physical handling, which can be distracting for the audience and the presenter, unless handled very smoothly. There is, too, always a risk of technical breakdown, which renders the aid useless: the format is not readily adaptable.

6.2 Presentation software – Microsoft PowerPoint

Programs for presentations allow the user to build up a series of graphical displays or images which can be used for presentation. With additional hardware, this type of software can be used to produce 35 mm slides for an on-screen slideshow or storyboard (which can be synchronised with a sound track). The slides that your lecturer uses on the overhead projector may well be produced by similar means using, for example, the Microsoft PowerPoint package. You have also no doubt seen PowerPoint-type presentations running continuously on computers in shops, telling you about the features of the computer itself or of a software package.

Quite commonly now lecture halls and conference theatres are equipped with a large VDU type screen and the person giving the presentation simply has to plug his or her laptop PC into the hall's system to give a computerised display of their slides, allowing a certain amount of **animation** (the slides 'build', point by point, as you watch) and professional looking transitions between slides, so that one can dissolve into the next, or fold into itself to reveal the next and so on. If you are presenting to a large peer group, you may find that you use a hall or lecture room with these facilities.

Here is an example of a set of slides produced using Microsoft PowerPoint. Note that professional looking **design templates** can be applied at the click of a mouse button. You would simply need to specify matters such as font type and size and colours wanted.

BPP
LEARNING MEDIA

6.3 Using visual aids

Whether using overhead slides or Microsoft PowerPoint, visual aids are **versatile** with regard to content. On either of the two formats, you might use maps, diagrams, flowcharts, verbal notes, drawings, photographs and so on.

In general you need to consider the following.

(a)   Visual aids are **simplified and concrete**: they are easier to grasp than the spoken word, giving the audience both motivation and time to absorb complex relationships and information.

(b)   They are **stimulating** to the imagination and emotions, and therefore useful in gaining attention and recall. They can be 'worth a thousand words' in time-saving on lengthy explanation and description.

(c)   Visual aids can also be **distracting** for the audience – and for the presenter, who has to organise/operate them. They can add complexity and ambiguity to the presentation, if not carefully designed for relevance and clarity.

(d)   Visual aids impose **practical requirements**.

   (i)   **Skill, time and resources** must be available for any pre-preparation of aids that may be required in advance of the presentation.

   (ii)   **The equipment, materials and facilities** you require must be available in the venue, and you must **know** how to **use** them. (No good turning up with film when there is no overhead projector.)

6.4 Guidelines for effective use of visual aids

(a)   Ensure that the aid is:

   (i)   **Appropriate** to your message, in content and 'style' or mood
   (ii)   **Easy to see** and understand
   (iii) Only used when there is **support** to be gained from it

(b)   Ensure that all **equipment** and materials are **available and working** and that you can (and do) operate them efficiently and confidently. This includes having all your slides/acetates/notes with you, in the right order, the right way up and so on.

(c)   Ensure that the aid does not become a **distraction**.

   (i)   Show each image **long enough** to be absorbed and noted, but not so long as to merge with the following idea.

   (ii)   Maintain **voice and eye contact** with your audience, so they know that it is you who are the communicator, not the machine.

   (iii) **Introduce** your aids and what they are for, placing the focus on the verbal presentation.

7 Delivery

Delivery of a presentation is equivalent to 'style' and 'presentation' in writing.

Here we will look briefly at some of the dynamics of communication between a speaker and audience.

7.1 Pre-presentation nerves

Stage-fright can be experienced before making a phone call, going into an interview or meeting, or even writing a letter, but it is considerably more acute, for most people, before standing up to talk in front of a group or crowd of people. Common fears are to do with **making a fool of oneself**, forgetting one's **lines**, being unable to answer **questions**, or being faced by blank incomprehension or **lack of response**. Fear can make vocal delivery hesitant or stilted and **body language** stiff and unconvincing: this may give the audience the impression that you are lying, or uninterested, or unsure of what you are saying. (Or worse: fainting, incoherence, memory lapse and physical fumbling can be caused by fear, in what is called a **self-fulfilling prophecy**: because you **think** the worst is going to happen, fear creates conditions which **make** it happen.)

A **controlled amount of fear**, or stress, is actually **good for you**: it stimulates the production of **adrenaline**, which can contribute to alertness and dynamic action. Only at excessive levels is stress harmful, degenerating into **strain**. If you can **manage your stress** or stagefright, it will help you to be **alert** to feedback from your audience, to think 'on your feet' in response to questions, and to project vitality and enthusiasm.

Some people are simply **more prone** to strain than others. If you tend to be crippled by nerves, you need to learn to relax, using techniques such as breathing exercises, physical exercise, visualisation of positive outcomes and so on. By and large, however, you can **control** your nervousness by the following simple means.

(a) **Reduce uncertainty and risk**. This means:

    (i) **Preparing thoroughly** for your presentation, including rehearsal, and anticipating questions.

    (ii) **Checking** that equipment, seating, conditions and so on are as required and expected.

    (iii) **Preparing** whatever is necessary for your own confidence and comfort (hayfever medication, glass of water, handkerchief, note cards etc).

    (iv) **Ensuring** that you – and the audience – have the correct venue details and start time.

    (v) **Keeping your notes to hand**, and in order, during your presentation. Keep a marker (say, your finger) on the point you've reached, so you need not fear losing your place.

(b) **Ensure that you look and feel your best**: presentable appearance, sleep the night before, no hangover and so on.

(c) **Have confidence in your message**. Forget fear of failure, and concentrate on the desired outcome: that is why you are there. Believe in what you are saying. It will also make it easier to project enthusiasm and energy.

(d) **Control physical symptoms**. Breathe deeply and evenly. Control your gestures and body movements. Put down the piece of paper that is visibly shaking in your hand. Pause to collect your thoughts if necessary. Smile, and maintain eye contact with members of the audience. If you **act** as if you are calm, the calm will **follow**.

7.2 The presenter's appearance

The dress and mannerisms of the presenter are part of the delivery of his speech, and are often the first and most readily-judged aspects of the presentation as a whole. There are two major pitfalls.

(a) **You may lose credibility if your dress and general appearance are untidy or careless**. Dress and grooming are a **reflection** of individual personality, and it is important for the speaker to feel comfortable and at ease in whatever he is wearing. However, poor grooming can be distracting to the audience, and may convey a **negative impression** of the speaker's taste, attitude to the presentation and audience, and organisational culture. The important thing is to show that you care about your appearance and the impression it will make on others, no matter what your personal style.

(b) **Your non-verbal signals may convey unease or lack of confidence**. Again, exaggerated or repeated mannerisms may simply be distracting or irritating to the audience, but non-verbal cues are also **interpreted** to imply attitudes, as discussed below.

Any number of factors may contribute to a speaker **looking** confident and relaxed, or nervous, shifty and uncertain. **Cues** which indicate confidence – without arrogance – may be as follows.

(a) An upright – but not stiff – **posture**: slouching gives an impression of shyness or carelessness.

(b) **Movement** that is purposeful and dynamic, used sparingly: not constant or aimless pacing, which looks nervous.

(c) **Gestures** that are relevant, purposeful and flowing: not indecisive, aggressive, incomplete or compulsive. Use gestures **deliberately** to reinforce your message, and if possible keep your hands up so that gestures do not distract the audience from watching your face. Watch out for habitual, irrelevant gestures you may tend to make such as rubbing your nose or taking off your glasses.

(d) **Eye-contact** with the audience. This is vital, not just to maintain credibility, giving an impression of honesty and sincerity, but to maintain the involvement of the audience. Eye-contact should be **established immediately**, when you stand up to speak or acknowledge any introduction you may have been given. It should be **re-established** immediately after periods when you have had to look away, to consult notes or use visual aids.

Staring at a single individual or group can make them uncomfortable, but a fixed gaze on 'space', or a wandering gaze avoiding the audience's eyes, makes you look shifty, dishonest or as if you are trying to make up your message as you go along. The most effective technique is to meet the eyes of **each person** in the audience, one by one.

Your gaze is thus wandering – but **purposefully** – across the whole audience, **involving** them all, without intimidating anybody: establish eye-contact long enough for it to be registered, to accompany a point you are making, and then move on. Eye-contact is also a way of inviting and seeking feedback: an important guide to how the audience is receiving and responding to your message.

7.3 Delivery techniques

In Chapter 9 we considered oral communication and the ability to speak to other people in general terms. You should refer back to that chapter to refresh your memory on the main points.

In addition, there are some tips which can help you in the specific context of giving presentations, so do not overlook these:

(a) Relate to the audience: look at people, ask if they can hear you at the back

(b) Speak clearly and avoid the temptation to speak too quickly. Remember that although you may feel that you know your script backwards, the audience may be grappling with the concepts you are introducing for the first time. You must give them time to absorb what you are saying.

(c)   Don't walk through or stand in the beam of an overhead projector while it is switched on: your shadow will be projected onto the screen, and it is not usually flattering

(d)   Don't read your notes out loud: if you think that you are likely to do that, make small cards instead with the key points, and use them as an aide memoire

(e)   Try to respond to your audience: if their expressions are becoming glazed, try to vary the speed of your delivery and the intonation, or ask a question in general terms to stimulate interest

8 Taking questions

The Information Pack guidelines refer to the fact that you should be prepared to answer questions and provide explanations when requested. If you do not want to be interrupted during the presentation (which does create a risk that you will be put off your flow) you should say at the beginning that you will be happy to take questions at the end.

Inviting or accepting questions can be a helpful – if slightly nerve-wracking – part of a presentation.

(a)   In informative presentations, questions offer an opportunity to **clarify** any misunderstandings, **or gaps** that the audience may have perceived.

(b)   In persuasive presentations, questions offer an opportunity to **address and overcome** specific doubts or resistance that the audience may have, which the speaker may not have been able to anticipate.

8.1 Tackling questions

The manner in which you **field questions** may be crucial to your credibility. Everyone knows you have prepared your **presentation** carefully: ignorance, bluster or hesitation in the face of a question may cast doubt on your expertise, or sincerity, or both. Moreover, this is usually the last stage of the presentation, and so leaves a **lasting impression**.

The only way to tackle questions effectively is to **anticipate** them. Put yourself in your audience's shoes, or, more specifically, in the shoes of an ignorant member of the audience and a hostile member of the audience and a member of the audience with a particular axe to grind: what questions might **they** ask and why? When questions arise, listen to them carefully, assess the questioner's manner, and draw the questioner out if necessary, in order to ascertain exactly **what** is being asked, and **why**. People might ask questions:

(a)   To **seek additional information** of particular interest to them, or to the group – if you have left it out of your talk

(b)   To **seek clarification** of a point that is not clear

(c)   To **add information** of their own, which may be relevant, helpful and accurate – or not

(d)   To **lead the discussion** into another area (or away from an uncomfortable one)

(e)   To **display** their own knowledge or cleverness

(f)   To **undermine** the speaker's authority or argument, to 'catch him out'

If you have anticipated questions of the first two kinds (a) and (b) in the planning of your talk, they should not arise: incorporate the answers in your outline.

8.2 How to answer

The important points about answering questions are as follows.

(a) You may seek **feedback** throughout your talk, as to whether your message is getting across clearly – and it is common to **invite the audience** to let you know if anything is unclear – but by and large, you should encourage questions only at the **end** of your presentation. That way, disruptive, rambling, hostile and attention-seeking questions will not be allowed to **disrupt** your message to the audience as a whole.

(b) You should **add or clarify information** if required to achieve your purpose. An honest query deserves a co-operative answer.

(c) You need to maintain your **credibility and authority** as the speaker. **Strong tactics** may be required for you to stay in control, without in any way ridiculing or 'putting down' the questioner.

    (i) If a question is based on a false premise or incorrect information, **correct it**. An answer may, or may not, then be required.

    (ii) If a question is **rambling**: **interrupt**, clarify what the question, or main question (if it is a multiple query) is, and answer that. If it is completely irrelevant, say politely that it is outside the scope of the presentation: you may or may not offer to deal with it informally afterwards.

    (iii) If a question is **hostile** or argumentative, you may wish to show understanding of how the questioner has reached his conclusion, or why he feels as he does. However, you then need to reinforce, repeat or **explain your own view**.

    (iv) If a question tries to **pin you down** or 'corner' you on an area in which you do not wish to be specific, be **straightforward** about it.

    (v) If a question **exposes an area** in which you do not know the answer, **admit** your limitations with honesty and dignity, and invite help from members of the audience, if appropriate.

    (vi) Try and answer **all questions** with points **already made** in your presentation, or related to them. This reinforces the impression that your speech was in fact **complete and correct**.

(d) **Repeat** any question that you think might not have been audible to everyone in the room.

(e) **Clarify** any question that you think is lengthy, complex, ambiguous or uses jargon not shared by the audience as a whole.

(f) Answer **briefly**, keeping strictly to the point of the question (while relating it, if possible, to what you have already said). If your answer needs to be lengthy, structure it as you would a **small talk**: introduce what you are going to say, say it, then confirm what you have said!

(g) Keep an eye on the overall **time-limit** for your talk or for the question-and-answer session. **Move on** if a questioner is taking up too much time, and call a halt, courteously, when required.

'I'll take one more question ... ' or 'I'm afraid that's all we have time for' is standard practice which offends few listeners. Indeed, leaving an audience wishing there was time for more is a sign of their interest and your success: unanswered questions tend to be taken away with the listener, which may increase the impact of your message.

Exercise 2

When you have time, watch a television programme such as the BBC's Question Time or an equivalent political discussion programme in your own country. See how questions are fielded and dealt with. Politicians are very skilled in dealing with questions, but also look at how the host deals with both audience and guests. The whole show is based on questions. This is a very useful exercise for you.

Exercise 3

Here are two examples of questions and how they can be handled. Which response do you think is the more effective?

Example 1

Questioner: So do you think that there is no future for any of the business class only airlines?

Presenter: (*Laughing*) No, no, of course I don't think that's the case: that's a ridiculous suggestion. Of course some of them will survive, but......

Questioner: But what criteria would you apply for a successful business class only airline?

Presenter: Well the problem with them is that there is a long-term cash outflow, so of course the banks wonder when they'll start to see any return on their investment.

Example 2

Questioner: So do you think that there is no future for any of the business class only airlines?

Presenter: Of course that's the question which worries a lot of people at the moment, and it receives a lot of coverage in the press. I don't think that there is no future at all: rather I think that only the better ones will survive.

Questioner: But what criteria would you apply for such an airline to be successful?

Presenter: I think there are several criteria:
A clear feasible cashflow forecast
Realistic assumptions in the production of budgets
Definite clearcut financing agreements
Motivated management
Recognition of external factors, such as fuel prices

Answer

In Example 1, the presenter makes the unforgiveable mistake of patronising and ridiculing the questioner. The likely effect of this is to make the rest of the audience hostile and to detract from the overall impression given by the presentation. The presenter also fails to answer the question, and instead turns it back to his particular hobbyhorse.

In Example 2, the presenter manages to appear to compliment the questioner on the question, which will go down well with the audience, and also clearly answers the second question by producing a list of points.

9 Feedback

Many people find it very difficult to respond to feedback and make the best use of it, because it is usually viewed as a form of criticism. This is especially so when the feedback relates to a presentation as opposed to written work, as:

(a) It is more immediate, coming as it does straight after the presentation

(b) It seems more personal, because you will have put a great deal of highly personal effort into your presentation, which will have involved you standing alone in front of an audience

9.1 Feedback from the mentor

Remember that it is part of the role of the mentor to question you on the work done, and it is a critical part of his role to report to Oxford Brookes University that you have delivered a presentation and answered questions on it.

You should try to accept his comments in that very positive light, and take the view that they are helping you to achieve your ultimate goal, which is your degree in Applied Accounting.

If your mentor gives you constructive criticism, he or she is not saying that you are wrong in what you have said, or that your ideas are no good. The criticism is designed to help you to improve your presentational skills and it will be invaluable when drafting your Skills and Learning Statement, as you have to state what went well and what could have been improved.

If your mentor provides you with detailed suggestions as to how to do some aspect differently in the future, it will precisely fulfil one of the precise purposes of the Skills and Learning Statement. Your mentor will tell you whether your ideas have not come across properly, whether the sequence is not easy to follow or where the train of logical thought breaks down. It may be that you cannot see the wood for the trees, and have not realised that your arguments do not hang together. Without the mentor, you would not necessarily realise this, and you would not then achieve your full potential in the Research and Analysis Project.

9.2 Feedback from your peer group

The emphasis within the feedback from your peer group is likely to be different from that received from your mentor. Your peer group does not have a specific responsibility to report that you have completed the stages of the Research and Analysis Project. To put it at its most basic, the members of it are listening to your presentation because you will then be listening to theirs.

Whereas your mentor will be familiar with your thought processes and the content of your Research Project from the two previous meetings, your peer group will have had no prior knowledge of it. This will mean that their feedback will probably concentrate on the mechanics of your presentation (audibility, confidence, effective use of visual aids) rather than the technical content.

This can be as useful as the more measured feedback from your mentor. When writing up your Skills and Learning Statement, you must consider all aspects of the presentation and scope for improvement. Members of the peer group are likely to reflect upon the quality of your presentation in the light of their own, so that they come up with more practical points.

When receiving peer group feedback, bear in mind that they are learning from the process too, as you will learn from watching their presentation and providing feedback on it to them.

Chapter roundup

- You are required to prepare and deliver a fifteen minute presentation as part of your Research and Analysis Project.

- The key to a successful presentation is planning, of both the content and also the physical logistics of delivering the presentation.

- The way in which you deliver your presentation can be almost as important as what you actually say.

- Taking questions and responding to feedback are an important part of the procedure.

Part D:

The Research Project

chapter 11

INTRODUCTION

Having done all of your planning, research and analysis, you may now feel that you are facing the hardest task of all, which is to write the Research Project. You need not worry: once you have started (which is the hardest step of all) you should find that all your preparatory work will fall into place and you will produce the report with relative ease.

However, there are certain skills attached to report writing, and this chapter aims to familiarise you with them. They are critical, as one of the criteria for assessment set out in the Information Pack guidelines is a pass in communication skills.

The Information Pack guidelines recommend the following format for the Research Project.

TITLE PAGE

CONTENTS PAGE

PART 1
PROJECT OBJECTIVES AND OVERALL RESEARCH APPROACH – 1,000 words

PART 2
INFORMATION GATHERING AND ACCOUNTING/BUSINESS TECHNIQUES – 1,500 words

PART 3
RESULTS, ANALYSIS, CONCLUSIONS AND RECOMMENDATIONS – 4,000 words

LIST OF REFERENCES

APPENDICES

1 Establishing the structure of the Research Project

The **structure** of your Research Project can make all the difference between passing and failing.

(a)   A confidently presented, sensibly structured and well laid out Research Project will attract the approval of the assessor, who will be far more likely to look favourably upon your efforts.

(b)   A scrappy and ill thought out Research Project, on the other hand, will mean that the assessor is more likely subconsciously to think that such poor presentation reflects poor preparation and confused thinking.

The external examiner has commented that candidates have failed the project because they have failed to follow the structure set out in the Information Pack guidelines. It is not sufficient just to describe the topic without the related analysis.

1.1 Overall design of the Research Project

The Information Pack guidelines set out the requirements.

(a)   Overall structure for the main body of the Research Project. This is as follows.

TITLE PAGE
CONTENTS PAGE

1.   Project objectives and overall research approach – 1,000 words
2.   Information gathering and accounting/business techniques – 1,500 words
3.   Results, analysis, conclusions and recommendations – 4,000 words

LIST OF REFERENCES
APPENDICES

(b)   Word count and appendices

You must stay within the maximum word count as Oxford Brookes University reserves the right to fail Research Projects which contain more than the maximum 6,500 words.

The 6,500 word limit **excludes** the

*   Title page
*   Contents page
*   List of References
*   Appendices

The 6,500 word count also **excludes**

*   Words used in tables and graphs and other forms of data presentation.

Note that section headings are **included** in the 6,500 word count.

Page 1: Title page

Title
Author
Date
Word count

An example is shown below:

Oxford Brookes University

Research and Analysis Project

The effects of technological change on staffing costs in organisation XYZ

By: Paul Smith

October 20X8

6,488 words

1.2 Page 2: Contents

Table of contents

Outline the contents of the Research Project in numbered sections

Here is an example. Note that this is indicative only.

Contents	Page no.
Introduction	
1 Terms of reference	X
Information gathering	
2 Primary sources	X
3 Secondary sources	X
4 Analysis	X
5 Conclusion	X
Appendix A – questionnaire	
Appendix B – spreadsheet	

1.3 Pages 3 and 4: Part 1 – Project objectives and overall research approach

You are limited to 1,000 words in Part 1 and you must be quite rigorous in observing this. This part will set the scene and will include

- the reasons for choosing your topic
- your objectives and research questions
- your research approach.

Here is an example taken from a student project on the communication of company environmental data and the use of environmental cost accounting and environmental performance indicators.

BPP
LEARNING MEDIA

1.4 Example

Introduction

1   **Reasons for choosing topic area and overall research approach**

I chose to study the topic of environmental disclosure because I am aware of 'green' issues gaining increasing importance through media exposure and environmental events. This is filtering through to businesses where a rise in interest and concern about the environment has been reflected in new demands for information (Butler, 1992). The Advisory Committee on Business and the Environment (1996) explain:

'Deeper knowledge of a business's environmental performance would help analysts, fund managers and other key players to form more accurate judgements of its risk profile and worth.' (pp36). However, the 'Business and the Environment' journal (August 1997) indicates that this is not as straightforward as may first appear: 'In less than a generation, society will look back at the availability of environmental performance information today and be amazed at the gaps, clutter and noise.' (pp 4) This hints that a study in this area will provide several issues for discussion.

This project will focus on environmental impact disclosures made by companies to external audiences. I will achieve this by analysing the current state of environmental reporting which will then be taken one step further by introducing two methods of disclosing such information and the benefits they may achieve.

2   **Aims and objectives of the project**

My project will attempt to solve the following concerns.

- How and why companies currently disclose their environmental impact information, including a consideration of:

    (1)   The methods utilised
    (2)   The extent of the data content
    (3)   The vehicle of communication used for this distribution and its effectiveness
    (4)   The audience they are aiming at
    (5)   Their motivations for disclosing
    (6)   The influence wider accountability has on their motivations – if any

- Does the management cost accounting tool of activity based costing lend itself to be adapted to environmental cost disclosure and help external readers understand a company's environmental situation?

- Do environmental performance indicators, as a form of environmental reporting, help external readers understand a company's environmental situation?

- Which of ABC or EPIs offer a better foundation for company environmental disclosure?

- Is a standard environmental disclosure methodology possible? If so, what barriers will be incurred?

Note that this is just a brief which is indicative and not intended to reflect the actual word count required. Here is another example of a slightly more 'chatty' style, on the contribution of reward systems to company success.

1.5 Example

Introduction

This project evolved from a year's work in the statistics and finance department in Q Ltd. During the year I spent much of my time analysing sales and contribution figures for individual areas and for the whole company. The other half of my job was to calculate commission payments each month and to authorise bonuses.

I was particularly interested in how the accounting and control systems within Q Ltd influenced behaviour and in turn what result these changes in behaviour had on the firm. At the same time as this it was clear that Q Ltd was experiencing deteriorating sales and declining contribution.

Therefore I set myself the aim to explore how effective different reward systems (which require accounting and control systems to operate) have been and could be used in improving sales performance, contribution and ultimately the profit of the company. Conclusions are hard to prove but theory, opinion and logic can lead to some recommendations.

Structure of the report

Initially a chapter on the theory of reward systems will set the foundation for comments made throughout the text. Next, a short chapter on the structure and performance of Q Ltd should help the reader to understand and appreciate later references to the company in the main body of the project.

Rewards for salesmen will then be analysed in the next chapter. This will include a section on targets, due to their function as a basis for rewarding salesmen. Several pay schemes will be analysed in Chapter 6 followed by a short chapter on competitions and incentives.

Chapter 8 will discuss how managers and executives are rewarded. After a short introduction, a section on the theory of truth inducing incentives will help reveal the behavioural problems which can arise in setting targets. Management pay schemes within Q Ltd will then be looked at followed by a longer section on executive incentives.

All these points will be brought together in the concluding chapter.

1.6 Information gathering

This section will include the sources of information you used, and explain why you used them. It will explain the methods used to gather the information. It will explain where your conclusions have come from. The Information Pack guidelines include this because one of the purposes of the Research and Analysis Project is to demonstrate your ability to gather information and then apply that information.

It is possible to show how information has been gathered in a tabular format, if the subject matter warrants it. If, for example, your report is examining results or activities over a period of time, and your work is carried out alongside, it could be a time and word-effective way of explaining what you have done to present it as a chart.

1.7 Example

Monthly progress	Sept	Oct	Nov	Dec	Jan	Feb	Mar	Apr	May
Project proposal									
Preliminary research									
Exploratory interview									
Further interviews (× 4)									
Primary research									
Findings analysed									
Written report									

As you have seen in earlier chapters, there are two types of information: primary information and secondary information.

(a) Primary information is data which is collected specifically for a given project, for example the management accounts of the particular company you are writing about.

(b) Secondary information is that which can also be used for some purpose other than the specific task in hand, for example statistics for an industry in general. Secondary information can be regarded more as background information.

You need to consider in what order you will present the information you have obtained. If you need to set the scene and provide background information for the industry you are dealing with, and then move on to the precise results of the company under scrutiny, you should discuss your secondary information first. If, however, you are taking specific information relating to one company, and extrapolating or applying it elsewhere, then it may be better to present the primary information first.

We set out here an example, taken from a dissertation on performance measurement, which shows what information gathering techniques were used.

1.8 Example

Description of methods used to gather information

This describes in detail the procedure under which the research into this project was carried out. The research was broken down into two distinct sections – secondary research and primary research.

(a) **Secondary research**

The secondary research consisted of two different methods.

(i) **Conventional library research**. Reading through both books and journals, sorting out materials which covered operations management and management accounting areas, and following up references with various libraries. Facilities used for obtaining this data included: Oxford Brookes University, public libraries (ie Slough Central Library) and inter-library loan facilities (ie Thames Valley University).

(ii) **Electronic research**. Searching through a variety of business related databases such as Searchbank, Financial Times, Economist and ABI. This initially proved to be a relatively quick way of finding and providing up-to-date information. However, it took considerable time to find articles with relevant data. The search yielded approximately fifty articles (1996-1999) drawn from journals in five disciplines: performance, measurement, dealer performance measurement (motor industry), forklift truck industry, balanced scorecard and customer satisfaction measurement. Once the information was found, this proved to be a very successful research method. Consequently, secondary research enabled the writer to achieve the project objectives in several ways.

Firstly, it helped guide the writer in building up a good knowledge of the subject. An effective performance measurement model therefore could be devised.

Secondly, it was also used as justification to evaluate the HDPMS critically in the Data Analysis section.

(b) **Primary research**

Primary data were obtained through the company's internal materials and interviews.

Internal materials. Corporate literature and internal reports were kindly provided by a number of Z plc departments such as Dealer Development, Finance, Marketing and Credit Control. The internal materials consisted of Z plc Annual Reports, Z plc Dealer Annual Business Plan, Z plc European Project List Reviews, Customer Support Surveys and Monthly Awareness Reports.

The internal data was utilised to examine the present HDPMS. This information was the foundation of the findings chapter (Chapter 4).

1.9 Results and analysis

This is the most important part of the Research Project, as it will contain the real meat of your argument.

The main content of the Research Project should follow numbered sections and numbered paragraphs, in the same sort of style as this textbook.

Each section should begin on a new sheet of paper. This makes it easier if you subsequently amend an early section at a later stage, as you will avoid having to repaginate the whole thing. Write on one the side of the paper only.

Page ?: Conclusions

In the conclusion you are asked to present your findings, and use your judgement as to what the data means. The conclusion should be supported by the arguments in your report. The Information Pack guidelines state that a grade A can be achieved by a report which can engage the reader in a professional manner and produce a relevant and coherent report in an appropriate structure.

To force yourself to ensure your conclusions are backed up by evidence, refer to relevant paragraph numbers in the main body of the report.

1.10 Example

Report

1   Meldarks Ltd's ROCE has fallen from 15% to 10% in the past five years.

2   Net cash flows have switched from a net inflow of £3m to a net outflow of £0.5m.

3   Meldarks Ltd has kept buildings in the accounts at historical cost even though they are worth a lot more on a market value basis.

Conclusion

Meldarks' deteriorating ROCE (para 1) is made to look less obvious by low fixed asset valuations (para 3). This and the deteriorating cash flow (para 2) suggest that the company is in difficulties.

1.11 Pages ? to ?: Appendices

Put into the appendices anything the user does not have to know immediately to understand the contents of the Research Project. The most obvious item to put into an appendix is the spreadsheet.

Appendices may also include:

- Calculations underpinning your narrative
- Facts of borderline relevance (but you should not have too many of those!)

1.12 Example

Text	Appendices
Over the past three years, reported ROCE has increased from X% to Y% largely as a result of the financial engineering: the continued use of fully depreciated fixed assets and a policy of non replacement (See Appendix A).	Here could go detailed calculations for the past three years, with workings to show how it is lower asset valuation rather than increased operating performance that has caused the improvement.

Remember that the appendices are limited to 8 sides, excluding any extracts from financial statements, so you must be selective about their contents. Restrict yourself to the **spreadsheet** which you must produce, and maybe one other.

Make sure that your appendices make sense, and are not just jumbled workings with no logical structure. Otherwise their impact will be lost and you will derive no benefit from producing them.

2 Planning the detailed contents

This can be one of the most time-consuming tasks in producing a report such as this, but it is worth taking as much time as you need and not rushing. Much will depend on the extent to which you managed to organise your information at the information gathering and analysis stages. Once a detailed plan has been produced, the rest of the Research Project should slot into place.

Sometimes, you may be completely at a loss, so here are some basic rules.

2.1 Basic rule 1: look at the requirement

If you think that the **requirement** falls into **logical parts**, allocate separate sections for each requirement.

2.2 Basic rule 2: think of a structure

If you need to follow a line of reasoning, **identify the most logical way of making the data clear**.

If you are at a loss for ideas, then structure your requirements in a sensible and logical order based on, for example:

- Functions of the business (eg sales, marketing)
- Timescale
- Balanced scorecard categories
- Markets and customer bases
- Strategic business units

2.3 Basic rule 3: plan what you want to say

One approach is to jot down all the things you want to say as a series of headings, with perhaps a little expansion of some points. Then look at them together and, by experiment if necessary, put them into a logical order by putting numbers against each. Only if you are very certain that your thoughts are logical and coherent should you omit putting them on paper as a plan – apart from any other reason, you are likely to forget vital material if you do not have a plan.

You might try writing 'network' notes to present your headings visually (see the diagram).

A network note

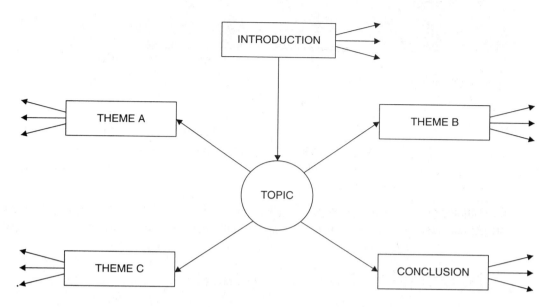

2.4 Basic rule 4: separate pages for new sections

Start each section on a separate piece of paper. This means that you can alter some sections without having to repaginate all the other ones.

2.5 Basic rule 5: number every paragraph

Give each section a number, and number every paragraph in that section in a hierarchy, like the paragraph numbering in this textbook. This makes cross-referencing very easy.

3 Format

The Research and Analysis Project will be assessed and graded as either a pass from grades A to C or a fail. Here is a table which shows the criteria on which presentation will be judged for each grade.

Research Project	Pass – grade A	Pass – grade B	Pass – grade C	Fail – grade F
Technical and professional skills				
Understanding of accountancy/business models	Highly appropriate choice of theory/concepts. Very clear relevance and shows evidence of wider reading.	Appropriate choice of theory/concepts. Significant evidence of understanding.	Some, but limited, choice and use of theory/concepts. Some evidence of understanding.	Poor choice of theory/concepts, very limited understanding. Reliance of narrow range of material.
Application of accountancy/business models	Insightful and critical application of models to the project topic.	Mostly correct application of theory to the project topic.	Some application of theory, but lacking a coherent approach.	Poor use of theory/models and confused understanding of application.

Research Project	Pass – grade A	Pass – grade B	Pass – grade C	Fail – grade F
Technical and professional skills				
Evaluation of information, analysis and conclusions	High level of critical thought shown in the analysis and a rigorous approach to the evaluation of information.	Strength shown in some areas of critical review of the information. Good evaluation of information.	Some analysis but a tendency towards description rather than analysis and evaluation.	Descriptive and lacking in analysis. Inaccuracies. Little or no critical evaluation.
Presentation of project findings	Can engage reader in a professional manner and produce a relevant and coherent project report with appropriate structure.	Can communicate effectively in a format appropriate to the report. Clear and concise manner with all relevant information.	Some communication is effective. Can report practical applications in a structured way.	Communication is only partially effective and project is poorly structured.

Exercise 1

Here is a paragraph containing some facts about Carnelian Ltd, in no particular order. This paragraph illustrates two things.

- It will show you quite how irritating unstructured and unformatted data is to read and make sense of. The marker may be under time pressure, so don't annoy him or her.

- It introduces you to the concept of format and structure.

Carnelian Ltd was founded over a century ago. 50% of its sales are exports to Germany. It has two principal shareholders, Ms Underwood and Mr Mongrove, who each own 50% of the issued share capital. Net assets are £150,000. The company specialises in making artificial flowers for sale. The Finance Director is Mr Mace. There are 20 employees, of whom five are employed in marketing (reporting to Ms Underwood). The production department reports to Mr Mongrove. Turnover per annum is £1m. Issued share capital is 1,000 ordinary shares of £1 each. The company used to market by mail order, but now mainly promotes itself through its website. The two people who work in accounts and the IT expert report to Mr Mace. The best selling flower is the silk orchid accounting for 30% of turnover. Profit before tax was £50,000 in 20X1. No one customer accounts for more than 1% of turnover.

Required

Produce a report about Carnelian Ltd incorporating all the data above.

Answer

You could have chosen a number of different formats. At the very least, you could have organised the data in logical order.

Report

To: The marker
From: A Candidate
Date:

Re: Carnelian Ltd

Contents

1   Summary
2   Products and markets
3   Organisation and management
4   Financial position

Appendix A: customers
Appendix B: financial position

1   Summary

1.1   Carnelian Ltd is a long established, privately owned company specialising in the manufacture of artificial flowers for sale worldwide, employing a functional departmentation structure.

2   Products and markets

2.1   Turnover from artificial flowers is £1m per annum.
2.2   £300,000 derives from one product, the silk orchid.
2.3   Exports to Germany account for 50% of turnover.
2.4   No one customer accounts for 1% of turnover. See Appendix A for a list of customers.
2.5   The main marketing activity is the website, which has replaced mail order.

3   Organisation and management

3.1   The company employs 23 people, including the directors.

3.2   The company is divided into three departments.

- Marketing – 5 personnel reporting to Ms Underwood.
- Production – 12 personnel reporting to Mr Mongrove.
- Finance and IT – three personnel reporting to Mr Mace.

4   Financial position and capital structure

4.1   The company makes a profit margin of 5% and a return of assets of 33%. See Appendix B for workings.

4.2   The sole shareholders are Ms Underwood and Mr Mongrove, each of whom own 500 of the issued share capital of 1,000 ordinary shares of £1 each.

Appendix A

List of customers

Appendix B: financial position

B.1   Profit margin

Profit £50,000/turnover £1m = 5%

B.2	ROCE
	£50,000/£150,000 = 33%; Turnover: £1m
	Net assets £150,000

Comment on the answer

You will note that the very requirement to produce a report structuring the data suggested some useful analysis such as calculating ROCE and profit margins. We are not saying that this is perfect by any means, but you can tell that the data about Carnelian Ltd is much easier to grasp than it was before. You may have chosen a different structure of course.

4 Different audiences

Before you start to write the Research Project itself, you should consider the **style and tone which you should adopt**. This may depend on the identity of the potential readers of the Research Project.

(a)   The main readers of your project will be the different individuals involved in the marking and moderation of Oxford Brookes projects. This may include the first marker, a project moderator, the BSc programme director and the Oxford Brookes project external examiner. The purpose of the marking and moderation processes is to reach an agreed view of the standards you have achieved in your project.

(b)   You will also be required to make a presentation on your Research Project to your mentor, and probably also your peer group of other candidates, where your mentor has more than one student. Techniques for preparation and presentation to your mentor and peer group were covered in Chapter 10, but you should bear in mind that you may be **supplying your audience with extracts from your Research Project, and consider this when writing it**.

4.1 Project markers and moderators

Oxford Brookes employs a number of appropriately qualified individuals to mark and moderate Research and Analysis Projects. Many teach accounting, finance and business subjects in UK higher education institutions including Oxford Brookes. Others are professional qualified accountants from a range of business backgrounds. You can assume that markers and moderators do not need to have general technical terms explained in your project.

However, you should think carefully about the subject matter of your Research Project. You may have to provide more background material or explanation of terms in the following circumstances.

(a)   You will prepare your project on a specific organisation. You may have to provide additional information about the organisation itself in order to give the markers and moderators enough background to understand the context of your project work.

(b)   If you decide to use a specialist financial or statistical technique, then you should define and explain any terminology specific to your approach. It is very important to put this in the context of your report and explain how it has been applied to the organisation which is the focus of your project.

(c)   There may be factors or circumstances specific to your own country that have had a strong influence or impact on your project work and findings. You should give a brief explanation of these issues in your Research Project.

5 Language

When starting your research work and planning for your Project, you may feel that 6,500 words is a lot, and wonder how you will manage to produce that much. By the time you come to write it, you may wonder how you are going to manage to say everything you need to within only 6,500 words, especially given the breakdown given by the Information Pack. This allows you

(a)   Up to 1,000 words for the project objectives and overall research approach
(b)   Up to 1,500 words for the information gathering and accounting / business techniques
(c)   Up to 4,000 words for the results, analysis, conclusions and recommendations

Remember that these figures are a maximum number allowed. If you consider that the word count for this chapter alone is 7,195, you will appreciate that 6,500 is not a very great number.

One way to keep your word count under tight control is to be as efficient as possible in your use of language. Practise the use of concise and precise language in all your written work, not just the Research Project.

5.1 Stylistic requirements

There are certain stylistic requirements in the writing of reports, formal or informal.

Coupled with this, you may have time management problems with your writing. In the context of this Research Project, however, you do have the luxury of taking as much time as you need, unlike in your ACCA exams.

Consider the following actual extract from an exam script submitted for a past exam paper for the Chartered Institute of Marketing (Pearson, 1993). Note in particular the writing times.

(a)   Proposals for change in the organisational structure.

(b)   Creation of 'strategic business units' centred around each terminal

This would allow each terminal to be represented at board level with each manager having his own operational and commercial staff beneath him. This will involve a huge restructuring of the organisation and individual job roles/responsibilities, however this move is necessary in order that commercial and operations staff work alongside each other and cooperate to solve problems in the most effective way, to the benefit of EAL in serving the needs of its customers. All commercial versus operations conflicts would be solved lower down the hierarchy which will in turn be flattened out as a result of restructuring. Each terminal general manager must have beneath him his appropriate support staff for his commercial and operations roles eg catering manager, retail operations manager, quality control engineers.'

Total words = c 140   **Total writing time = 8 minutes**

Keeping the same heading we might change the section to read as follows.

Each terminal to become an SBU under a general manager with his own support staff (catering, retail operations, quality control etc).

BENEFIT

Although requiring much restructuring and reformulation of job descriptions:

(a)   Commercial and operations staff would work together in meeting the needs of the customer
(b)   All commercial v operations conflicts would be solved lower down the hierarchy
(c)   Each terminal would be represented at board level

Total words = c 70   **Total writing time = 4 minutes**

The re-wording cuts the original word length in half.

- It is **easier to understand and mark**.
- **It takes half the time to write, leaving you more time to think and to make extra points**.
- It takes up less of your precious ration of words.

5.2 Basic principle: 'Less is more'

Rule	Example		
	No		**Yes**
Keep words simple	Expenditure	vs	Cost
	Aggregate	vs	Total
Short words are quicker to write	Terminate	vs	End
Avoid words you don't need to write	I would be grateful		Please
	Due to the fact that		Because
	In the not too distant future		Soon (better: give a time scale)
	At this point in time		Now (or currently)
	In the majority of instances		In most cases (or usually)
	It is recommended that A Ltd should consider		A Ltd should consider
	36 words (55 syllables)		14 words (18 syllables)

5.3 Jargon

Be **careful** of jargon: jargon is **technical language with a precise meaning** and therefore has its uses. Keep in mind the needs and likely response of your audience. Do not try to blind the assessor with technological jargon. If you do, the assessor may question whether you understand it yourself.

Be precise. Be careful of 'very' 'fairly' 'partly', unless you are unable to state facts.

Avoid patronising language

(a)   There is a fine line between explaining technical vocabulary or situations which may not be familiar to the reader, and 'dumbing down'. By that we mean reducing the level of your writing to something well below the assumed competence of your audience.

(b)   You do not need to explain routine technical terms. You can assume that your audience has a reasonable awareness of factors such as the current state of the domestic and international economy, the debate over the UK's adoption of the euro, the advance of e-commerce, increasing fuel and food prices and so forth.

(c)   Your meetings with your mentor and your presentation could provide a suitable forum for you to discuss the style of language which you have adopted. You could receive some constructive feedback.

5.4 Spelling and grammar checkers

The Research and Analysis Project is designed to enable you to demonstrate your IT skills, among others. The main means of doing this is to show that you have accessed online information, and that you have used a spreadsheet or other software. However, you should remember that there are other IT tools which can help you, and which you will be expected to use.

The spelling and grammar checker is one of the most useful elements in a word processing package, and can help both the poor speller and the clumsy typist. It is similar in most packages. If you are working in Word, click on Tools and then Spelling and Grammar, and Word will work right through your document seeing if the spelling matches the spelling of words in the computer's dictionary. If not, it will suggest alternatives from which you click on the best one to replace what you have typed.

For example, if you have typed 'drp' the choices you are offered include 'drip', 'drop', 'dry' and 'dip'. You also have the option to add what you have typed to the computer's dictionary, so that unusual technical or foreign words are not thrown up repeatedly.

You must bear in mind, however, that the **spellchecker will only pick up words which do not match an entry in the computer's dictionary**: it will not recognise the fact that you have merely typed in the wrong word, for example 'from' instead of 'form'. Take care also if you are an overseas candidate whose spelling and grammar checker is set to another language, including one of the nine variations of English included in many standard word processing packages. As the Research Project must be written in English, you should set the spellchecker to UK English.

You still need to read through what you have written, for sense and correct language. Some people like to do this on the screen at the end of each section or paragraph, while others prefer to print out at intervals and read the hard copy. It really does not matter which you do, as long as you do one of them.

Having reached the stage you have in your academic and professional careers, your standard of grammar should be quite high. Most spellcheckers also incorporate a grammar check which is still useful as it enables you to stand back and see the wood from the trees.

The grammar check will perform tasks such as:

(a)   Detecting sentences where you have omitted the verb

(b)   Detecting sentences where you have used mixed singular and plural subject and verb (for example 'two of the main reasons for the development of the multinational company is ....'.)

(c)   Indicating sentences which are unduly long or have too many clauses, potentially confusing the reader

You can specify in the grammar check what style of language you are using, such as 'casual' 'technical' and 'standard'. You can also use a grammar option that gives the readability statistics of your work. This is a useful tool in that it can indicate when your language is becoming over obscure.

Thesaurus

If you think your use of words is becoming repetitive, try the thesaurus. This will suggest alternatives and can also supply meanings.

6 Example report

This is an example of a report compiled from given data. It is obviously shorter than the one you will be expected to produce, and there is far less data to deal with, but it will give you a good illustration in miniature of the way in which information can be used to produce a report.

You are the management accountant of a company which specialises in producing dairy products for the slimming market. The results of your latest research have just been published.

Data

Market Research Results

This research was carried out from January to June 2002, using in-depth interviews in the respondents' homes, recorded on tape and interpreted by ourselves, 'The XYZ Research Agency', specialists in market research for the food industry.

Sample size: 500
Age range: 15-55
Socio-economic groups: ABC1*
Locations: Bristol, Manchester and Greater London
Sex: Males and Females

Three broad categories were tested and the results are as follows:

	% of respondents with weight problems mentioning
Motives for wanting to lose weight	
To feel good physically	68
For health reasons	67
To stay fit	43
Because I want to live longer	25
To stay mentally alert	23
To be more attractive	21
To be more popular	15
Methods for weight control	
Avoid certain foods, eat 'slimming items'	32
Eat and drink less	23
Play sports, keep 'fit'	22
'Have certain diet days'	7
Take medicines, stimulants	3
Food which people dislike giving up	
Cakes, pies, bakery products	31
Sweets, sugar	23
Beer, alcoholic beverages	17
Meat, sausages etc	15
Chocolate	13
Cream	9
Fruit juices	9
Potatoes	9
Pasta	9

In general, the comments also revealed that dieting means a loss of pleasure at mealtimes, causes problems when one can't eat the same as the family and also one is regarded as being 'ill' when dieting.

* Socio-economic groupings:

A   Higher managerial, Chief Executives etc.
B   Managerial, Executives etc
C1 Higher clerical, Supervisory etc

Required

Write a short formal report to the Marketing Director, Mr David Forsythe, highlighting the conclusions drawn from this research. Your recommendation will be used to help identify new products for possible development in this market.

Suggested answer

To: Marketing Director
From: Management Accountant
Date:

REPORT ON NEW PRODUCT DEVELOPMENT

1   Summary
2   Methods of research
3   Findings

1   Summary

This report highlights the conclusions drawn from market research into the 'slimming market' conducted by The XYZ Research Agency between January and June 2002. The report, to include recommendations for possible new product development and new promotion methods was requested by Mr David Forsythe, Marketing Director.

2   Method of research

2.1   This report has been compiled from research findings designed to show:

(a)   Respondents' motives for losing weight
(b)   Respondents' methods of weight control
(c)   Foods which respondents were reluctant to give up

2.2   Respondents were a sample group of 500 ABC1s aged 15-55 of both sexes in the Bristol, Manchester and Greater London areas. In-depth interviews were recorded in the respondents' homes, and analysed by XYZ Research: see Appendix A.

3   Findings

3.1   **Motives for losing weight (see Appendix A)**

Most respondents expressed their motives for losing weight as the desire for physical well-being (68%), health (67%) and fitness (43%), with related concerns, such as longevity and mental alertness, also scoring over 20%.

Perhaps unexpectedly, the motives most commonly associated with 'slimming' – increased attractiveness and popularity – scored comparatively low, with 21% and 15% respectively.

3.2   **Methods of weight control (see Appendix B)**

The most frequently-stated method of weight control (32%) was based on food selection: consuming 'slimming items' and avoiding certain foods. Reduced consumption in general (23%) and increased physical activity (22%) featured strongly, however, compared to the use of medicines and stimulants, mentioned by only 3% of respondents.

3.3   **Foods respondents disliked giving up (see Appendix C)**

A significant proportion of respondents were reluctant to give up foods in the high-calorie 'snack' categories: cakes, pies and bakery products (31%), sweets and sugar (23%). Alcohol (17%), meat (15%) and chocolate (13%) also featured significantly, compared to the more 'healthy' food groups such as fruit juice, potatoes and pasta (9% each). Cream was the only dairy product mentioned, (9%).

3.4   **General comments**

Respondents experienced 'dieting' as a loss of pleasure, an inconvenience when it comes to family meals, and a social stigma.

4   **Conclusions**

The prime reason for losing weight was health and fitness, mainly achieved through regulated food intake and increased activity. However, respondents felt deprived in general by the dieting process, and particularly disliked giving up snack foods and food generally regarded as 'unhealthy': processed foods, high in fats and sugars, low in fibre.

APPENDIX A: MOTIVES FOR WEIGHT LOSS

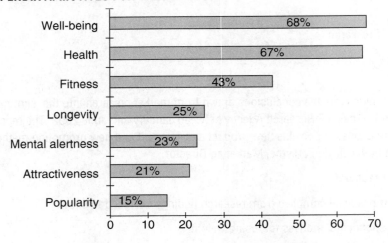

% of respondents with weight problems who mentioned each motive

APPENDIX B: METHODS OF WEIGHT CONTROL

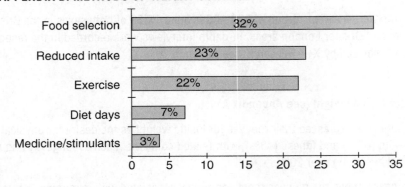

% of respondents with weight problems who mentioned each method

APPENDIX C: FOODS WHICH PEOPLE DISLIKE GIVING UP

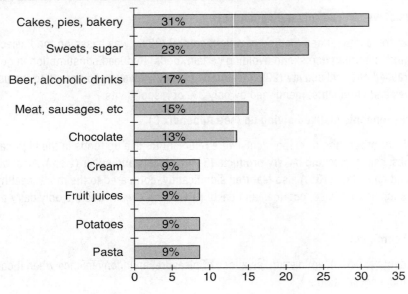

% of respondents with weight problems who mentioned each food

Debrief. What did you think of the report? Note that the report writer had constructed a graph of the data. You are required to submit a spreadsheet as part of your Research Project, but don't forget other ways of making your points clear, such as graphs and diagrams.

7 Referencing, citation and attribution of source material

The Information Pack guidelines explain how to reference your information sources.

- **Clear and accurate referencing**

    This is very important for Part 2 of your project i.e. the information gathering section.

- **Referencing of appropriate sources of information**

    Very clear guidance on references is provided in Appendix 3 of the Information Pack guidelines. The information is set out again here.

Guidance on referencing and constructing a List of References is given below partly extracted from Appendix 3 of the Information Pack.

Appendix 3: HOW TO REFERENCE YOUR WORK

This is an introduction to how to reference your work. You should read the full Oxford Brookes document "A guide to citing and referencing for Business School students" which is published on the ACCA BSc degree webpages.

Referencing

Whenever you are directly quoting or referring to one of your sources of information, you should acknowledge this in the text as you go along. References should be clearly set out using the Harvard System. It is important to double check that all references in your text appear in the List of References.

List of References

Your List of References comes at the end of your Report. It is a list of all the sources you have used in compiling your Report e.g. books, articles, company publications, newspaper articles etc. The List of References should be set out alphabetically using the Harvard System. It is not sufficient to merely include your sources of information in the List of References without including the proper reference in the text. Failure to do this will result in failure of the Research Project.

How to reference your work and construct a List of References

Correctly referencing your work is simple, and compulsory. You must reference all your sources of information. We do advise you to reference as you go along, rather than leaving it until the end of your research work. There is nothing more time consuming than constructing a List of References retrospectively.

References within your text

In the Harvard system references within the text are set out as follows:

Example

In any organisation made up of different interest groups some conflict over goals is inevitable (Needle, 1994).

In the List of References the reference shown above would appear in this way:

Example of a book reference

Needle, D. (1994) *Business in Context.* 2nd Edition, London, Chapman & Hall

NB: You only cite the edition if it is not the first. Please note that the title of the book is either underlined or emboldened.

Example of a journal or newspaper reference

Buxton, J. (1998) Management: The Growing Business: Co-operative's Wheels of Fortune. *The Financial Times*, February 24

NB: It's the title of the journal or newspaper that is either underlined or emboldened

Example of a journal article where no author is given

The Economist (1997) 'New technology is no snap', October 11, p125

Citing Electronic Sources

No standard agreed method has yet evolved for citing electronic sources. Electronic sources may include ftp sites, Telnet addresses, WWW and gopher pages, newsgroups and e-mail messages.

A simplified solution might be:

Author's last name, First name. Title of work. *Title of complete work if applicable in italics.* [protocol and address] [path] (date of message or visit).

Example

Walker, Janice R. MLA-Style Citations of Electronic Sources. http://www.columbia.edu/cu/cup/cgos/idx_basic.html (visited 1 April 2008)

You must observe these conventions, as the assessor will be looking for evidence of it. The logic is that in the main body of your Research Project you refer to anyone whose work you are quoting or using, for example (Smith, 2002). Should the reader want to know more about that point, or read the book itself, they can turn to the List of References to obtain full information about it. There it might be presented as

Smith, G. S. (2002) *Management Accounting Can Be Fun*, 3rd Edition, London, Business Book Publishers.

If you have a variety of sources, you may want to split them into categories for your List of References. A logical split might be:

(a)   **Direct references**: publications etc to which you have referred specifically in the text
(b)   **Further reading**: additional reading undertaken but not directly referred to in the text

Referencing correctly is also vital because it provides comfort that you have not plagiarised the work of anyone else. Whenever you mention thoughts or words of other people, you must attribute the source in the text and then give it in full in the List of References. The external examiner has commented that in some cases students don't use enough external references, and in others they don't reference them properly. This can cause you to fail the project.

You may see in one book you are reading a reference to a source that the author has used and you may want to refer to that source yourself. In such a situation, you should make every effort to find a copy of the quoted source, so that you can quote it directly. If that is not possible (for example it is out of print or your library cannot locate a copy to borrow for you) you can refer to the book as follows:

Raimond, P. (1993) *Management Projects,* London, Chapman and Hall. Cited in Saunders, M., Lewis, P. and Thornhill, A. (2000) *Research Methods for Business Students* 2nd Edition, Harlow, Financial Times Prentice Hall

This indicates clearly to the reader that you are citing something you have not read yourself, merely seen cited in another book. As far as possible you should try to obtain the original book and refer to it directly.

Chapter roundup

- Having completed this chapter, you should be able to establish the structure and form that your Research Project will take.

- You are best advised to keep to the limits outlined by Oxford Brookes University as a guide to structure.

- You will have time to pay careful attention to language and structure.

Part E:

The Skills and Learning Statement

chapter 12

The Skills and Learning Statement

INTRODUCTION

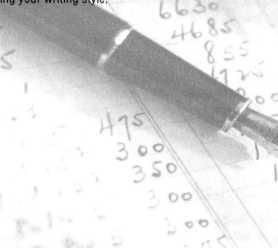

The Skills and Learning Statement is the second element of the Research and Analysis Project, and is as vital as the Research Project. Do not give in to the temptation of overlooking its importance, assuming that you do not need to do much work on it and treating it as an afterthought. The requirements for the Statement are very precise, and you may find it quite challenging to include all of the required components in the limited number of words permitted.

The Skills and Learning Statement also requires you to describe and then reflect upon the meetings with your mentor, and it will provide evidence to the University of your skills of communication and self-reflection. We will also consider the writing of the Skills and Learning Statement itself. Remember that it is quite a short document consisting of answers to four questions of approximately 500 words each, and you will need to be disciplined regarding your writing style.

1 Purpose and significance of the Skills and Learning Statement

The Information Pack guidelines give a lot of guidance on the preparation of the Skills and Learning Statement. The basic introduction is set out here.

> The Skills and Learning Statement (SLS) is the opportunity for you to demonstrate that you have developed the key 'graduate' skills of self-reflection and communication. You will provide evidence of self-reflection by answering a number of questions. Your communication skills will be developed through the preparation and delivery of a presentation to your Project Mentor. You will submit a copy of the PowerPoint presentation or overhead slides that you used in your presentation to your Project Mentor as evidence of skills development.
>
> Your SLS must be based on the following four questions:
>
> - What did you learn from the meetings with your Project Mentor, including the presentation that you gave to your Project Mentor?
>
> - How well do you think that you have answered your research question(s)?
>
> - How have you demonstrated your interpersonal and communication skills during the project work?
>
> - How has undertaking the RAP helped you in your accountancy studies and/or current employment role?

1.1 Purpose

The requirement to produce a Skills and Learning Statement (SLS) is included to ensure that you extract the maximum value from the preparation of the Research Project and from the Research and Analysis Project as a whole. Although the end requirement is a structured piece of writing, it encompasses evidence of skills such as preparation, questioning, listening, responding to questions, public presentation and self assessment.

Demonstration of these skills will show that you have not just the ability to write, but also to **communicate** in a variety of ways.

The University makes it clear that the production of the Skills and Learning Statement is to be a **learning process**. Much of the Statement you produce will consist of reflection on the process for the production of the Research Project. There is scope for identifying how you could have improved on aspects of this, for example what could have been improved in your presentation.

As part of the self-assessment process, you will be expected to exercise **honesty and integrity**, and identify your weak areas as well as your areas of strength. This critical self-evaluation is one of the essential procedures in gaining your degree.

1.2 Self reflection

One of the key graduate skills being tested in the Skills and Learning Statement is self reflection. So what is meant by self reflection? The Information Pack gives the following outline.

Self reflection, or critical reflection as it may also be called, is a key academic and professional skill. Reflection requires you to review and evaluate the experiences you have had and the learning you have acquired. You should note the emphasis on evaluation. Your Skills and Learning Statement should not be a description of what you did – it must be an evaluation of your experiences of doing your project work. You must try to make some meaning of what you have experienced, and make a judgement of how well you have achieved your objectives, and come to a conclusion about the value of undertaking your RAP.

Your evaluation should be honest. There is no model answer or right answer to any of these four questions. Not all your experiences will necessarily be positive, as things may not always go to plan or happen in the way that you might want them. Your evaluation should reflect on what actually happened, not an idealised version of what you might want Oxford Brookes to think did happen. We know that applied research can be messy and unsatisfying at times, though we strongly believe that what you learn from doing this research will be valuable to you. We hope this will be reflected in your Skills and Learning Statement.

1.3 Preparing your SLS answers

The Information Pack has the following to say about the preparation of your Skills and Learning Statement answers.

An important aspect of study or working life is to actively evaluate your own performance and to identify your own personal development needs. Have you achieved what you intended to achieve? If not, then why not and what do you need to do better in the future? You may have to work with others to achieve your work or study objectives and your ability to make the best use of your resources – and to communicate effectively – are important personal attributes. Your ACCA education will give you knowledge of accountancy and business, and undertaking research will enhance your practical skills. What have been the benefits for you of doing the RAP?

By answering the SLS questions you will gain some important personal insight into these issues. Although there are four questions with a total word limit of 2,000 words, you do not have to write exactly 500 words to answer each of the four questions. You may find that you want to write more about one or two particular questions. You may write between 350 and 650 words on each question within the total word limit of 2,000 words.

1.4 Assessment

The Information Pack gives the following guidelines.

Your Skills and Learning Statement will be assessed as 'satisfactory' or 'not satisfactory', it will not be given a grade. However you should give it equal importance to the Research Project since you must submit a 'satisfactory' SLS in order to pass the Research and Analysis Project overall.

To pass the 'self-reflection' component of the SLS, you have to make a reasonable attempt to address all of the four SLS questions. If you do not, then you will not pass the SLS. You must demonstrate your ability to reflect on the judgements that you have made and the actions that you have taken while undertaking your RAP work. We want to see you provide evidence that you recognise your strengths and weaknesses. If you only provide a description of what happened while you were doing your RAP, then you will not pass the SLS.

1.5 Skills required

The skills that must be evidenced for your Skills and Learning Statement to be satisfactory can be summarised as follows:

Skills and Learning Statement	Satisfactory	Not satisfactory
Self reflection	Makes a reasonable attempt to address all four questions. Shows ability to reflect on judgements made/actions taken during project work. Evidence of recognising own strengths and weaknesses.	Overly focused on only one or two questions. Emphasis on description of events, little evaluation of self-development etc. Little discussion of own strengths and weaknesses.
Communication skills	A copy of the presentation to the project mentor is included. Presentation has appropriate structure. Content is clearly linked to project report findings.	A copy of the presentation to project mentor has not been included. Presentation is poorly structured and/or content is not relevant to project report findings.

2 Preparing the Skills and Learning Statement

2.1 Sources of SLS evidence

When you plan your project research work you should also plan to collect evidence to contribute to your Skills and Learning Statement, so that some of your self-reflection will 'fall out' of the activities undertaken for your Research Project. One important set of activities will be the three meetings with your Project Mentor. If you think about what happened in each of these meetings soon after they have taken place and record your thoughts, then you will be well on the way to writing your responses to two of the four questions.

Other sources of evidence could include meetings with individuals who you may interview as part of your project research or conversations / correspondence that you may have during your information gathering. You should think of every aspect of your project research work and how this may provide evidence for you to write your Skills and Learning Statement.

2.2 Communication skills

You will give a presentation on your Research Project to your Project Mentor in your final meeting. The preparation of this presentation will further develop your ability to present the concepts and findings of an accounting / business research report to an audience. As evidence of this you must submit a copy of your presentation in your Skills and Learning Statement.

You will pass 'communication skills' if a copy of the Research Project presentation is included in the SLS and your presentation's structure and content is clearly linked to the Research Project findings. There are many sources of advice (online and hard copy) on how to prepare an effective presentation and we recommend that you follow best practice.

It is possible that your Project Mentor may comment on the quality of your presentation and suggest that improvements would be possible. If you wish to revise your presentation after the meeting with your Project Mentor, then that is acceptable to Oxford Brookes. You should include a reference to this process and what you learned in your response to the first SLS question.

2.3 Style

The style of writing in the Skills and Learning Statement will be different from that in the Research Project. In the latter, your style will be quite formal. The purpose is to convey information, analyse that information and come to a conclusion based upon it. Much of the language used is likely to be technical and complex, and apart from the Introduction where you set out what you have tried to achieve in writing the Research Project, it will largely be written in the third person.

This means that you will not refer to yourself as such, but rather to the Research Project and its results.

2.4 Example

First person: I discovered that 67% of the finance directors who responded to my questionnaire felt that their company accounting procedures had benefited from the existence of internal audit.

Third person: It was noted that 67% of the finance directors who responded to the questionnaire felt that their company accounting procedures had benefited from the existence of internal audit.

The Skills and Learning Statement demands a different approach. You will be setting out **your own assessment of your own abilities**, and in some cases you will have to be fairly critical. You will be expected to recognise weaknesses which you have identified and consider how they can be remedied or improved. Such self-evaluation and criticism can often be a difficult experience, and writing about it even more so. There is a risk that you will lack confidence in carrying out this exercise, and that this will be reflected in your style of writing.

You will be writing in the first person (ie using 'I' and referring specifically to your own experiences) and this in itself can cause you to feel vulnerable, as it is often easier to immerse oneself in anonymity. You must maintain your confidence in doing this, and ensure that you highlight the good points. **Where you identify weaknesses, counter them by saying how you will improve upon them.**

Imagine yourself in this scenario

Exercise 1

1   Your presentation to your mentor and a peer group of eight other Research and Analysis Project students has not gone well.

2   Just before delivering your presentation, you discovered that three of the other students had chosen exactly the same research topic as you, an analysis of the financial position of Marks and Spencer plc and the impact of its trading decisions on its suppliers. This made you feel nervous and exposed, as you would be faced with a highly knowledgeable audience.

3   Once the presentation started, you had too much to say, and had to bring proceedings to a fairly abrupt halt after 20 minutes, when the mentor indicated that you had taken up too much time. This meant that your conclusions remained largely unsaid.

4   During the brief period for questions allowed at the end, you were completely floored by a question on a complex accounting ratio from one of the other students researching Marks and Spencer, and became flustered and confused, unable to come up with an answer.

5   You feel that the presentation has been an unmitigated disaster, and wonder how you can possibly reflect this in the relevant section of your Skills and Learning Statement.

Spend five minutes thinking of how you can accentuate the positive things to come out of this experience.

Answer

The section of your Skills and Learning Statement dealing with the presentation could look something like this.

Presentation

1   I delivered my presentation to my mentor and a group of eight fellow students on 30 November 20X9.

2   Three of my audience were also engaged in research on the position of Marks and Spencer. This provided a stimulating challenge for me, as it meant that I was delivering to a knowledgeable audience. It generated both advantages and disadvantages.

Advantage

3   There would be more scope for discussion and debate, and my presentation would not be limited to my speaking to the audience with limited feedback.

Disadvantages

4   The fact that there were others present with a detailed knowledge dented my confidence and made me feel exposed on certain complex aspects of my presentation. This made me unduly nervous during my opening remarks, and detracted from the content of the presentation. During questions, I was asked a very unexpected question to which I had no prepared response.

5   I realise that I should have prepared for my presentation in greater depth, as I had assumed that no one would have a detailed knowledge of my subject matter. When asked the difficult question, I should have taken the opportunity to open up debate and canvas the opinions of my fellow students, rather than react negatively because I could not answer the question.

Timing

6   Once I had established the flow, the presentation went well and I felt confident. However, I had to stop short, as my notes were too detailed and I exceeded the time limit. On another occasion, I will practise the whole presentation and amend it as necessary to ensure that the timing is better organised.

Conclusion

7   I have learned from this exercise that planning is of paramount importance in preparing for a presentation. That would give me greater confidence to deal with the unexpected and thus make the presentation more effective.

(298 words)

3 Communication

3.1 Use of a communication model

This diagram shows the classic *communication model*.

In the context of this diagram:

(a)   You the student are the **sender**

(b)   Your mentor is the **receiver** (although of course these two roles can be reversed)

(c)   The **coded message** is both verbal (what you actually say) and non-verbal (your body language)

(d)   The **medium** is the meeting (or presentation in Meeting 3)

(e)   The **decoded message** is your mentor's (or your) interpretation of the message

(f)   **Feedback** will come from your mentor to you (and *vice versa* when the roles are reversed)

However, the process of communication is not always as simple as that. There are barriers to communication and this diagram shows how they can affect the process.

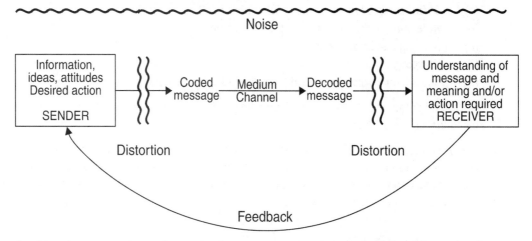

You should review your notes and records of your mentor meetings in the light of these two diagrams. You may prefer to use one of the diagrams of the communication model in one of the recommended texts, so that you can refer specifically to it, for example that in Guirdham (1995). You can of course use the models set out in this text, which are equally valid.

Do you think that your communication with your mentor is accurately summarised by these two models? Problems are most likely to have occurred in the decoding of the message and in the receiver's understanding of the message, although there is also the risk of distortion at the input stage.

Exercise 2

Ask yourself these questions:

1   Did your mentor have to ask you to rephrase a question or repeat it for any reason (even if only because an aircraft was passing overhead)?

2   Did a response given by your mentor indicate to you that he or she had misunderstood your comment or question?

3   Was there any form of interruption to any of your meetings, for example the telephone ringing, knocks at the door, external noise, the need to go and photocopy one of your documents?

4   Did you have to ask the mentor for further clarification of a point made because you did not at first understand it?

If the answer to any of those is 'yes' and you and your mentor could have done something to prevent it (for example done the photocopying beforehand, diverted phone calls etc) you should identify it as a factor which could have caused your communication to falter or fail. Where appropriate you can indicate what you would differently in the future.

If you honestly believe that none of these potential problems arose, you can be very positive in your self-evaluation, and show that your communication skills are good.

3.2 Key elements of successful communication

If communication is to be successful, the message must be:

(a)   **Credible** (inspiring trust and/or belief)

(b)   **Congenial** (appearing pleasant or compatible with the recipient)

(c)   **Of the correct length** (not overloaded, but still with sufficient depth)

(d)   **Relevant** (so that it is the 'correct' message)

(e)   Sent via a **suitable medium**

(f)   **Correctly interpreted**

(g)   Capable of **acknowledging the needs and expectations** of the receiver.

Do you think that those descriptions could be used to describe the communication process in **your** meetings with **your** mentor?

If your mentor or members of your peer group question the comments you make, or seem to disagree with them or require further clarification, it is arguable that the interaction between you does not correspond with the key elements of successful communication. If this is the case, you need to acknowledge this in your self-evaluation and recognise it as a potential problem.

4 Oral communication

Oral communication means communication **by speech, or word of mouth**. In the context of your Research and Analysis Project and the writing of the Skills and Learning Statement, you will mainly be involved in two different types of oral communication:

(a)   Meetings with your mentor to discuss your Research Project and progress to date

(b)   Your presentation to your mentor

You may also experience different forms of oral communication, for example if part of your research involves verbal questioning or discussion, or the distribution and explanation of a questionnaire.

An earlier chapter has dealt in depth with the presentation you are required to make, so this section covers oral communication in more general terms.

Face-to-face oral media include:

- Conversations
- Interviews
- Meetings
- Public addresses or briefings

Oral communication can also take place when sender and receiver are not physically face-to-face, through:

- Telephone calls
- Intercom
- Audio/video tape recordings
- Video conferencing

Oral communication is the most basic and generally used way of sending a message to another person.

4.1 Advantages and disadvantages of oral communication

Advantages of oral communication

(a)   It is a **swift and direct medium**. There is little or no time lapse between the sending and receiving of the message.

(b)   It is therefore suitable for **'interactive' communication**: the exchange of ideas, opinions, attitudes on the spot. Decisions can be arrived at and action taken more swiftly than is possible through lengthy correspondence. All parties present are able to contribute.

(c)   This creates **greater flexibility**: circumstances and attitudes can be changed more easily, especially since the personality, voice and manner of the parties involved can be employed in persuasion and motivation.

(d)   **Instant feedback** is obtainable to overcome doubts or misunderstandings. The sender will be able to ascertain immediately whether his message has been received and correctly interpreted.

(e)   In face-to-face oral communication, there is the added advantage of being able to *see* as well as hear the other party. Verbal meaning may be reinforced and feedback given by non-verbal cues.

(f)   Face-to-face communication allows for the **sensitive handling of personal messages**, such as bad news, reprimand or conflict resolution. Parties can respond flexibly to the situation, offering support, sympathy, encouragement or directness as required.

Disadvantages of oral communication

(a)   **Technical noise**, such as background sounds or bad telephone lines, can interfere with effective transmission.

(b)   **Memory is untrustworthy, and perceptions differ**. A written confirmation and record of an oral event will be required, so that both parties can check that they agree on what has been decided, can recall the details later, and can produce evidence if necessary.

(c)   **Less time is usually available for planning** the message's general content, let alone the exact wording. Inferior decisions may be made, because they had to be thought through on the spot in a meeting or on the phone, without sufficient planning or information. Time may be wasted and misinterpretation caused by ill-conceived or thoughtless utterances, 'putting one's foot in it'.

(d)   Face to face, **strong personalities** may 'swamp' and overrule weaker ones, however valid their respective ideas. A louder voice on the telephone may hinder the two-way process. Clash of personalities may become a crippling barrier to effective communication.

(e)   Where a large number of people is involved, it is even more **difficult to control** the process, and ensure that it is effective.

Skills in oral communication

You spend much of your time in oral communication of some sort, either speaking or listening. You probably take it very much **for granted**: it is something you have always done, and got by with. Think, however, of the consequences of **failure** in oral communication.

(a)   If you do not speak with **precision and clarity**, you will not be understood correctly.

(b)   If you do not speak with **tact and sensitivity**, you will not get a positive response.

(c)   If you do not speak with **persuasiveness**, you will not get your desired response.

(d)   If you do not **listen attentively**, you will not get feedback, messages etc.

Here are some basic communication skills

(a)   Defining the **purpose** of the communication

(b)   Anticipating factors likely to affect the reception of the message by the **audience**

(c)   Judging how much to say, and **structuring** your message so that it reinforces your main idea

(d)   Adapting your **style** – vocabulary, sentence structure and tone – to your purpose and the needs of the recipient

(e)   **Listening** attentively when you are on the receiving end of communication, and using **non-verbal cues** to aid understanding

(f)   Seeking and offering **feedback**

(g)   Anticipating potential **barriers** to communication

(h)   Appreciating the **roles**, relationships and constraints particular to business communication

These all apply equally to spoken communication.

The same stages apply in oral communication as in written: a message is conceived, encoded, transmitted, decoded, interpreted and acknowledged. In face-to-face oral communication, however, you are sending and receiving messages at the same time, or very close together. You **switch rapidly** between speaking and listening, and all the time your relationship with the other person, your tone of voice, your expressions and gestures, are modifying, qualifying or confirming the messages you are sending and your response to messages received.

4.2 Words at work

Some communications experts argue that using phrases like 'no problem', 'no worries' in a conversation sets the other person thinking that there **might** be problems or worries that you are keeping quiet about.

Here's a list of words and phrases that are thought to be very persuasive.

Delighted
Assured
Confident
Peace of mind
Enjoy
Pleasure
Satisfied
Appeal
Happy
Special
Valued
Normal
However
Good
Popular
Substantial
You're welcome
You'll be pleased to hear

Certainly
Yes
Please
Thank you
You
Help
Look after
Straightforward
Situation
Position
Recommended
Easier for you
Better for you
Quicker for you
Significant
I will organise that for you
Glad I could help

Articulation

We learn to speak **instinctively**. Babies imitate their parents; children pick up words wherever they hear them; adults enlarge their vocabulary and absorb the styles of speech that they are used to hearing. Our speech patterns become **deeply ingrained**, and although we may notice (and admire or dislike) the way others speak, we rarely pay attention to our **own articulation** and pronunciation until we have encountered a real problem. (You know you have a problem when someone has to ask you to repeat your message several times, and then spell it out.)

Listen to other people speaking. Do they speak clearly, so that you never have trouble understanding them? Do they speak with a strong regional or foreign accent which makes it difficult to understand them sometimes? Do they speak exaggeratedly, in a would-be 'posh' style, which sounds false and affected and distracts from what they say?

Exercise 3

Dictate the following sentences to someone else, allowing them time to write each sentence down, but speaking at your normal pace, and reading each item only once. (Alternatively, record yourself reading, and come back later and try to transcribe the sentences yourself.)

What a little pop, pet.
Jo gave George a rum for his money.
That stuff isn't it.
You have an aim and a dress.
They are having pea stalks.
He grows great vines.
Why choose 'Glow in the dark'?
You'll hear the waiter speak.
Will we have passed her at dinner?

Write down the alternative ways of hearing these sentences. What did you have to do in the way of articulation, pronunciation and intonation to make yourself clear?

People tend to have a certain image about **patterns of speech** and accents: the mode of speech is a **badge** of belonging to a like-speaking group with which the individual can **identify**. This can be an almost exclusive identification, based on the assumption that 'people who speak differently, think differently'. In most countries of the world hostility between groups is perpetuated by accent and speech mannerisms.

The important thing is that you **desire to communicate effectively**.

(a)   Clear articulation is vital, not because it is associated with a particular region, section of society or level of education, but because you want to be understood immediately and unambiguously by **any other person**, in order to get a response that you require.

(b)   A dialect or accent may be attractive to listen to and perfectly comprehensible within a certain community, but unless the speaker can make himself readily understood by someone who does not share it (over a long-distance telephone line, say, or in a gathering of people from various countries and regions) it will prevent him from communicating effectively to those outside his own community.

(c)   Be considerate to the recipient of your message: don't use or pronounce words in a way that he will not understand.

(d)   If you are satisfied that your speech is clear, unambiguous and not mannered just for the sake of it: fine.

4.3 Delivery

Volume and pitch. If you are articulating clearly, you will be much more audible, but you will also have to consider how to **project** your voice. Speaking softly or even at a normal level will be ineffective in a large room with a high ceiling and heavy curtains: the sound of your voice will be absorbed by everything except the person x yards away whom you are trying to inform or persuade, and whose attention you want to grab and hold. Stand or sit straight, keep your chin up and pitch your voice to travel to the **furthest** listener. Try not to shout, grate or squeak: find your own best pitch. You project your image when you project your voice: get it right.

One to one or in a small group, particularly if in an intimate or informal context, you will not create a good impression by aggressive voice projection. The same is true in small rooms. You do not want to appear brash, insensitive, rude or deaf. Look for **feedback** indicating that you are clearly but not painfully audible, and stick to that pitch and volume.

Intonation and pace affect how your message reaches its recipient, as much as volume affects whether it does.

(a)   Be aware of how the placing of **emphasis** on different words alters the meaning of a sentence: the stress **implies** something to the listener.

(b)   Likewise, notice how **inflexion** and **tone** alter meaning, when you raise or lower your voice, lift at the end of a question, lift and drop in an exclamation etc.

(c)   How do you make your voice sound cheery, gloomy, disapproving, encouraging, affectionate, enthusiastic, indifferent, hostile?

Experiment with the simple sentence: 'Nobody is available to see you.'

(a)   Try stressing each word in turn, and consider the implications of each change.

(b)   Try each as a statement, and as a question (not all combinations will work).

(c)   Try making the statement with each of the emotional overtones mentioned in Paragraph 4.3 (c) above.

Pace and pauses are further elements in fluent but clear delivery. Don't garble your words or string together long breathless sentences.

You do **not** have to pause frequently and at length: if you do, your audience may not stay with you. If you need time in which to frame your next idea, there are phrases and expressions you can use almost without thought, to preserve the fluency of your message. Notice how your vocabulary consists not only of single words, but of blocks of words which have become associated in your mind. Here are some examples.

'Of course it's really a matter of'
'I wonder if I might just'
'On the other hand, it wouldn't surprise me if'
'in fact', 'not at all', 'thank you very much'
etc.

Don't: use blocks of words that are so firmly established as to be clichéd: 'to coin a phrase' 'to err is human'.	Don't: resort to 'stabilisers' like 'um', 'ah', 'you know', or 'sort of like', 'you know what I mean?'

5 Writing the Skills and Learning Statement

It is now time to get down to writing the 2,000 words of your Skills and Learning Statement. You will need to address all four questions with equal depth and thought.

5.1 The main difficulty

Arguably the most difficult aspect of writing the Skills and Learning Statement will be covering all four questions in sufficient depth but with the necessary brevity as you are only permitted 2,000 words in total.

(a)   The best way to overcome this difficulty is to ensure that you **allow yourself enough time to prepare the statement**. If you rush you will find it very difficult to produce a statement which fulfils the requirements of the Information Pack guidelines, and that could cause you to fail the Research and Analysis Project regardless of the merits of your Research Project.

(b)   Use the time to **plan the Skills and Learning Statement in as much detail as possible**. Decide precisely what you are going to say for each of the questions and what examples you are going to use from your experiences. If you have a choice of examples of equal relevance choose the one which you will be able to describe in fewer words, so that you have some flexibility in your word count.

(c)   You will probably need to **prepare at least three drafts of your Statement** to hone it down to its most concise and cogent form. Make sure that you allow yourself enough time to do this and do not get frustrated at the seemingly slow progress in doing this. Each draft you prepare will improve the Statement immeasurably and will make you more familiar with the contents making the next draft much easier to write.

5.2 Assessment criteria

Before starting to write your Statement let's just have a quick reminder of the assessment criteria for a satisfactory Statement and one which is judged to be not satisfactory.

Satisfactory Skills and Learning Statement

- It makes a reasonable attempt to address all four questions
- It shows an ability to reflect on judgements made and actions taken during the project work
- There is evidence of recognition of the individual's weaknesses as well as strengths
- A copy of the presentation to the project mentor is included
- The presentation has an appropriate structure and its content is clearly linked to the project report findings.

Not satisfactory Skills and Learning Statement

- Overly focused on only one or two questions
- Emphasis of description of events rather than evaluation of self-development
- Little discussion of the individual's strengths and weaknesses
- No copy of the presentation to the project mentor included
- A poorly structured presentation whose content is not relevant to the project findings.

5.3 Answering the questions

The total word count is 2,000 words which averages at 500 words per question. However there is no requirement to write exactly 500 words for each question. You may in fact write between 350 and 650 words on each question within the total word limit of 2,000 words.

So now we will consider each of the four questions individually to give you some ideas about your approach.

5.4 What did you learn from the meetings with your project mentor, including the presentation that you gave to your project mentor?

This one may be the easiest question to answer particularly if you have kept and filed notes of those meetings and your thoughts and feelings about them afterwards as suggested.

Think about some of the following to determine where your strengths and weaknesses lie:

- Were you properly prepared for each meeting?

- Had you planned what you were going to talk about at each meeting?

- Particularly for the second and third meetings had you scheduled them for a time when you had completed an appropriate amount of work on your Research Project?

- Did you get out of the meeting what you intended to?

- Did you feel that each meeting went well or were you unhappy with the outcome?

- Did your presentation run to time? If not why not?

- Did you cover all the points that you intended to in your presentation?

- Did your project mentor ask questions which showed he understood what your presentation had been about?

5.5 How well do you think that you have answered your research question(s)?

This is perhaps a little harder to answer than the first question. Remember that you are required to reflect on judgements made and actions taken during the project work. You do not need to describe those actions but to reflect on whether they were appropriate, necessary and sufficient.

Think about some of these questions to give you a few ideas of where to go with this question:

- In retrospect was your choice of project topic a good one?
- Were you prepared for your first meeting with your project mentor?
- How did you decide what research to do for your project?
- Do you think you did enough research?
- Did you have enough primary and secondary data to analyse for your project?
- Was the conclusion the one that you expected when starting the project?
- If your conclusion was different to that which you expected how did you react to this?

5.6 How have you demonstrated your interpersonal and communication skills during the project work?

We have spent some time looking at communication and particularly oral communication earlier in this chapter so think back to some of the areas covered there.

Ask yourself some of the following questions:

- Did you carry out personal interviews designed to find information during the project work? If you did do you feel that learnt enough relevant information from these interviews?

- Did you design and send out a questionnaire during your project work? If so was the response adequate and useful?

- Do you feel that you ask good questions or is this an area that you need to improve?

- Do your feel that you are good listener or is this an area that you need to improve?

- How have you developed/improved your questioning skills?

- How did you respond to questions at the end of your presentation?

5.7 How has undertaking the Research and Analysis Project helped you in your accountancy studies and/or current employment role?

This is probably the hardest question of them all to answer. However remember that in order to have a "satisfactory" Skills and Learning Statement you must make a reasonable attempt at all four questions so you need to be aiming for at least 350 words in answer to this question.

Think about what you have done in academic terms for this project as well as what you have learned in other areas. Think about some of the following questions that you could ask yourself:

- How did the academic content of the project help with either your studies or your current employment role?

- Do you now have a greater insight into a particular area of accounting and finance?

- How has the process of applied academic research affected the way you either study or approach your work?

- How will you be able to use any of the interpersonal or communication skills that you have learned during the project work in your current employment?

- Would you now feel confident to make a presentation to colleagues in your work place?

Chapter roundup

- The Skills and Learning Statement is a critical part of your Research and Analysis Project.

- It requires you to reflect on the communication process, and the skills you have learned.

- Oral communication, in the form of meetings with your mentor, is as important as written communication.

- You must make a reasonable attempt to answer all four questions in the Skills and Learning Statement.

BPP
LEARNING MEDIA

Appendix

Referencing exercise

It is essential that you reference your sources throughout your Research Project, and also construct a List of References.

Referencing techniques using the Harvard system are explained in Chapter 11 of this book, and are also covered in Appendix 3 of the Information Pack guidelines.

Note that Appendix 3 states that correctly referencing your work is compulsory.

The List of References must indicate all the sources you have used, including newspaper articles, company publications and Internet resources.

In order to give you some practice at these techniques, we set out in this appendix an exercise in referencing, which will help you to make the connection between writing the text and constructing the List of References.

The extracts which follow are from a book about Walt Disney. [1]

The bibliography included at the end of the book is also reproduced.

From the pages of text, **attempt these activities**.

1   List the authors to whom Bryman refers.

2   Check these in the bibliography and make a list of the different type of resources that Bryman used.

3   Did he read all the material he quotes?

4   From the bibliography, identify:

    (a)   An 'Introduction'
    (b)   Articles written by unknown authors. Why are they unknown?

[1] Bryman, A. (1995) *Disney and his Worlds*, Routledge

However, one of the issues with which Weber was especially concerned was how charismatic leadership can be transformed into a relatively stable force. Weber recognized that charismatic leadership was inherently transitory and that it needed to be placed on a stable footing for it to persist beyond the specific circumstances that give rise to the charismatic leader's ascendancy or beyond the leader's lifetime. Weber employed the term 'routinization of charisma' to describe the process by which charismatic leadership becomes an enduring force, arguing that a failure to routinize a leader's charisma will almost inevitably result in the dissipation of that charisma. In fact, the issue of the routinization of charisma occupied Weber's attentions more than the nature and genesis of charismatic leadership as such because he recognized that without routinization charisma is bound to be ephemeral. There are two main aspects to the routinization of charisma in Weber's writings (Bryman, 1992, 1993). One is that charismatic leaders have to create a structure which incorporates and enshrines their charisma. This will establish continuity for the visions of charismatic leaders and provide a sense of security for their followers. Thus, the *development of structure* is one aspect of the process whereby permanence can be given to charismatic leadership. Second, there is the issue of the *succession* to the charismatic leader. In other words, what will happen when the charismatic leader dies or leaves the organization or movement? Weber delineated a number of different ways whereby succession might take place: the charismatic leader designates a successor; charisma becomes associated with a bloodline; the successor is 'revealed'; or charisma becomes associated with an 'office' or position. Weber recognized that charisma is changed by the process of routinization, since it becomes something that can be transferred and as such no longer attaches to a special person by dint of his or her extraordinary qualities.

Weber's notion of charismatic leadership was developed out of the religious context where charisma means 'gift of grace'. He applied it to a variety of religious leaders and then broadened it further to encompass political figures as well. In recent years, a number of writers have sought to explore the notion within business organizations (for example, Bass, 1985; Biggart, 1989; Bryman, 1992, 1993; Conger, 1989, 1993; Gaines, 1993). It was suggested in Chapter 1 that Walt Disney fits fairly well the image of a charismatic leader in the business sphere, but how successfully was his charisma routinized? Of course, in the first of the two senses of the idea of routinization, Walt did routinize his charisma in that he created an organization and a culture that embodied his visions. In fact, it is hard to envision a charismatic leader in the business context for whom at least the creation of an organization does not apply. As to the second aspect of routinization, it is clear that Walt did not specifically nominate a successor. When founders of organizations, such as Steve Jobs of Apple Computer, leave (or die) there is a profound sense of loss among those left behind (Rose, 1989), and it is apparent that Walt's passing engendered a similar sense of despair. While Roy was an obvious successor, it has to be remembered that he was over eight years older than his brother and that he had been considering retirement at the time of Walt's death. He was able to continue as part of the Disney troika and it seems that, for the five years of their reign, this triumvirate successfully routinized Walt's charisma, in large part due to the continued presence of a Disney in the leadership. The troika also had the advantage of a stream of activities that Walt had set in motion so that they were to a significant extent executing his visions.

Roy's death in 1971 ushered in a period in which there was no longer a Disney at the helm. It is also clear that neither Tatum nor Walker enjoyed charisma of office, in that they were not able to bathe in the glow of positions which were viewed as emblematic of Walt's charisma. To make matters worse, as Potts and Behr (1987), have observed, Walt's successors were trapped by a 'strong culture'. In the early 1980s, a number of management writers pointed to the advantages to organizations of having a strong culture and the importance of having leaders who foster such a culture (for example, Deal and Kennedy, 1982; Peters and Waterman, 1982), although later evidence suggests the need for a much more cautious assessment of the advantages of strong culture s (for example, Kotter and Heskett, 1992). In the case of Disney, it is easy to see why greater caution might be necessary. The company had developed a strong culture which was an extension of Walt's vision for the company – a preoccupation with quality, perfectionism, and a commitment to providing family entertainment. To this was harnessed a belief in customer satisfaction which would be particularly relevant to the operation of the theme parks, while the Disney University became the vehicle

Extract 2

opened, the visitor was able to purchase a block of tickets for rides and attractions, which had been graded according to their popularity. Each block would have a certain number of tickets for each grade of ride. Even this approach was dropped when in 1982 the passes which are still used today were introduced and allowed unlimited access to the rides in any park. At Disney World, visitors typically purchase multi-park tickets which allow access to all the rides in all the parks (and the minor parks depending on the type of pass) over a set number of days. Findlay (1992) suggests that the continuous exchange of money in the early Disneyland years gave the impression of a visit being expensive. It may be that one of the concerns was that this 'psychologically bad situation', as one of the Disney Imagineers called it (Bright, 1987: 109), inhibited people's preparedness to spend money on merchandise. While the significance of the consumption of merchandise and food at the parks has grown greatly since 1955, it is likely that Walt and his associates were profoundly aware of its profitable nature, particularly in the light of its importance in the studio's early years (see Chapter 1).

A second register of consumerism at the Disney theme parks revolves around an observation that has been made in a number of guises previously, namely, that some of the corporate-sponsored attractions in the parks relate to the goods and services that they sell. In presenting to us pictures of past and future revolving around electrical goods (Carousel of Progress) and cars (World of Motion), the good life is construed in terms of our identities as consumers – we are what we buy. The new Innoventions buildings at Disney World can be viewed more appropriately as showcases for the electronics, information technology and computer products of companies such as IBM, Sega and AT&T. Kuenz (1993) suggests that a major reason for the frequent allusion to the family in the parks is that it is the chief locus of consumption. Stimulating this image acts as a prompt to remind the visitor of his/her identity as consumer of both the corporation's products and the Disney merchandise itself, though this is not to suggest that visitors are unreflective automata who rush to buy character dolls and tee-shirts as soon as they can, but that the image is a convenient, self-serving one.

The third context of consumerism relates to consumption at the parks themselves. Some commentators have written as though the parks are simply shopping milieux. Yoshimoto (1994) suggests that the point of providing guests with narratives to mould their experiences of the parks is to naturalize consumption, so that people consume without being aware of what they are doing. By making consumption part of the experience itself, its nature as consumption is not fully revealed. In Yoshimoto's view, the 'ingenuity of Disney magic lies in its attempt to integrate shopping as part of the attractions without destroying the autonomy of the latter' (1994: 187). It is not surprising, therefore, that more and more shopping malls are adopting a Disney approach to retailing, so that shopping takes place in themed environments. Increasingly, it is difficult to distinguish large malls with themed environments from theme parks. The most frequently cited illustration of this trend is the West Edmonton Mall in Alberta, Canada; to all intents and purposes it is a shopping mall which increasingly resembles a theme park (Crawford, 1992; Shields, 1989). In fact, West Edmonton Mall's publicity tries to give the impression that it provides a great deal more than a Disney theme park:

> Imagine visiting Disneyland, Malibu Beach, Bourbon Street, the San Diego Zoo, Rodeo Drive in Beverly Hills and Australia's Great Barrier Reef . . . in one weekend – and under one roof. . . . Billed as the world's greatest shopping complex of its kind, the Mall covers 110 acres and features 828 stores, 110 restaurants, 19 theaters . . . a five-acre water park and a glass dome that is over 19 storeys high. . . . Contemplate the Mall's indoor lake complete with four submarines from which you can view sharks, octopi, tropical marine life, and a replica of the Great Barrier Reef. . . . Fantasyland Hotel has given its rooms a number of themes.
> (Travel Alberta publicity material, quoted in Urry, 1990: 147)

However, even less extreme cases than this, such as the Metro Centre in Gateshead, sometimes exhibit this tendency to narrativize shopping by creating themed locations, such as a Mediterranean Village (Chaney, 1990). In large part, of course, the aim of theming the experience of shopping is to keep the shopper in that role for as long as possible and for shopping to become an attraction in its own right. Crawford (1992) argues that the advantage of theming is that mundane goods reap the benefit of 'adjacent attraction', whereby their display in exotic contexts renders them more glamorous and interesting. This is especially

Bibliography

Abercrombie, N., Hill, S., and Turner, B.S. (1980) *The Dominant Ideology Thesis*, London: Allen & Unwin.

Adamson, J. (1975) *Tex Avery: King of Cartoons*, New York: Da Capo.

Adler, S. (1983) 'Snow White for the defense: why Disney doesn't lose', *American Lawyer*, March: 32–5.

Aldridge, A. (1994) 'The construction of rational consumption in *Which?* magazine: the more blobs the better?' *Sociology*, 28: 899–912.

Alexander, G. (1994) 'Power play in the magic kingdom', *The Sunday Times* (Section 3), 28 August: 5.

Alexander, J. (1953a) 'The amazing story of Walt Disney: Part 1', *Saturday Evening Post*, 31 October: 24–5, 80, 84–6, 90, 92.

——— (1953b) 'The amazing story of Walt Disney: Part 2', *Saturday Evening Post*, 7 November: 26–7, 99–100.

Allan, R. (1985) 'Alice in Disneyland', *Sight and Sound*, Spring: 136–8.

Allen, H. and Denning, M. (1993) 'The cartoonists' front', *South Atlantic Quarterly*, 92: 89–117.

Alvesson, M. (1990) 'Organization: from substance to image?', *Organization Studies*, 11: 373–94.

Andrae, T. (1988) 'Of mouse and the man', in *Walt Disney's Mickey Mouse in Color*, New York: Pantheon.

Ang, I. (1990) 'Culture and communication: toward an ethnographic critique of media consumption in the transnational media system', *European Journal of Communication*, 5: 239–60.

Anon. (1932) 'Mickey Mouse's fourth birthday finds organization world-wide', *Motion Picture Herald*, 1 October: 42–3, 51.

——— (1934) 'The big bad wolf', *Fortune*, November: 88–95, 142–8.

——— (1948) 'The mighty mouse', *Time*, 25 October: 33.

——— (1950) 'Money from mice', *Newsweek*, 13 February: 84–9.

——— (1954) 'Father Goose', *Time*, 27 December: 30–4.

——— (1962) 'The wide world of Disney', *Newsweek*, 31 December: 48–51.

——— (1965) 'Disney's live-action profits', *Business Week*, 2 July: 78–82.

——— (1967) 'Disney without Walt', *Forbes*, 1 July: 39–40.

Apple, M. (1983) 'Uncle Walt', *Esquire*, December: 164–8.

Arlidge, J. (1992) 'Disney casts recruits for European venture', *Independent*, 7 January: 3.

Bailey, A. (1982) *Walt Disney's World of Fantasy*, New York: Everest House.

Barker, M. (1989) *Comics: Ideology, Power and the Critics*, Manchester: Manchester University Press.

—— (1993) 'Seeing how far you can see: on being a "fan" of 2,000AD', in D. Buckingham (ed.), *Reading Audiences: Young People and the Media*, Manchester: Manchester University Press.

Barley, S.R., Meyer, G.W., and Gash, D.C. (1988) 'Cultures of culture: practitioners and the pragmatics of normative control', *Administrative Science Quarterly*, 33: 24–60.

Barrier, M. (1974) 'Of mice, wabbits, ducks and men: the Hollywood cartoon', *AFI Report*, 5: 18–26.

—— (1979) '"Building a better mouse": fifty years of Disney animation', *Funnyworld*, 20: 6–15.

Bass, B.M. (1985) *Leadership and Performance Beyond Expectations*, New York: Free Press.

Baudrillard, J. (1983) *Simulations*, New York: Semiotext(e).

—— (1993a) 'I don't belong to the club, to the Seraglio: interview with Mike Gane and Monique Arnaud', in M. Gane (ed.), *Baudrillard Live: Selected Interviews*, London: Routledge.

—— (1993b) 'Hyperreal America', *Economy and Society*, 22: 243–52.

Bauman, Z. (1992) *Intimations of Postmodernity*, London: Routledge.

Beard, R. (1982) *Walt Disney's Epcot Center*, New York: Harry N. Abrams.

Bendazzi, G. (1994) *Cartoons: One Hundred Years of Cinema Animation*, London: John Libbey.

Bierman, J.H. (1976) 'The Walt Disney robot dramas', *Yale Review*, 66: 223–36.

—— (1979) 'Disneyland and the "Los Angelization" of the arts', in M. Matlaw (ed.), *American Popular Entertainment*, Westport, Conn.: Greenwood Press.

Biggart, N.W. (1989) *Charismatic Capitalism: Direct Selling Organizations in America*, Chicago: University of Chicago Press.

Billig, M. (1994) 'Sod Baudrillard! Or ideology critique in Disney World', in H.W. Simons and M. Billig (eds), *After Postmodernism: Reconstructing Ideology Critique*, London: Sage.

Birmingham, S. (1964) 'The greatest one-man show on earth: Walt Disney', *McCall's*, 91: 98–101, 121.

Birnbaum, S. (1989) *Walt Disney World: The Official Guide*, New York: Avon Books.

Blake, P. (1972) 'Walt Disney World', *Architectural Forum*, 136: 24–41.

Blocklyn, P.L. (1988) 'Making magic: the Disney approach to people management', *Personnel*, 65: 28–35.

Boehme, L.R. (1975) 'The Magic Kingdom: is it really magic?', *American Opinion*, May: 13–20, 85–90.

Boorstin, D.J. (1961) *The Image: A Guide to Pseudo-events in America*, New York: Harper & Row.

Boyer, P.J. (1991) 'Katzenberg's seven-year itch', *Vanity Fair*, November: 64–79.

Bragdon, C. (1934) 'Mickey Mouse and what he means', *Scribner's*, July: 40–3.

Bright, R. (1987) *Disneyland: Inside Story*, New York: Harry N. Abrams.

Bristol, G.T. (1938) 'Snow White: inanimate characters become a new force in merchandising', *Dun's Review*, April: 13–17.

Brophy, P. (1991) 'The animation of sound', in A. Cholodenko (ed.), *The Illusion of Life: Essays on Animation*, Sydney: Power.

Bryman, A. (1992) *Charisma and Leadership in Organizations*, London: Sage.

—— (1993) 'Charismatic leadership in business organizations', *Leadership Quarterly*, 4: 289–304.

Bryson, B. (1993) 'Of mice and millions', *Observer Magazine*, 28 March: 16–23.

Budd, M., Entman, R.M., and Steinman, C. (1990) 'The affirmative character of U.S. cultural studies', *Critical Studies in Mass Communication*, 7: 169–84.

Bukatman, S. (1991) 'There's always Tomorrowland: Disney and the hypercinematic experience', *October*, 57: 55–78.

Cabarga, L. (1988) *The Fleischer Story*, New York: DaCapo.

Calás, M.B. (1993) 'Deconstructing charismatic leadership', *Leadership Quarterly*, 4: 305–28.

Carlzon, J. (1987) *Moments of Truth*, New York: Ballinger.

Carr, H. (1931) 'The only unpaid movie star', *American*, March: 55–7, 122–5.

Chamberlain, M. (1981) 'How the world of Disney is building for the future', *Marketing Week*, 11 December: 28–37.

Chaney, D. (1990) 'Subtopia in Gateshead: the MetroCentre as a cultural form', *Theory, Culture and Society*, 7: 49–68.

—— (1993) *Fictions of Collective Life: Public Drama in Late Modern Culture*, London: Routledge.

Chase, M. and Shaw, C. (1989) 'The dimensions of nostalgia', in C. Shaw and M. Chase (eds), *The Imagined Past: History and Nostalgia*, Manchester: Manchester University Press.

Churchill, D.W. (1934) 'Now Mickey Mouse enters art's temple', *New York Times Magazine*, 3 June: 13, 21.

—— (1938) 'Disney's philosophy', *New York Times Magazine*, 6 March: 9, 23.

Clegg, S. (1990) *Modern Organizations: Organization Studies in the Postmodern World*, London: Sage.

Cohen, E. (1979) 'A phenomenology of tourist experiences', *Sociology*, 13: 179–201.

—— (1988) 'Traditions in the qualitative sociology of tourism', *Annals of Tourism Research*, 15: 29–46.

Condit, C.M. (1989) 'The rhetorical limits of polysemy', *Critical Studies in Mass Communication*, 6: 103–22.

Conger, J.A. (1989) *The Charismatic Leader: Beyond the Mystique of Exceptional Leadership*, San Francisco: Jossey-Bass.

—— (1993) 'Max Weber's conceptualization of charismatic authority: its influence on organizational research', *Leadership Quarterly*, 4: 277–88.

Cooke, P. (1990) *Back to the Future: Modernity, Postmodernity, and Locality*, London: Unwin Hyman.

Corner, J., Richardson, K., and Fenton, N. (1990) *Nuclear Reactions: Form and Response in Public Issue Television*, London: John Libbey.

Cox, G.D. (1989) 'Don't mess with the Mouse', *National Law Journal*, 11, 31 July: 1, 26–7.

Crafton, D. (1982) *Before Mickey: The Animated Film, 1989–1928*, Cambridge, Mass.: MIT Press.

Crawford, M. (1992) 'The world in a shopping mall', in M. Sorkin (ed.), *Variations on a Theme Park: The New American City and the End of Public Space*, New York: Noonday.

Culhane, J. (1976) 'The old Disney magic', *New York Times Magazine*, 1 August: 11, 32–6.

Culhane, S. (1986) *Talking Animals and Other People*, New York: St Martin's Press.

Curran, J. (1990) 'The new revisionism in mass communication research: a reappraisal', *European Journal of Communication*, 5: 135–64.

Custen, G.F. (1992) *Bio/Pics: How Hollywood Constructed Public History*, New Brunswick, N.J.: Rutgers University Press.

Davidson, B. (1964) 'The fantastic Walt Disney', *Saturday Evening Post*, 7 November: 66–74.

Davis, S.O. (1980) 'Wish upon a falling star at Disney', *New York Times Magazine*, 16 November: 144–52.

Deal, T.E. and Kennedy, A.A. (1982) *Corporate Cultures*, Reading, Mass.: Addison-Wesley.

Debord, G. (1994) *The Society of the Spectacle* (1967), New York: Zone Books.

deCordova, R. (1994) 'The Mickey in Macy's window: childhood, consumerism, and Disney animation', in E. Smoodin (ed.), *Disney Discourse*, New York: Routledge.

Dennett, A.S. (1989) 'A postmodern look at EPCOT's American Adventure', *Journal of American Culture*, 12: 47–53.

De Roos, R. (1963) 'The magic worlds of Walt Disney', *National Geographic*, August: 159–207.

Dickson, E.J. (1993) 'Who's afraid of the big bad mouse?', *The Sunday Times Magazine*, 28 March: 30–4.

Disney, R. (1969) 'My unforgettable brother, Walt Disney', *Reader's Digest*, March: 133–9.

Disney, W. (1931) 'Mickey Mouse: how he was born', *Windsor Magazine*, October: 641–5.

—— (1934) 'The life story of Mickey Mouse', *Windsor Magazine*, January: 259–63.

—— (1941) 'Growing pains', *American Cinematographer*, March: 106–7, 139–42.

Doctorow, E.L. (1972) *The Book of Daniel*, London: Macmillan.

Dorfman, A. and Mattelart, A. (1975) *How to Read Donald Duck: Imperialist Ideology in the Disney Comic*, New York: International General.

Eckert, C. (1978) 'The Carole Lombard in Macy's window', *Quarterly Review of Film Studies*, 3: 1–22.

Eco, U. (1986) *Travels in Hyperreality*, London: Pan.

Eddy, D. (1955) 'The amazing secret of Walt Disney', *American*, August: 28–9, 110–15.

Edwards, R. (1979) *Contested Terrain: The Transformation of the Workplace in the Twentieth Century*, London: Heinemann.

Eisen, A. (1975) 'Two Disney artists', *Crimmer's: The Harvard Journal of Pictorial Fiction*, Winter: 35–44.

Eisman, R. (1993) 'Disney magic', *Incentive*, September: 45–56.

Eliot, M. (1993) *Walt Disney: Hollywood's Dark Prince*, New York: Birch Lane.

Elliott, H. (1994) 'Disney goes for older generation', *The Times*, 3 May: 5.

Ewen, S. (1988) *All Consuming Images: The Politics of Style in Contemporary Culture*, New York: Basic Books.

Eyssartel, A.-M. and Rochette, B. (n.d.) *Des mondes inventés: les parcs à thèmes*, Paris: Les Éditions de la Villette.

Featherstone, M. (1991) *Consumer Culture and Postmodernism*, London: Sage.

Feifer, M. (1985) *Going Places*, London: Macmillan.

Feild, R.D. (1942) *The Art of Walt Disney*, New York: Macmillan.

Fessier, M. (1967) 'Legacy of a last tycoon', *Los Angeles Times West*, 12 November: 16–23.

Fielding, H. (1992) 'Teach yourself post-modernism', *Independent on Sunday*, 15 November: 21.

Finch, C. (1973) *The Art of Walt Disney: From Mickey Mouse to the Magic Kingdoms*, New York: Harry N. Abrams.

Findlay, J.M. (1992) *Magic Lands: Western Cityscapes and American Culture after 1940*, Bekeley, Cal.: University of California Press.

Fiske, J. (1989) *Understanding Popular Culture*, London: Unwin Hyman.

Fjellman, S.M. (1992) *Vinyl Leaves: Walt Disney World and America*, Boulder, Col.: Westview Press.

Fleischer, R. (1993) *Just Tell Me When to Cry: Encounters with the Greats, Near-Greats and Ingrates of Hollywood*, New York: Carroll & Graf.

Flower, J. (1991) *Prince of the Magic Kingdom: Michael Eisner and the Re-making of Disney*, New York: John Wiley.

Ford, B. (1989) *Walt Disney*, New York: Walker.

Ford, G. (1975) 'Warner Brothers', *Film Comment*, 11: 10–16, 93, 96.

Forgacs, D. (1992) 'Disney animation and the business of childhood', *Screen*, 33: 361–74.

Francaviglia, R.V. (1981) 'Main Street USA: a comparison/contrast of streetscapes in Disneyland and Walt Disney World', *Journal of Popular Culture*, 15: 141–56.

France, V.A. (1991) *Window on Main Street*, Nashua, N.H.: Laughter Publications.

Freedland, J. (1994) 'Mighty mouse in magic kingdom', *Guardian*, 31 January: 8–9.

Fushaho, A. (1988) 'Disneyland's dreamlike success', *Japan Quarterly*, 35: 58–62.

Gaines, J. (1993) '"You don't necessarily have to be charismatic . . .": an interview with Anita Roddick and reflections on charismatic processes in The Body Shop International', *Leadership Quarterly*, 4: 347–59.

Galbraith, J.K. (1992) *The Culture of Contentment*, New York: Houghton Mifflin.

Garfield, B. (1991) 'How I spent (and spent and spent) my Disney vacation', *Washington Post*, 7 July: B5.

Gergen, K.J. (1992) 'Organization theory in the postmodern era', in M. Reed and M. Hughes (eds), *Rethinking Organization: New Directions in Organization Theory and Analysis,* London: Sage.

Gindin, R. (1984) 'The mystique of training at Disney World', *Restaurant Business,* 10 February: 242.

Giroux, H.A. (1994) 'Beyond the politics of innocence: memory and pedagogy in the "Wonderful World of Disney"', *Socialist Review,* 23: 79–107.

Goff, N. (1979) 'Disney: all gassed up and ready to go', *Financial World,* 1 September: 14–18.

Goldberger, P. (1972) 'Mickey Mouse teaches the architects', *New York Times Magazine,* 22 October: 40–1, 92–9.

Gomery, D. (1994) 'Disney's business history: a reinterpretation', in E. Smoodin (ed.), *Disney Discourse,* New York: Routledge.

Gordon, M. (1958) 'Walt's profit formula: dream, diversify – and never miss an angle', *Wall Street Journal,* 4 February: 1, 12.

Gottdiener, M. (1982) 'Disneyland: a Utopian urban space', *Urban Life,* 11: 139–62.

—— (1986) 'Recapturing the center: a semiotic analysis of shopping malls', in M. Gottdiener and A.P. Lagopolous (eds), *The City and the Sign,* New York: Columbia University Press.

Gottlieb, A. (1982) 'Americans' vacations', *Annals of Tourism Research,* 9: 165–87.

Gould, S.J. (1979) 'Mickey Mouse meets Konrad Lorenz', *Natural History,* 88: 30–6.

Greene, K. and Greene, R. (1991) *The Man Behind the Magic: The Story of Walt Disney,* New York: Viking.

Grossman, C.L. (1993) 'Vegas deals new hand of family fun', *USA Today* (International Edition), 11 August: 5A.

Grover, R. (1991) *The Disney Touch: How a Daring Management Team Revived an Entertainment Empire,* Homewood, Ill.: Irwin.

—— (1994) 'Jeffrey Katzenberg: no more Mr Tough Guy?', *Business Week,* 31 January: 46–7.

Haden-Guest, A. (1973) *The Paradise Program: Travels through Muzak, Hilton, Coca-Cola, Texaco, Walt Disney and other World Empires,* New York: Morrow.

Halas, J. and Manvell, R. (1959), *The Technique of Film Animation,* London: Focal Press.

Halevy, J. (1958) 'Disneyland and Las Vegas', *The Nation,* 7 June: 510–13.

Hall, S. (1980) 'Encoding/decoding', in S. Hall, D. Hobson, A. Lowe, and P. Willis (eds), *Culture, Media, Language,* London: Hutchinson.

Hand, D.D. (n.d.) *Memoirs: David Dodd Hand,* privately printed.

Harmetz, A. (1985) 'The man re-animating Disney', *New York Times Magazine,* 29 December: 13–18, 3, 37, 42–3.

Harrington, M. (1979) 'To the Disney station: corporate socialism in the Magic Kingdom', *Harper's,* January: 35–44, 86.

Harvey, D. (1989) *The Condition of Postmodernity,* London: Basil Blackwell.

Hayes, T.C. (1984) 'Trouble stalks the Magic Kingdom', *New York Times,* 17 June: 1, 12.

Heydebrand, W.V. (1989) 'New organizational forms', *Work and Occupations*, 16: 323–57.

Holleran, A. (1992) 'The mouse and the virgin', in *Fodor's 93: Walt Disney World*, New York: Fodor's.

Holliss, R. and Sibley, B. (1988) *The Disney Studio Story*, New York: Crown.

Hollister, P. (1940) 'Genius at work: Walt Disney', *Atlantic Monthly*, December: 689–701.

Horton, J.O. and Crew, S.R. (1989) 'Afro-Americans and museums: towards a policy of inclusion', in W. Leon and R. Rosenzweig (eds), *History Museums in the United States*, Urbana, Ill.: University of Illinois Press.

Howell, J.M. and Avolio, B.J. (1992) 'The ethics of charismatic leadership: submission or liberation?', *The Executive*, 6: 43–54.

Hulett, S. (1992) 'Walt Disney's *Pinnochio*', in *1992 Screen Cartoonists Annual*.

Hunt, P. and Frankenberg, R. (1990) 'It's a small world: Disneyland, the family and the multiple re-presentations of American childhood', in A. James and A. Prout (eds), *Constructing and Reconstructing Childhood: Contemporary Issues in the Sociological Study of Childhood*, London: Falmer.

Iacocca, L. (1984) *Iacocca: An Autobiography*, New York: Bantam.

Jackson, K.M. (1993) *Walt Disney: A Bio-bibliography*, Westport, Conn.: Greenwood.

Jackson, T. (1994) 'Disney seeks solutions to the park's midlife and identity crises', *Tampa Tribune* (Business and Finance section), 8 August: 8–9.

Jacobs, L. (1939) *The Rise of the American Film: A Critical History*, New York: Harcourt, Brace.

Jacobson, G. and Hillkirk, J. (1986) *Xerox: American Samurai*, New York: Collier.

Jameson, F. (1991) *Postmodernism, or, The Cultural Logic of Late Capitalism*, London: Verso.

Jenkins, I. (1992) 'French turn on "fascism" at Disney', *The Sunday Times* (section 3), 16 February: 6.

Jermier, J.M. (1993) 'Introduction – charismatic leadership: neo-Weberian perspectives', *Leadership Quarterly*, 4: 217–33.

Johnson, D.M. (1981) 'Disney World as structure and symbol: re-creation of the American experience', *Journal of Popular Culture*, 15: 157–65.

Jones, C. (1991) 'What's up, down under?', in A. Cholodenko (ed.), *The Illusion of Life: Essays in Animation*, Sydney: Power.

Kapsis, R.E. (1989) 'Reputation building and the film art world: the case of Alfred Hitchcock', *Sociological Quarterly*, 30: 15–35.

Kasindorf, J. (1991) 'Mickey Mouse time at Disney', *New York*, 7 October: 32–42.

Kasson, J.F. (1978) *Amusing the Million: Coney Island at the Turn of the Century*, New York: Hill & Wang.

Keat, R., Whiteley, N. and Abercrombie, N. (1994) 'Introduction', in R. Keat, N. Whiteley, and N. Abercrombie (eds), *The Authority of the Consumer*, London: Routledge.

King, M.J. (1981) 'Disneyland and Walt Disney World: traditional values in futuristic form', *Journal of Popular Culture*, 15: 116–40.

—— (1983) 'McDonald's and Disney', in M. Fishwick (ed.), *Ronald Revisited: The World of Ronald McDonald*, Bowling Green, Ohio: Bowling Green University Popular Press.

—— (1991) 'The theme park experience: what museums can learn from Mickey Mouse', *The Futurist*, November–December: 24–31.

King, P. (1986) 'The marketing challenge: backstage at Walt Disney World', *Food Management*, July: 74–8, 142–8.

Kinney, J. (1988) *Walt Disney and Assorted Other Characters: An Unauthorized Account of the Early Years at Disney's*, New York: Harmony.

Klein, N.M. (1993) *Seven Minutes: The Life and Death of the American Animated Cartoon*, London: Verso.

Kottak, C.P. (1982) 'Anthropological analysis of mass enculturation', in C.P. Kottak (ed.), *Researching American Culture*, Ann Arbor, Mich.: University of Michigan Press.

Kotter, J. and Heskett, J.L. (1992) *Corporate Culture and Performance*, New York: Free Press.

Kuenz, J. (1993) 'It's a small world after all: Disney and the pleasures of identification', *South Atlantic Quarterly*, 92: 63–88.

Lang, G.E. and Lang, K. (1988) 'Recognition and renown', *American Journal of Sociology*, 94: 79–109.

Langer, M. (1992) 'The Disney–Fleischer dilemma: product differentiation and technological innovation', *Screen*, 33: 343–60.

Langley, W. (1993) 'Euro-dismal', *The Sunday Times*, 22 August: 9.

Lash, S. (1990) *Sociology of Postmodernism*, London: Routledge.

Lawrence, E.A. (1986) 'In the Mick of time: reflections on Disney's ageless mouse', *Journal of Popular Culture*, 20: 65–72.

Leerhsen, C. (1989) 'How Disney does it', *Newsweek*, 3 April: 14–20.

Lenburg, J. (1993) *The Great Cartoon Directors*, New York: Da Capo.

Lennon, P. (1993) 'Priest who took Mickey for a ride', *Guardian* (section 2), 25 October: 2–3.

Leyda, J. (1942) 'The dimensions of Disney', *Saturday Review*, 6 June: 5.

Lloyd, C. (1994) 'Airport rides ready for take-off', *The Sunday Times* (section 3), 10 July: 10.

Long, K.H. (1994) 'Quiet region debates value of theme park', *Tampa Tribune* (Travel section), 31 July: 1.

Lowenthal, D. (1985) *The Past is a Foreign Country*, Cambridge: Cambridge University Press.

—— (1989) 'Nostalgia tells it like it wasn't', in C. Shaw and M. Chase (eds), *The Imagined Past: History and Nostalgia*, Manchester: Manchester University Press.

Lowenthal, L. (1944) 'Biographies in popular magazines', in P.F. Lazarsfeld and F. Stanton (eds), *Radio Research: 1942–1943*, New York: Duell, Sloan & Pearce.

Lutz, E.G. (1920) *Animated Cartoons: How They Are Made, Their Origin and Development*, New York: Scribner.

Lyotard, J.-F. (1984) *The Postmodern Condition: A Report on Knowledge*, Manchester: Manchester University Press.

MacCannell, D. (1976) *The Tourist: A New Theory of the Leisure Class*, New York: Schocken.

—— (1992) *Empty Meeting Grounds: The Tourist Papers*, London: Routledge.

McDonald, J. (1966) 'Now the bankers come to Disney', *Fortune*, May: 138–41, 223–4.

McGuigan, J. (1992) *Cultural Populism*, London: Routledge.

Maltin, L. (1973) *The Disney Films*, New York: Crown.

—— (1987) *Of Mice and Magic: A History of American Animated Cartoons*, revised edition, New York: Plume.

Mann, A. (1934) 'Mickey Mouse's financial career', *Harper's*, 168: 714–21.

Marin, L. (1984) *Utopics: Spatial Play*, London: Macmillan.

Marling, S. (1993) *American Affair*, London: Boxtree.

Martin, J. (1992) *Cultures in Organizations: Three Perspectives*, New York: Oxford University Press.

Massie, J. (1992) 'How we got here', *1992 Screen Cartoonists Annual*.

Masters, K. (1994) 'A house divided', *Vanity Fair*, 57 (November): 122–8, 156–60.

Mechling, E.W. and Mechling, J. (1981) 'The sale of two cities: a semiotic comparison of Disneyland with Marriott's Great Adventure', *Journal of Popular Culture*, 15: 166–79.

Medved, M. (1993) 'Still wishing on a star', *The Sunday Times*, 8 August: 24–5.

Merritt, R. and Kaufman, J.B. (1992) *Walt in Wonderland: The Silent Films of Walt Disney*, Perdenone: Edizioni Biblioteca dell'Imagine.

Meyer, M. (1994) 'Of mice and men', *Newsweek*, 5 September: 40–7.

Miller, D. Disney (1956) *The Story of Walt Disney*, New York: Dell.

Mills, S.F. (1990) 'Disney and the promotion of synthetic worlds', *American Studies International*, 28: 66–79.

Mintzberg, H. (1991) 'The entrepreneurial organization', in H. Mintzberg and J.B. Quine (eds), *The Strategy Process: Concepts, Contexts, Cases*, Englewood Cliffs, N.J.: Prentice-Hall.

Mooney, J. (1994) 'Disney on the edge?', *Empire*, November: 78–84.

Moore, A. (1980) 'Walt Disney World: bounded ritual space and the playful pilgrimage center', *Anthropological Quarterly*, 53: 207–18.

Morison, E.E. (1983) 'What went wrong with Disney's world's fair', *American Heritage*, 35: 70–9.

Morley, D. (1980) *The 'Nationwide' Audience*, London: British Film Institute.

—— (1993) 'Active audience theory', *Journal of Communication*, 43: 13–19.

Mosley, L. (1986) *The Real Walt Disney: A Biography*, London: Grafton.

Mulkay, M. and Chaplin, E. (1982) 'Aesthetics and artistic career', *Sociological Quarterly*, 23: 117–38.

Murdock, G. (1989a) 'Cultural studies: missing links', *Critical Studies in Mass Communication*, 6: 436–40.

—— (1989b) 'Critical inquiry and audience activity', in R. Dervin, L. Grossberg, B.J. O'Keefe, and E. Wartella, *Rethinking Communication, vol. 2: Paradigm Exemplars*, Newbury Park, Cal.: Sage.

Nadler, D.A. and Tushman, M.L. (1990) 'Beyond the charismatic leader: leadership and organizational change', *California Management Review*, 32: 77–97.

Natale, R. (1986) 'Prince of the Magic Kingdom: Michael Eisner re-animates Disney', *California Business*, December: 18–23.

Neff, R. (1990) 'In Japan, they're Goofy about Disney', *Business Week*, 12 March: 39.

Nelson, S. (1986) 'Walt Disney's EPCOT and the world's fair performance tradition', *Drama Review*, 30: 106–46.

—— (1990) 'Reel life performance: the Disney–MGM Studios', *Drama Review*, 24: 60–78.

Nye, R.B. (1981) 'Eight ways of looking at an amusement park', *Journal of Popular Culture*, 15: 63–75.

Olins, R. (1993) 'Dynamic duos – or terrible twins?', *The Sunday Times* (section 3), 30 May: 8.

Peary, D. and Peary, G. (eds) (1980) *The American Animated Cartoon: A Critical Anthology*, New York: Dutton.

Peters, T. and Austin, N. (1985) *A Passion for Excellence*, New York: Random House.

Peters, T. and Waterman, R. (1982) *In Search of Excellence: Lessons from America's Best-run Companies*, New York: Harper & Row.

Potts, M. and Behr, P. (1987) *The Leading Edge: CEOs who Turned Their Companies Around*, New York: McGraw-Hill.

Reader, I. (1993a) 'Introduction', in I. Reader and T. Walter (eds), *Pilgrimage in Popular Culture*, London: Macmillan.

Reader, I. (1993b) 'Conclusions', in I. Reader and T. Walter (eds), *Pilgrimage in Popular Culture*, London: Macmillan.

Real, M.R. (1977) *Mass-mediated Culture*, Englewood Cliffs, N.J.: Prentice-Hall.

Relph, E. (1976) *Place and Placelessness*, London: Pion.

Ritzer, G. (1993) *The McDonaldization of Society*, Thousand Oaks, Cal.: Pine Forge.

Roberts, E.A. (1994) 'History is different from Disneyhistory', *Tampa Tribune* (Commentary section), 31 July: 1.

Robertson, R. (1990) 'After nostalgia? Wilful nostalgia and the phases of globalization', in B.S. Turner (ed.), *Theories of Modernity and Post-modernity*, London: Sage.

Rojek, C. (1993a) 'Disney culture', *Leisure Studies*, 12: 121–35.

—— (1993b) *Ways of Escape: Modern Transformations in Leisure and Travel*, London: Macmillan.

Rose, F. (1989) *West of Eden: The End of Innocence at Apple Computer*, London: Business Books.

—— (1990) 'Taking care of business', *Premiere*, November: 104–12.

Rosenau, P.M. (1992) *Post-modernism and the Social Sciences: Insights, Inroads, and Intrusions*, Princeton, N.J.: Princeton University Press.

Ross, I. (1982) 'Disney gambles on tomorrow', *Fortune*, 4 October: 62–8.

Rowe, C. and Koetter, F. (1978) *Collage City*, Cambridge, Mass.: MIT Press.

Rugare, S. (1991) 'The advent of America at EPCOT Center', in R. Diprose and R. Ferrell (eds), *Cartographies: Structuralism and the Mapping of Bodies and Spaces*, North Sydney, Australia: Allen & Unwin.

Sayers, F.C. (1965) 'Walt Disney accused', *Horn Book*, December: 602–11.

Sayle, M. (1983) 'Of mice and yen', *Harper's*, August: 36–45.

Schein, E.H. (1985) *Organizational Culture and Leadership*, San Francisco: Jossey-Bass.

Schickel, R. (1986) *The Disney Version: The Life, Times, Art and Commerce of Walt Disney*, revised edition, London: Pavilion.

Schiller, H.I. (1973) *The Mind Managers*, Boston, Mass.: Beacon.

—— (1989) *Culture, Inc.: The Corporate Takeover of Public Expression*, New York: Oxford University Press.

Schudson, M. (1979) 'Review essay: On tourism and modern culture', *American Journal of Sociology*, 84: 1249–58.

Schultz, J. (1988) 'The fabulous presumption of Disney World: Magic Kingdom in the wilderness', *Georgia Review*, 42: 275–312.

Sehlinger, B. (1994) *The Unofficial Guide to Walt Disney World*, New York: Prentice Hall.

Seldes, G. (1931) 'Mickey Mouse maker', *New Yorker*, 19 December: 23–7.

—— (1937) 'No art, Mr Disney?', *Esquire*, September: 91, 171–2.

Sertl, W.J. (1989) 'Hollywood divine: Disney–MGM Studios in Orlando', *Travel and Leisure*, 19: 140–6, 192–6.

Shearer, L. (1972) 'How Disney sells happiness', *Parade*, March 26: 4–6.

Shields, R. (1989) 'Social spacialization and the built environment: the West Edmonton Mall', *Environment and Planning D: Society and Space*, 7: 147–64.

—— (1991) *Places on the Margin: Alternative Geographies of Modernity*, London: Routledge.

—— (1992) 'The individual, consumption cultures and the fate of community', in R. Shields (ed.), *Lifestyle Shopping: The Subject of Consumption*, London: Routledge.

Simons, C. (1990) 'Business and leisure', *Landscape Architecture*, 80: 42–5.

Smith, R.C. and Eisenberg, E.M. (1987) 'Conflict at Disneyland: a root-metaphor analysis', *Communication Monographs*, 54: 367–80.

Smoodin, E. (1993) *Animating Culture: Hollywood Cartoons from the Sound Era*, Oxford: Roundhouse.

Snyder, N.H., Dowd, J.J., and Houghton, D.M. (1994) *Vision, Values and Courage: Leadership for Quality Management*, New York: Free Press.

Solomon, C. (1989) *Enchanted Drawings: The History of Animation*, New York: Alfred A. Knopf.

—— (1990) 'The new toon boom', *Los Angeles Times Calendar*, 19 August: 8–9, 94–5.

—— (1993) 'Disney's daughter attacks book', *Los Angeles Times*, 17 July: F14.

Sorkin, M. (1992) 'See you in Disneyland', in M. Sorkin (ed.), *Variations on a Theme Park: The New American City and the End of Public Space*, New York: Noonday.

Spanier, D. (1994) 'Poker with the plastic pirates', *The Financial Times*, 22 January: xi.

Stanley, L. (1993) 'On auto/biography in sociology', *Sociology*, 27: 41–52.

Starobinski, J. (1966) 'The idea of nostalgia', *Diogenes*, 54: 81–103.

Stephanson, A. (1987) 'Regarding postmodernism – a conversation with Fredric Jameson', *Social Text*, 17: 29–54.

Susman, W. (1989) 'Did success spoil the United States?: dual representations on postwar America', in L. May (ed.), *America: Culture and Politics in the Age of Cold War*, Chicago: University of Chicago Press.

Sutton, R.I. (1992) 'Feelings about a Disneyland visit: photography and the reconstruction of bygone emotions', *Journal of Management Inquiry*, 1: 278–87.

Taylor, J. (1987) *Storming the Magic Kingdom: Wall Street, the Raiders and the Battle for Disney*, New York: Viking.

Terrell, J. (1991) 'Disneyland and the future of museum anthropology', *American Anthropologist*, 93: 149–53.

Tester, K. (1993) *The Life and Times of Post-modernity*, London: Routledge.

Thomas, B. (1976) *Walt Disney: An American Original*, New York: Simon & Schuster.

—— (1991) *Disney's Art of Animation from Mickey Mouse to Beauty and the Beast*, New York: Hyperion.

Thomas, F. and Johnston, O. (1981) *Disney Animation: The Illusion of Life*, New York: Abbeville.

Thomas, M. (1969) 'The men who followed Mickey Mouse', *Dun's Review*, 94: 34–8.

Tichy, N.M. and Devanna, M.A. (1986) *The Transformational Leader*, New York: John Wiley.

Tietyen, D. (1990) *The Musical World of Walt Disney*, Milwaukee, Wis.: Hal Leonard.

Toth, M.A. (1981) *The Theory of the Two Charismas*, Washington D.C.: University Press of America.

Toufexis, A. (1985) 'No Mickey Mousing around', *Time*, 11 March: 40.

Turner, B.S. (1987) 'A note on nostalgia', *Theory, Culture and Society*, 4: 147–56.

Turner, R. (1991) 'Hollywood blues as Disney stumbles', *The Sunday Times*, 17 November: 7.

Turner, V. and Turner, E. (1978) *Image and Pilgrimage in Christian Culture*, New York: Columbia University Press.

Urry, J. (1990) *The Tourist Gaze: Leisure and Travel in Contemporary Societies*, London: Sage.

Van Maanen, J. (1991) 'The smile factory: work at Disneyland', in P.J. Frost, L.F. Moore, M.R. Louis, C.C. Lundberg and J. Martin (eds), *Reframing Organizational Culture*, Newbury Park, Cal.: Sage.

—— and Kunda, G. (1989) '"Real feelings": emotional expression and organizational culture', *Research in Organizational Behavior*, 11: 43–103.

Wakefield, N. (1990) *Postmodernism: The Twilight of the Real*, London: Pluto.

Waldrep, S. (1993) 'The contemporary future of tomorrow', *South Atlantic Quarterly*, 92: 139–55.

Wallace, I. (1949) 'Mickey Mouse and how he grew', *Collier's*, 9 April: 20–36.

Wallace, K. (1963) 'The engineering of ease', *New Yorker*, 7 September: 104–29.

Wallace, M. (1981) 'Visiting the past: history museums in the United States', *Radical History Review*, 25: 63–96.

—— (1985) 'Mickey Mouse history: portraying the past at Disney World', *Radical History Review*, 32: 33–57.

Waller, G.A. (1980) 'Mickey, Walt and film criticism from *Steamboat Willie* to *Bambi*', in D. Peary and G. Peary (eds), *The American Animated Cartoon: A Critical Anthology*, New York: Dutton.

Walsh, K. (1992) *The Representation of the Past: Museums and Heritage in the Post-modern World*, London: Routledge.

Wanger, W. (1943) 'Mickey Icarus, 1943', *Saturday Review*, 4 September: 18–19.

Warde, A. (1994) 'Consumers, identity and belonging: reflections on some theses of Zygmunt Bauman', in R. Keat, N. Whiteley, and N. Abercrombie (eds), *The Authority of the Consumer*, London: Routledge.

Warren, S. (1994) 'Disneyfication of the metropolis: popular resistance in Seattle', *Journal of Urban Affairs*, 16: 89–107.

Wasko, J., Phillips, M., and Purdie, C. (1993) 'Hollywood meets Madison Avenue: the commercialization of US films', *Media, Culture and Society*, 15: 271–93.

Wasserman, A. (1983) 'Un and loathing at EPCOT', *Industrial Design Magazine*, March/April: 34–9.

Weber, B. (1969) 'The Disney troika', *California Business*, 20 October: 7, 18–19.

Weber, M. (1968) *Economy and Society* (1925), 3 vols, eds G. Roth and C. Wittich, New York: Bedminster.

Weinstein, R.M. (1992) 'Disneyland and Coney Island: reflections on the evolution of the modern amusement park', *Journal of Popular Culture*, 26: 131–64.

Welsh, T. (1994) 'Best and worst corporate reputations', *Fortune*, 7 February: 32–6.

Westley, F.R. and Mintzberg, H, (1989) 'Visionary leadership and strategic management', *Strategic Management Journal*, 10: 17–32.

Wiener, J. (1993) 'Murdered ink', *The Nation*, 256: 743–50.

Willis, S. (1993) 'Disney World: public use/private state', *South Atlantic Quarterly*, 92: 119–37.

Wilson, A. (1992) *The Culture of Nature: North American Landscape from Disney to the Exxon Valdez*, Cambridge, Mass.: Basil Blackwell.

Wolf, J.C. (1979) 'Disney World: America's vision of Utopia', *Alternative Futures*, 2: 72–7.

Yoshimoto, M. (1994) 'Images of empire: Tokyo Disneyland and Japanese cultural imperialism', in E. Smoodin (ed.), *Disney Discourse*, New York: Routledge.

Zehnder, L.E. (1975) *Florida's Disney World*, Tallahassee, Fla.: Peninsular Publishing.

Zukin, S. (1990) 'Socio-spatial prototypes of a new organization of consumption: the role of real cultural capital', *Sociology*, 24: 37–56.

—— (1991) *Landscapes of Power: From Detroit to Disney World*, Berkeley, Cal.: University of California Press.

Index

List of References

List of references

Cameron, S. (2002) *Business Students' Handbook: learning skills for study and employment.* 2nd Edition, Harlow, Financial Times/Prentice Hall

Guirdham, M. (2002) *Interpersonal Skills at Work,* 2nd Edition, London, Prentice Hall

Hayes, J. (2002) *Interpersonal Skills at Work.* 2nd Edition, Hove, Routledge

Honey, P. (1988) *Face to Face: A Practical Guide to Interactive Skills* 2nd Edition, Aldershot, Gower

Hussey, J. Hussey, R. (1997) *Business Research.* Basingstoke, Macmillan

Kolb, D. A., I. M. Rubin and J. M. McIntyre (1973) *Organisational Psychology: An Experiential Approach.* Englewood Cliffs, NJ, Prentice Hall

Luck, M. (1999) *Your Student Research Project.* Aldershot, Gower

Northedge, A. (1990) *The Good Study Guide.* Milton Keynes, Open University

Pearson, D. (1993) *Strategic Marketing Management: Analysis and Decision.* London, BPP Publishing

Pedler, M. Burgoyne, J. Boydell, T. (1994) *A Manager's Guide to Self Development.* Maidenhead, McGraw Hill

Saunders, M. Lewis, P. Thornhill, A. (2003) *Research Methods for Business Students.* 3rd Edition, Harlow, Financial Times/Prentice Hall

Shea, G. F. (1992) *Mentoring: A guide to the basics.* London, Kogan Page

REVIEW FORM & FREE PRIZE DRAW

All original review forms from the entire BPP Learning Media range, completed with genuine comments, will be entered into one of two draws on 31 January 2009 and 31 July 2009. The names on the first four forms picked out on each occasion will be sent a cheque for £50.

Name: _____   **Address:** _____

_____

_____

How have you used this Tutorial Text?
(Tick one box only)

☐ Home study (book only)

☐ On a course: college _____

☐ Other _____

Why did you decide to purchase this Text?
(Tick one box only)

☐ Have used BPP Texts in the past

☐ Recommendation by friend/colleague

☐ Recommendation by a lecturer at college

☐ Saw advertising

☐ Other _____

During the past six months do you recall seeing/receiving any of the following?
(Tick as many boxes as are relevant)

☐ Our advertisement in *Student Accountant*

☐ Our advertisement in *Pass*

☐ Our brochure with a letter through the post

Which (if any) aspects of our advertising do you find useful?
(Tick as many boxes as are relevant)

☐ Prices and publication dates of new editions

☐ Information on Text content

☐ Facility to order books off-the-page

☐ None of the above

Your ratings, comments and suggestions would be appreciated on the following areas and features of this book

	Very useful	Useful	Not useful
Self assessment (Chapter 2))	☐	☐	☐
Overview (Chapter 3)	☐	☐	☐
Project definition (Chapter 4)	☐	☐	☐
Project management (Chapter 5)	☐	☐	☐
Research and analysis (Chapters 6 and 7)	☐	☐	☐
Synthesis (Chapter 8)	☐	☐	☐
Report writing (Chapter 9)	☐	☐	☐
Mentor meetings (Chapters 10 and 11)	☐	☐	☐
Presentation (Chapter 12)	☐	☐	☐
Key Skills Statement (Chapter 13)	☐	☐	☐
Examples	☐	☐	☐
Exercises	☐	☐	☐
Proforma forms	☐	☐	☐
Checklists	☐	☐	☐

	Excellent	Good	Adequate	Poor
Overall opinion of this Tutorial Text	☐	☐	☐	☐

Do you intend to continue using BPP Learning Media Study Texts/Kits?   ☐ Yes   ☐ No

Please note any further comments and suggestions on the reverse of this page.

Please return to: Stella Dinenis, BPP Learning Media, FREEPOST, London, W12 8BR or email your comments to stelladinenis@bpp.com

REVIEW FORM & FREE PRIZE DRAW (continued)

Please note any further comments and suggestions below

FREE PRIZE DRAW RULES

1   Closing date for 31 January 2009 draw is 31 December 2008. Closing date for 31 July 2009 draw is 30 June 2009.

2   Restricted to entries with UK and Eire addresses only. BPP employees, their families and business associates are excluded.

3   No purchase necessary. Entry forms are available upon request from BPP Learning Media. No more than one entry per title, per person. Draw restricted to persons aged 16 and over.

4   Winners will be notified by post and receive their cheques not later than 6 weeks after the relevant draw date.

5   The decision of the promoter in all matters is final and binding. No correspondence will be entered into.